The Fish & Shellfish
Cookbook

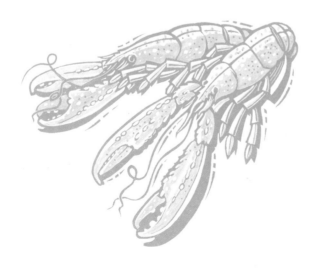

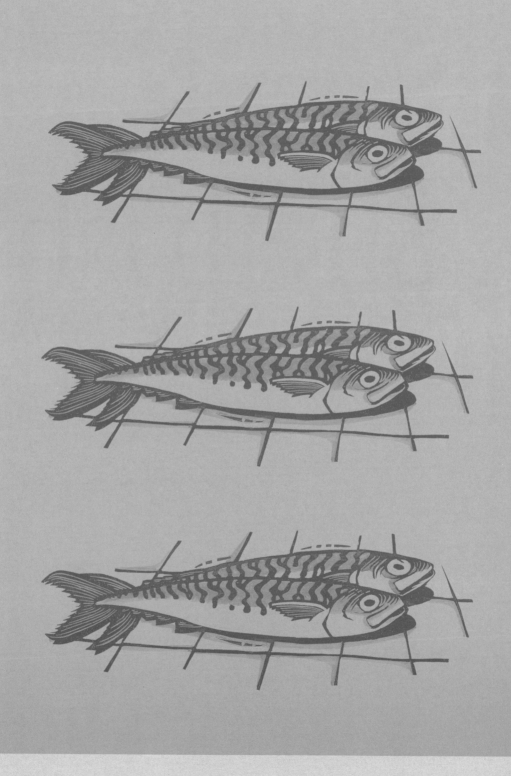

The Fish & Shellfish

Cookbook

Kate Whiteman

HERMES
HOUSE

This edition is published by Hermes House
Hermes House is an imprint of Anness Publishing Ltd
Hermes House, 88–89 Blackfriars Road, London SE1 8HA
tel. 020 7401 2077; fax 020 7633 9499; info@anness.com

© Anness Publishing Ltd 2003

A CIP catalogue record for this book is available from the British Library.

Publisher : Joanna Lorenz
Managing Editor : Linda Fraser
Editor: Susannah Blake
Jacket and Text Design: Chloe Steers
Tyesetting :Jonathan Harley
Illustrations:Angela Wood
Production Controller : Joanna King

Recipes : Katherine Atkinson, Alex Barker,Carla Capalbo,Carole Clements,
Trish Davies,Brian Glover,
Rosamund Grant, Lesley Mackley, Jane Milton,Sallie Morris,Liz Trigg, Kate Whiteman,
Elizabeth Wolf -Cohen, Jeni Wright

1 3 5 7 9 10 8 6 4 2

Note
Bracketed terms are intended for American readers
For all recipes, quantities are given in both metric and imperial measures and where appropriate,
measures are also given in standard cups and spoons.
Follow one set, but not a mixture, because they are not interchangeable.

Standard spoon and cup measures are level
1tsp=5ml, 1tbsp=15ml,1 cup=250ml/8fl oz

Australian standard tablespoon are 20ml. Australian readers should use 3tsp in place of 1 tbsp for
measuring small quantities of flour, salt, etc

Medium(US large) eggs are used unless otherwise stated

Contents

INTRODUCTION

There is no doubt that fish is exceptionally good for you. All fish and seafood is low in fat and high in proteins, minerals and vitamins; oily fish can actually improve your health by lowering cholesterol levels and unclogging arteries. The Japanese, whose diet consists largely of fresh raw fish, have the lowest incidence of heart disease in the world.

Good health is only one of many reasons to eat fish, however. When properly prepared and cooked, it can be among the most delicious foods imaginable. Really fresh fish and shellfish need little cooking or embellishment and most takes very little time to prepare – a huge bonus for the modern cook whose time is often very limited. It is easy to rustle up the most elegant and impressive fish dish in under half an hour.

Every fish and shellfish has its own unique flavour, offering something for all tastes. It is unlikely that there is a recipe for a piscatorial dessert, but fish and shellfish can feature in every other part of a meal, including appetizers, main courses, salads and savouries.

It is hard to understand why fish has been undervalued for so long. Perhaps it has something to do with the fact that it was traditionally eaten on fast days, as a substitute for meat, so is associated with self-denial and penance. In times of plenty, easily obtainable seafoods, such as salmon and oysters, were regarded as foods fit only for the poor. Medieval apprentices complained bitterly and refused to eat oysters more than three times a week. Bland, easily digested white fish was perceived as invalid food and rejected by those with more robust constitutions.

Probably the main reason for people eschewing fish, however, was lack of understanding of how to prepare it. Skinning, filleting, scaling and shelling all seemed like rather hard work. Nowadays, despite the demise of many fish-mongers, there is no need to do all the hard work yourself. Just visit your local supermarket and choose ready-prepared fish. Better still, follow the instructions given in this book, which will guide you through the complexities of handling and preparing all kinds of fish and shellfish.

Fish and shellfish are rewarding to cook and extremely versatile. Although some types have become scarce through overfishing, and therefore very expensive, the price of others has plummeted, thanks to advances in fish farming. Salmon, for example, has come full circle. Once despised as being too common, its subsequent rarity made it one of the most expensive and sought-after fish. Now, once again, it has become one of the cheapest types of fish available. Be wary, however, of buying very cheap farmed fish. Careless farming results in poor-quality specimens. Poor fish farming can also promote diseases, which may spread to other sea creatures in their natural habitat. Consumers must not repeat the mistakes of the past, when demand for ever-cheaper meat and other foods had disastrous consequences in terms of health and ecology. Fish and shellfish are superb natural foods and should remain so. That said, well-managed fish and shellfish farms produce healthy specimens and help counteract the disastrous effects of over-fishing of wild stocks.

One of the greatest pleasures when travelling is to visit the local fish market and see the dazzling array of brightly coloured fresh fish and seafood set out on the stalls. However strange their shapes and forms, all have a unique beauty and character. Modern methods of fishing and transportation have made sea creatures from all over the world accessible to adventurous cooks, so allow yourself the pleasure of experimenting, and enjoy the infinite variety of textures, flavours and colours of the fruits of the sea.

KATE WHITEMAN

EQUIPMENT

Preparing and cooking fish and shellfish is very easy once you know how. There are a number of pieces of kitchen equipment that will make the process much easier and give a better result. Some, such as the fish kettle, take up quite a lot of storage space; other gadgets, such as the fish scaler, are quite tiny, but all will prove invaluable for fish and shellfish cookery.

KNIVES, SCISSORS AND SCALERS

It is vital that you keep your knives and scissors sharp – sharpen them regularly along the whole blade.

Chef's knife A large, heavy knife with a 20–25cm/8–10in blade, often made of stainless steel, is essential for cutting fish steaks and splitting open crustaceans, such as crayfish and lobster.

Filleting knife For filleting and skinning fish, you will need a sharp knife with a flexible blade that is at least 15cm/6in long. This type of knife can also be used for opening some kinds of shellfish. It is essential to keep a filleting knife razor sharp so that you can make clean cuts.

Oyster knife This short, stubby knife – sometimes called a shucker – has a wide, two-edged blade to help prise open the shells of oysters and other bivalves. Make sure that it has a safety guard above the handle to protect your hands in case the blade slips.

Kitchen scissors A sturdy, sharp pair of scissors that have a serrated edge are needed for cutting off fins and trimming tails.

Fish scaler This resembles a small, rough grater. It will make short and relatively painless work of a task that few relish.

PANS

There are a huge range of pans to choose from nowadays, so be sure to invest in the best ones that you can.

Fish kettle This long, deep pan has rounded ends, a handle at either end, and a tightly-fitting lid. Inside is a perforated rack with handles on which to lay the fish. Most modern fish kettles are made of stainless steel, but they also come in aluminium, enamelled steel and copper with a tin-plated interior. Fish kettles are used on the hob (stovetop) and are invaluable for cooking whole large fish, such as salmon. Fish kettles can also be used for steaming other foods.

Oval frying pan This large, practical pan enables you to cook whole fish flat instead of bending them to fit a round pan and spoiling their shape.

Griddle pan A ribbed, cast-iron griddle pan is ideal for searing and grilling fish. It can be round, oval or rectangular. Some large griddles need to be used over two electric rings or gas burners on top of a stove.

Wok A 35cm/14in wok with a lid will be large enough for most fish and will prove invaluable in the kitchen. There is no need to reserve this piece of equipment for stir-frying; a wok also makes an effective steamer and can be used for deep-frying.

STEAMERS

If you steam food frequently, a stainless steel steamer set is a good investment. It has a lidded, deep outer pan and a perforated inner basket. Choose the widest type that you can find. Chinese bamboo steaming baskets are an economical alternative. These baskets can be stacked on top of each other so that several layers of food can be cooked at one time. Cheapest of all is a small, collapsible, perforated, stainless steel steamer, which unfolds like a flower to fit any pan.

OTHER USEFUL UTENSILS

You will need to buy some of these utensils specially, but others you will have around the home already.

Fish lifter Resembling an elongated fish slice or spatula, this curved and perforated turner is useful for flipping over whole fish.

Spatula Two spatulas with sturdy, flexible blades are good for turning over most fish.

Lobster pick Choose a pick with a two-pronged fork at the end to extract the flesh from lobster and crab legs.

Lobster crackers These look very similar to hinged nutcrackers (often made in the shape of lobster claws) with ridges on the inside to give a good grip.

Mallet This is useful for cracking crustacean claws and for flattening fish escalopes.

Pins Use dressmakers' pins with round heads to extract winkles and whelks from their shells. For safety's sake, stick them in a cork when not using.

Tweezers Use these to extract small bones and pin bones from fish fillets.

SPECIALIST ITEMS

As well as the everyday equipment that you may need for preparing and cooking fish and shellfish, there are several other pieces of specialist equipment that are invaluable for certain cooking techniques.

Barbecue grilling racks A large, hinged rack in the shape of a fish makes cooking – and turning – a single large fish relatively easy. Also available are shaped racks designed to hold 6–12 sardines. These racks can be round or rectangular. More useful for general purposes is a double-sided hinged grilling rack. These can be rectangular or square and have long handles so that several fish steaks or small whole fish can be barbecued and turned over simultaneously. However, the flat sides do tend to squash the delicate flesh of some fish. Grilling racks should always be well oiled before use to prevent the fish from sticking to them and falling apart during cooking.

Smoker The cheapest type of home-smoker is a lidded metal box with a rack to hold the fish. Smoke produced by placing dampened aromatic wood chippings or herbs on the coals gives extra flavour. (Hickory and oak wood chips impart a particularly good flavour.) More convenient, though much more expensive, are electric smokers. Stove-top smokers are also available and can be used indoors.

Buying & Preparing Fish

F ish is only worth buying if it is absolutely fresh, and it is best if you eat it on the day you buy it. Fresh fish have shiny skin with a metallic glint. The eyes should be clear, bright and slightly bulging and the flesh should feel firm and springy when you press it lightly with your finger. An accommodating fishmonger will gut and clean your fish for you and even scale, skin and fillet it.

When shopping for fresh fish, always buy whatever looks best and freshest on the day. If you want a specific type of fish, always ask the fishmonger in advance. If buying frozen fish, get it home and into the freezer without delay. Allow about 175g/6oz fish fillet, cutlets or steaks and 300g/11oz whole fish per person.

Rinse fresh fish in very cold water. Pat dry and place on a plate. Cover with clear film (plastic wrap) and store at the bottom of the refrigerator for no more than a day. White fish can be stored in the freezer for three months and oily fish for two months.

Preparing Round Fish

If you have to prepare fish yourself, do not despair; it is really very easy, given a sharp, flexible knife and a little dexterity.

Scaling

Always scale fish before filleting if you are going to cook it with the skin on. Smooth-skinned round fish do not need scaling. Work in the sink, preferably under running water to prevent the scales flying around.

1 Wash the fish in cold water. Using sharp scissors, cut off the fins that run along the stomach, and the dorsal fins on the back.
2 Hold the fish by the tail. Working from tail to head, scrape against the scales with a fish scaler or the back of a round-bladed knife. Wash to detach any clinging scales.

Gutting/Cleaning Round Fish

You can gut a whole round fish: through the belly or through the gills. In either case, the gills should be removed before the fish is cooked, because they taste bitter. Do this by holding the fish on its back and opening the gill flaps. Push out the frilly gills and cut them off at the back of the head and under the jawbone with a sharp knife.

Cleaning Through the Belly

This is the more usual method for gutting round fish.

1 Starting at the site of the anal fin, slit open the belly from tail to head.
2 Gently pull out and sever the innards. Keep any roes and red mullet livers, which are considered a great delicacy, but discard everything else. Use a tablespoon to make sure the cavity is empty, removing any blood vessels adjacent to the backbone. Wash the cavity thoroughly, then pat the fish dry with kitchen paper.

Defrosting Fish

If possible, thaw the fish overnight in the refrigerator. However, if you are in a hurry, microwave the fish on the defrost setting. Separate the pieces as soon as they are thawed enough and then spread out in an even layer. Remove the fish from the microwave while still icy, as over-thawed fish will become dry.

Cleaning Through the Gills

If splitting the fish open to gut through the belly would spoil its appearance, this method of cleaning through the gills should be used instead.

1 Lay the fish on its back. Make an incision in the bottom of the belly, near the tail. Snip through the end of the innards.

2 Cut through the bone under the lower jaw. Open the gill flaps, insert your fingers into the cavity and gently pull out the innards. Wash the fish thoroughly, then pat dry with kitchen paper.

BONING BONY FISH

Having cleaned bony fish, either through the belly or the gills, they are ready to bone.

1 Open the fish out like a book and lay it on a board, with the skin-side up. Press down firmly with your fingers right along the length of the backbone.

2 Turn the fish over and carefully pull the backbone away from the flesh. Cut off the backbone at the tail and pick out any loose bones. Rinse the fish and pat dry.

FILLETING ROUND FISH

Two fillets can be obtained from round fish, one from each side.

1 Lay the fish on a board with the back away from you and the tail towards you. Lift the gill fin and make a diagonal cut behind the fin to the top of the head.

2 Insert the knife about halfway down the fish as close to the backbone as possible. Cut towards the tail keeping the knife flat to the bone. Lift up the released fillet, turn the knife towards the head and carefully slide it along the bone to free the fillet completely.

3 Repeat on the other side. Remove any small bones from the fillets with tweezers, or make a diagonal cut on either side of the line of bones. Remove the v-shaped piece of flesh together with the bones.

PREPARING FLAT FISH

Flat fish are easy to prepare and their bones are rarely troublesome.

GUTTING FLAT FISH

Trim off the fins. Make an incision just below the gills, then insert your fingers and pull out the innards, including the roe.

FILLETING FLAT FISH

Four fillets can be obtained from flat fish, two from each side.

1 Place the fish on a board with the dark skin facing up and the head pointing away from you. Use a large, sharp knife and cut around the head and down the centre line of the fish, taking the knife blade all the way through to the backbone.

2 Insert the point of the knife under the flesh at the head end. Starting with the left-hand fillet, hold the knife almost parallel to the bones and carefully free the fillet with long stroking movements of the knife.

3 Turn the fish so that the head is towards you and remove the second fillet in the same way. Repeat the process on the other side.

SKINNING WHOLE FLAT FISH

To cook flat fish on the bone, rather than as fillets, they should first be skinned.

1 Lay the fish on a board with the dark skin facing up and the tail towards you. Slit through the skin just below the tail and loosen the skin on both sides.

2 Hold the tail down firmly with one hand. Use the other hand to pull away the skin quickly and firmly towards the head.

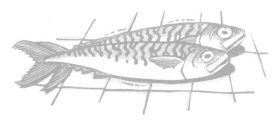

Cooking Fish

F ish is an extremely versatile food and there are many simple and delicious ways to cook it. Remember, however, that it is all too easy to overcook the delicate flesh and so destroy its wonderful flavour and texture. Apart from boiling, almost any cooking method suits fish and will give great results. Although fish should not be boiled, it can still be simmered for hearty soups.

Always take fish out of the refrigerator at least 30 minutes before cooking to ensure that it cooks evenly. Cooking times for fish depend on many factors, such as the thickness of fillets, whether they are much thinner at one end, and the type of fish. Fish is cooked when the internal temperature reaches about 63°C/145°F. You can use a meat thermometer to test this, but you can also judge by eye.

To test whether fillets are cooked, insert a knife into the centre and part the flesh; it should look opaque. Ease the flesh away from the bone; it should just come away, not fall off easily. Alternatively, press a fork into the thickest part of the fillet. If the prongs go in only halfway, cook the fish for a little longer. If they sink in, meeting a slight resistance near the bone, the fish is done.

Poaching
Cooking in a stock or court-bouillon brings out the flavour of fresh fish.

1 Place a whole fish in a fish kettle, and fish portions in a layer in a heatproof dish. Pour over cold court-bouillon or stock and add a few herbs and flavourings.

2 Lay baking parchment over the fish and heat until the liquid trembles. At this point, thin pieces of fish may be done. Continue to cook thicker pieces at a bare simmer until the flesh is just opaque. For 1kg/2¼lb fish allow 7–8 minutes. To serve the fish cold, leave to cool in the liquid.

Cooking "au bleu"
This method of cooking is mainly used for freshwater fish that are still alive or very fresh. It is good hot or cold.

1 Stun the fish, clean through the gills, then sprinkle with boiling vinegar – the fish skin will turn a steely blue colour.

2 Place the fish in a flameproof dish or fish kettle and pour over hot court-bouillon to cover. Cover the dish or kettle and simmer gently until the fish is just cooked through. If necessary, scale the fish before serving.

Making Fish Stock
For many recipes, a good fish stock is essential. White fish bones and trimmings make the best stock. Ask the fishmonger for these whenever you buy fish; they can be frozen for later use. To make 1 litre/ 1¾ pints/4 cups stock, you will need 1kg/2¼lb bones, heads and trimmings.

1 Wash the fish heads well and remove the gills. Chop the heads and bones `and put them in a large pan. Coarsely chop the white part of 1 leek, 1 onion and 1 celery stick and add to the fish.

2 Add 150ml/¼ pint/⅔ cup dry white wine, 6 white peppercorns, a bouquet garni, and 1 litre/1¾ pints/4 cups water to the pan. Bring the mixture to the boil, then simmer for just 20 minutes. Strain through a muslin-lined sieve.

STEAMING

This cooking method enhances the flavour of fish and gives a moist result. The fish retains its shape, even when overcooked. Steaming is the healthiest way to cook fish.
1 Half-fill the base pan of a steamer with water and bring it to the boil. Place the fish in one layer in the steamer basket, leaving room to let the steam circulate.
2 Lower the steamer into the base pan, making sure it stands well clear of the water.
3 Lay a sheet of baking parchment over the fish, then cover the pan tightly and steam until the fish is just cooked through. Check the water level during cooking and add more boiling water if necessary.

MICROWAVING

This is another healthy cooking method that helps to retain the nutrients found in fish. Whole fish can be microwaved, as long as they fit in the oven.
1 Slash the skin in several places to prevent it from splitting. Cook fillets in a single layer, thinner parts towards the centre.
2 Cover the whole fish or fish fillets with microwaveable clear film (plastic wrap). Microwave on full power (100%) for the shortest possible time, as recommended in your handbook, then allow to rest. It will finish cooking by residual heat.

Cooking time depends on the thickness of the fish. The following are guidelines for 500g/1¼lb fish in a 750 watt microwave, but test before the end of cooking.
• Whole round fish, thick fillets, steaks and cutlets: cook for 4–5 minutes, then leave to stand for 5 minutes. (Turn over whole fish halfway through cooking.)
• Flat fish and thin fillets: cook for 3–4 minutes, then rest for 3–4 minutes.
• Fish with denser flesh (shark, tuna, monkfish, skate etc.): cook for 6–7 minutes, then leave to stand for 5 minutes.

FRYING

Cooking fish in hot oil or butter gives it a great flavour, texture and colour. There are two main methods: shallow-, or pan-frying and deep-frying.

Shallow-frying or Pan-frying

For this popular cooking method, pieces of fish such as fillets, steaks or cutlets or small whole fish such as sardines are cooked in a little fat in a shallow pan to caramelize and colour the outside. This can either be used as a prelude to another cooking method or the fish can be fully cooked in the pan. Before frying, the fish can be coated with flour, breadcrumbs or oatmeal. Plain fish can be fried without fat using a non-stick pan, but it will have to be cooked very carefully to prevent drying out.

Frying fish in butter gives the best flavour, but it burns easily, so should be combined with a small amount of oil. Alternatively, use clarified butter or oil. Heat the butter and/or oil until very hot in a frying pan large enough to hold the fish pieces or whole fish. Put the fish in the pan and seal briefly on both sides. Lower the heat and cook gently until done. If the pieces are large, it may be necessary to finish cooking in a medium oven.

Deep-frying

Because fish is delicate, it must be coated in flour or batter before being deep-fried. This seals in the juices, so that the fish is crisp on the outside and moist inside. Most fish is suitable for deep-frying.

Use plenty of oil and make sure that it is really hot (180–190°C/350–375°F) before putting in the fish. Use an electric deep-fryer, a large, heavy pan or a large wok. Test the oil temperature by carefully dropping a cube of bread into the hot oil; if it browns within 30 seconds, the oil is hot enough. Larger pieces of fish should be cooked at a slightly lower temperature than small pieces like goujons. This allows the heat to penetrate to the centre before the outside burns. Only cook a few pieces at a time, or the temperature of the oil will drop. Dip the fish in seasoned flour, add to the oil and cook until golden. Drain the fish on kitchen paper before serving.

Oil used for frying fish should never be used for any other purpose.

Stir-frying

This quick Asian cooking method is perfect for fish, prawns (shrimp) and squid.
1 Cut fish or squid into bite-size strips; leave prawn tails whole, with the tail shells intact. Toss in a little cornflour (cornstarch) to prevent them falling apart as they cook.
2 Heat a little oil in a wok over a very high heat, add a few pieces of fish or shellfish and stir-fry for a few moments.

Searing

This method is best for thickish fillets that have not been skinned, or small whole fish.
1 Smear the base of a heavy frying pan or griddle with a little oil and heat until smoking. Lightly brush both sides of the fish with oil and put it into the hot pan.
2 Sear for 2–3 minutes, or until the skin is golden, then turn and cook the other side.

Cooking without Heat

Very fresh fish can be "cooked" without heat by being marinated or soused with lemon juice or white wine vinegar. The acids soften the flesh and turn it opaque. The classic dish of this type is ceviche, where cubes or strips of firm white fish are marinated in lemon juice, salt and finely chopped chilli for at least 2 hours, until the flesh turns pearly white.

Roasting

This method is more usually associated with meat, but it is an excellent way of cooking whole fish and "meaty" cuts such as monkfish tails and swordfish steaks. The oven should be preheated to 230°C/450°F/ Gas 8 with the roasting pan inside. The fish will then be seared by the heat of the pan and the juices will not escape. Cooking times will vary depending on thickness and density of the fish. As a general rule allow between 15 and 25 minutes.

Drizzle a little olive oil over the fish before roasting. For extra flavour, roast it on a bed of herbs or Mediterranean vegetables.

Baking

Whole fish and some chunky fish steaks and fillets, such as cod or halibut, are perfect for baking. Because the flesh is delicate, it is best to bake fish at a lower temperature than would be used for meat, and certainly no higher than 200°C/400°F/Gas 6. Cooking times vary depending on the thickness and density of the fish. As a general rule, allow between 20 and 40 minutes.

Baking *en papillote* is a healthy way of cooking, because it uses no fat and retains all the flavour of the fish. The fish is wrapped in baking parchment with vegetables and seasonings, and baked. Serve the fish still wrapped in paper.

BRAISING

This is another excellent cooking method for whole fish or large fillets.

1 Butter a flameproof dish and make a thick bed of thinly sliced or shredded vegetables, such as carrots, onions, fennel and celery.

2 Place the fish on top and pour on enough white or red wine and/or fish or chicken stock to come nearly halfway up the fish.

3 Scatter over 15ml/1 tbsp of fresh chopped herbs, then cover with buttered baking parchment and bring to the boil. Braise the fish at a low temperature on top of the stove or in a preheated oven at 180°C/350°F/Gas 4, allowing about 20 minutes for a 1kg/2¼lb fish and 10–15 minutes for large fish fillets.

GRILLING AND BARBECUING

Fish steaks, thick fillets and relatively small whole fish such as sardines, red mullet or trout can be grilled (broiled) or barbecued, as can crustaceans. The grill (broiler) should be preheated to a very high heat so that the fish juices are sealed in quickly. Griddle pans are better than overhead grills, but either will do. Grilling on the barbecue can be a little more tricky, as the marinades or bastes used to keep the fish moist can drip on to the coals and cause flare-ups.

All grilled fish will benefit from being marinated for 1 hour in a mixture of oil and lemon juice before being cooked. If the fish is to be cooked whole, make several slashes down to the bone on either side before marinating. Brush the grill rack and fish with oil to prevent sticking.

Thin fillets need only be grilled on one side. Do not use a grill rack. Brush the grill pan with a little oil. Place the pan under the grill until hot, then pass both sides of the fish through the oil before grilling on one side only; the underside will cook at the same time from the heat of the pan.

SMOKING

Although most of the smoked fish we buy has been commercially smoked, it is easy to smoke your own at home.

Hot Smoking

This method cooks and smokes the food at the same time, using a special smoker filled with fragrant hardwood chips. Domestic smokers are small and easy to use. Some can be used indoors, but they are best suited to outdoor use. For large quantities, use a kettle barbecue. Heat the wood chips to 80–85°C/176–185°F, place the fish on the rack, put on the lid and smoke until the fish is the colour of pale burnished wood.

Cold Smoking

This method cures but does not cook the fish. It must first be salted in dry salt or brine, then hung up to drip dry before smoking at 30–35°C/86–95°F.

Tea Smoking

This Chinese method imparts a wonderful flavour to oily fish such as trout and sea-food such as scallops and prawns (shrimp).

1 Line a wok with foil and sprinkle in 30ml/2 tbsp each of raw long grain rice, sugar and aromatic tea leaves.

2 Place a wire rack on top of the wok and then arrange the fish in a single layer. Cover the wok with a lid or more foil and cook over a very high heat until you see smoke.

3 Lower the heat slightly and cook until the fish is done (some smoke should still escape from the wok). A mackerel fillet will take 8–10 minutes, large prawns 5–7 minutes.

Buying, Preparing & Cooking Shellfish

The term shellfish is here applied to seafood other than fish. This includes crustaceans (lobsters, crabs, crayfish, prawns and shrimp), molluscs (which include bivalves such as clams, mussels, cockles, oysters and scallops), as well as gastropods such as winkles, whelks and abalone and cephalopods (octopus, squid and cuttlefish), which have their "shells" inside their bodies rather than outside.

Crustaceans and molluscs need very little cooking to enhance their already superb flavour. Indeed, many molluscs can be eaten raw. Cephalopods need either very brief or long, slow cooking. Crustaceans of all types must be cooked; unlike fish, the larger specimens can be boiled.

CRUSTACEANS

These shellfish are invertebrates with a hard external shell or skeleton protecting their soft and tender flesh.

LOBSTERS AND CRABS

These can be sold live or cooked. Lobsters are the luxurious choice today while crabs can be cheaper.

Buying and Storing

Live lobsters or crabs should smell very fresh and still be lively and aggressive when picked up. The tails of lobsters should spring back sharply when they are opened out. Crabs should feel heavy for their size, but you should make sure this is not because there is water inside the shell. The shell should neither be soft nor should it contain any cracks or holes.

Check that lobsters and crabs have both claws – if one is missing, make sure the price is reduced. Allow 450g/1lb per person.

Live lobsters or crabs should be cooked on the day you buy them. If you cannot pop them straight into the pot, live crustaceans can be wrapped in slightly wet newspaper or covered in a very damp dishtowel and kept in the coldest part of the refrigerator.

Preparing and Cooking a Live Lobster

The most humane way to kill a live lobster is to render it unconscious by placing it in a freezerproof dish or tray and covering it with crushed ice. Alternatively, place the lobster in the freezer for 2 hours.

1 When the lobster is very cold and no longer moving, place it on a chopping board and drive the tip of a large, sharp heavy knife or a very strong skewer through the centre of the cross on its head.

2 Alternatively, put the lobster in a large pan of cold, salted water and bring slowly to the boil. It will expire before the water boils.

3 You can also add the comatose lobster to a large pan of boiling water. Plunge it in head first and immediately clamp on the lid. Bring the water back to the boil.

4 To cook, lower the heat and simmer for 15 minutes for the first 450g/1lb and then allow 10 minutes more for each subsequent 450g/1lb, up to a maximum of 40 minutes.

5 When cooked, the lobster will turn a deep brick red. Drain off the water and leave to cool, if not eating hot.

If cooking two or more lobsters in the same pan, bring the water back to the boil before adding the second one. Cook more than two lobsters separately.

Always buy cooked lobsters or crabs from a reputable supplier. The colour of the crustaceans should be vibrant and they should feel heavy for their size. Cooked lobsters should have their tails tightly curled under their bodies.

Removing the Meat from a Boiled Lobster

1 Lay the lobster on its back and twist off the large legs and claws. Crack open the claws with a wooden mallet or the flat blade of a heavy knife and remove the meat, keeping the pieces as large as possible. Scoop out the meat from the legs with a lobster pick.

2 On a chopping board, stretch out the body of the lobster so that its tail is extended. Turn it on to its back and, using a sharp, heavy knife, cut the lobster neatly in half along its entire length.

3 Discard the whitish sac and feathery gills from the head and the grey-black intestinal thread that runs down the tail.

4 Remove all the meat from the tail. Keep the greenish tomalley (liver) and the coral (roe). The roe is only found in the female lobster. The tomalley, roe and creamy flesh close to the shell can be used in sauces.

Grilling/Broiling Lobster

1 Preheat the grill (broiler) to high. Boil the lobster for 3 minutes only, then drain, split in half lengthways and clean.

2 Lay the lobster halves cut-side up in a grill (broiling) pan, brush with melted butter and grill for about 10 minutes, spooning on more melted butter halfway through.

If the lobster has already been killed by stabbing, it can be split in half and grilled for about 12 minutes without being parboiled first.

Preparing a Live Crab

To kill a crab humanely, chill it by submerging it in ice, or leave it in the freezer for about 2 hours until it is comatose.

1 Lay the comatose crab on its back, lift up the tail flap and look for a small hole at the base of a distinct groove. Drive an awl or sturdy skewer into this hole, then carefully push the skewer between the mouth plates between the eyes.

2 Alternatively, the live crab can be killed and cooked simultaneously. Either plunge it into a large pan of boiling salted water, bring the water back to the boil and cook for 10–12 minutes; or place it in a pan of cold salted water and bring it slowly to the boil. Calculate the cooking time from the moment that the water boils, and do not boil the crab for more than 12 minutes.

Removing the Meat from a Cooked Crab

1 Lay the cooked crab on its back. Hold firmly and break off the tail flap. Twist off the claws and legs.

2 Stand the crab on its head and insert a heavy knife between the body and shell. Twist the knife firmly to separate them so that you can lift the honeycomb body out, or hold the crab firmly and use your thumbs to ease the body out of the shell.

3 Remove and discard the feathery, grey gills which are attached to either side of the body. Press down on the top shell to detach the spongy stomach sac, which is behind the mouth. Cut the body into quarters.

4 Carefully pick out the white meat. Scoop out the creamy brown meat from the back shell, then scoop out the thin solid brown meat from inside the flaps.

5 Crack open the claws and legs with a mallet, then remove the claw meat in the largest possible pieces. Pick or scrape out the leg meat. The smallest legs can be kept whole and used to make a shellfish stock.

Prawns, Shrimps, Langoustines and Crayfish

In North America, prawns, shrimps and langoustines are known collectively as shrimp. In the rest of the world shrimps are a separate small species.

Buying and Storing

Prawns and shrimps are not sold alive, but crayfish must be. All fresh raw prawns and shrimps should have crisp, firm shells and a fresh smell. If you have to buy frozen shellfish, get them into your freezer as soon as possible after purchase.

If you buy them with the shells on, allow about 300g/11oz prawns or shrimps per serving. There will be a lot of wastage once the shells are removed so buy a generous amount. Reserve the shells to flavour sauces, stocks and soups.

Fresh prawns and shrimps should be eaten as soon as possible after purchase. It is best to purge crayfish after capture or purchase. Place them in a large bowl, cover with a very damp dishtowel and leave in the coldest part of the refrigerator for 24 hours.

Poaching Langoustines or Prawns

Raw langoustines or prawns are best poached in sea water. Failing that, use a well-flavoured fish stock or heavily salted water. Bring the poaching liquid to the boil in a large, deep pan, drop in the crustaceans and simmer for only a minute or two, depending on their size.

Peeling and Deveining Raw Prawns

Raw prawns and large shrimps are often peeled before cooking. Raw prawns must have their intestinal tracts removed before cooking. This is known as deveining.
1 Pull off the head and legs then carefully peel off the body shell with your fingers. Leave on the tail fan if you wish.

2 To remove the black intestinal vein, make a shallow incision down the centre of the curved back of the prawn, cutting from the tail to the head.
3 Carefully pick out and discard the thin black vein that runs the length of the prawn.

Grilling or Barbecuing Langoustines, Large Prawns or Crayfish

Both raw and cooked langoustines, prawns and crayfish can be grilled (broiled). This cooking method gives delicious results.
1 Preheat the grill (broiler) or barbecue to hot. Butterfly the shellfish by laying them on their backs and splitting them in half lengthways, without cutting right through to the back shell.
2 Open the shellfish out like a book and brush the cut sides all over with a mixture of olive oil and lemon juice.
3 Lay in a grill pan or on the barbecue rack. Grill raw shellfish for 2–3 minutes on each side and cooked shellfish for half that time.

Peeling Cooked Prawns, Langoustines and Crayfish

1 Twist off the heads and, in the case of langoustines, the claws.
2 Squeeze the shellfish along their length and pull off the shell and the legs.
3 To keep the tail fan, carefully peel off the last piece of body shell, otherwise, squeeze the end of the tail and remove.

Sea Urchins
These edible sea creatures do not fall into the standard categories of crustaceans, molluscs and cephalopods. They are a popular delicacy in France, where they are served raw, or lightly cooked in salted water and eaten like boiled eggs. The tops are sliced off and fingers of bread are then dipped into the coral flesh.

MOLLUSCS

These soft-bodied shellfish are covered by a hard shell in one or more pieces. They can be divided into two main categories – bivalves and gastropods.

BIVALVES (MUSSELS, CLAMS, OYSTERS AND SCALLOPS)

These have thin shells hinged together, which are closed by a strong muscle.

Buying and Storing

Most molluscs must be alive when you cook them. Scallops are an exception, as they are often sold already opened and cleaned. Bivalves should contain plenty of sea water and feel heavy for their size. Do not buy any that have broken shells. If the shells gape, give them a sharp tap on a hard surface. They should snap shut immediately; if they do not, do not buy them. Allow about 450g/1lb per person. Four or five scallops will serve one person.

The general rule is to eat bivalves within one day of purchase. Tip them into a large bowl, cover with a damp cloth and keep them in the coldest part of the refrigerator (at 2°C/36°F) until ready to use. Oysters can be kept for a couple of days, thanks to the sea water contained in their shells. Store them cupped-side down. Never store shellfish in fresh water. Ready-frozen bivalves should be kept in the freezer for no more than 2 months.

Preparing

Scrub bivalves under cold running water, using a stiff brush to remove any sand or dirt. Open the shellfish over a bowl to catch the delicious juice. This will be gritty, so must be strained before being used in a sauce or stock. Cockles usually contain a lot of sand. They will expel this if left overnight in a bucket of clean sea or salted water.

Cleaning Mussels

1 Scrub the mussels well in plenty of cold water. Scrape off any barnacles with a knife.
2 Give any open mussels a sharp tap and discard any that fail to close. Pull out and discard the fibrous "beard" between the two halves of the shell.

Steaming Mussels, Clams, Cockles and Razorshells

This method opens and cooks the shellfish at the same time.
1 Put a few splashes of white wine into a wide pan with some finely chopped onion and fresh herbs and bring to the boil.
2 Add the shellfish, cover the pan and shake over a high heat for 2–3 minutes. Remove the shellfish that have opened.
3 Replace the lid and shake the pan over a high heat for another minute or so. Remove the remaining opened shellfish and discard any that stay closed.
4 Strain the cooking liquid. It can be reheated and used as a thin sauce, or heated until it has reduced by about half. For a richer sauce, stir in a little cream.

Grilling Mussels and Clams

Steam open the molluscs and remove the top shell. Arrange in their half shells in a single layer on a baking tray. Spoon over melted butter, and chopped garlic and parsley. Top with fresh breadcrumbs, a little more melted butter and cook under a hot grill (broiler) until golden brown and bubbling.

Opening Clams and Razorshells

This method should be used if clams or razorshells are to be eaten raw.

1 Protect your hand with a clean dishtowel, then cup the clam in your palm, holding it firmly. Work over a bowl to catch the juices.

2 Insert a sharp-pointed knife between the shells. Run the knife away from you to open the clam, twisting it to force the shells apart.

3 Cut through the hinge muscle, then use a spoon to scoop out the muscle on the bottom shell. Discard this part.

Opening Scallops in the Oven

1 Preheat the oven to 160°C/325°F/Gas 3. Spread the scallops in a single layer on a baking sheet. Heat them until they gape, then remove them from the oven.

2 Grasp a scallop in a clean dishtowel, flat-side up. Using a long, flexible knife, run the blade along the inner surface of the flat shell to cut through the muscle.

3 Lift off the top shell. Discard the black intestinal sac and the yellowish membrane.

4 Cut the white scallop and orange coral from the bottom shell and wash briefly under cold running water. Discard the white ligament attached to the scallop flesh.

Cooking Scallops

Small scallops need to be cooked only for a few seconds; larger ones take a minute or two. Scallops can be grilled (broiled) pan-fried, steamed, poached and baked. Wrap scallops in thin strips of streaky bacon or pancetta before grilling, if you like.

Opening Oysters

You really need a special oyster knife to open oysters. If you haven't got one, use a strong knife with a short, blunt blade.

1 Scrub the shells. Wrap one hand in a clean dishtowel. Hold the oyster with the cupped shell down and the hinge towards you.

2 Push the point of the knife into the small gap in the hinge and twist it to and fro until the hinge breaks. Lever open the top shell.

3 Slide the knife along the inner edges of the top shell. Sever the muscle joining the oyster to the shell. Lift off the top shell, leaving the oyster in its juices in the bottom shell.

Cooking Oysters

Oysters are best eaten raw with just a squeeze of lemon or a dash of Tabasco sauce. If you prefer to cook them, do so very briefly. They can be poached or steamed for a minute or two and served with a white wine sauce; grilled (broiled) like mussels or clams or deep-fried in cornmeal batter.

GASTROPODS (ABALONE, WINKLES AND WHELKS)

These snail-like shellfish have only one shell. Small gastropods need only a quick rinse under cold running water. They are removed from the shell after cooking using a small fork or pin. Larger gastropods such as abalone must be removed from the shell and beaten to tenderize before cooking.

Cooking Abalone or Ormers

There are two ways of cooking abalone: marinate the flesh, then cook it briefly in butter, or cook it slowly for a long time. Be sure to beat the abalone thoroughly first.

Boiling Winkles or Whelks

Ideally, these should be boiled in sea water. Otherwise, use heavily salted water. Add the winkles or whelks to the boiling salt water and simmer for 5 minutes for winkles; 10 minutes for whelks.

To test whether winkles or whelks are ready, use a fork or dressmaker's pin to remove the body from the shell. It should come out easily. If not, cook for a little longer, but do not overcook.

Cephalopods (Octopus, Squid, Cuttlefish)

These marine molluscs do not have an external shell but contain a small "quill" inside their bodies.

Buying and Storing

Large octopus are usually sold already prepared. Small octopuses can be dealt with in much the same way as squid, but their flesh needs to be beaten with a wooden mallet before being cooked.

Most fishmongers and supermarkets now sell ready-cleaned squid, but cuttlefish are usually sold whole. Both are easy to clean. When buying fresh squid or cuttlefish, look for ones that smell fresh and salty, have good colour and are slippery.

As a general guide, 1kg/2¼lb octopus, squid or cuttlefish will be more than ample for six people. Store as for fish.

Cleaning and Preparing Octopus

1 Cut the tentacles off the octopus and remove the beak and eyes. Cut off the head where it joins the body and discard it. Turn the body inside out and discard the entrails. Rinse thoroughly under cold water.

2 Pound the body and tentacles with a mallet until tender, then place in a pan of boiling water and simmer very gently for at least 1 hour, or until tender. Serve with a flavoursome sauce.

Cleaning and Preparing Squid

1 Rinse the squid thoroughly under cold running water. Holding the body firmly in one hand, grasp the tentacles at the base with the other, and gently but firmly pull the head away from the body. As you do this the soft yellowish entrails will come away.

2 Use a sharp knife to cut off the tentacles from the head of the squid. Reserve tentacles but discard the hard beak inside.

3 Remove and reserve the ink sac, then discard the head. Peel the purplish-grey membrane away from the body. Pull out the "quill" and wash the body. Cut the body, flaps and tentacles to the required size.

Squid Ink

This black ink can be used as a flavouring and colouring for home-made pasta and risotto, or to make a rich sauce. Having removed the ink sac from the squid, put it in a small bowl. Pierce it with the tip of a knife to release the thick ink. Dilute this with a little water and stir until smooth. Use at once, or freeze for later use.

There is ink in an octopus too. It is found in the liver and is very strongly flavoured. Like squid ink, it should be diluted in water before being used.

Cooking Squid

Squid can be cut into rings and deep-fried, stewed, stuffed and baked, or stir-fried.

1 For stir-frying, slit the body from top to bottom and turn it inside out. Flatten it and score the inside lightly with a knife.

2 Cut each piece lengthways into ribbons. These will curl when stir-fried.

Cleaning and Preparing Cuttlefish

Cut off the tentacles and remove the beak from the cuttlefish. Along the length of the body you will see the dark line of the cuttle bone. Cut along this line and remove the cuttle bone. Prepare in the same way as squid. The body is usually left whole.

SEAFISH

There are two main categories of seafish: round and flat. The nutritious oil of white fish is concentrated in the liver. In oily fish, this oil is dispersed throughout the flesh. Oily fish tend to swim in shoals near the surface of the sea. Flat fish spend most of their time sitting on the sea bed and do very little swimming. Consequently they have delicate white flesh with little muscle tone.

ROUND WHITE FISH

There are many different families of fish within this large group of seafish, including sea bass, sea bream and cod.

THE SEA BASS AND GROUPER FAMILY

This large and important family of fish is known as *perciformes* because they all share some of the characteristics of perch. They have some spiny fins, a v-shaped tail and pectoral fins set high on the body. The pelvic fins have one spiny ray each.

Various species are found in the Indian and Pacific Oceans and the Caribbean, and also in Mediterranean and Atlantic waters.

Sea Bass (*Dicentrarchus labrax*)

These have an elegant, sleek shape and a silvery body with a darker back and a white belly. They can grow to a length of 90cm/36in and weigh up to 7kg/15½lb, although the average weight is 1–3kg/2¼–6½lb.

Habitat Sea bass are voracious predators that live in small shoals close to rocky coasts around Great Britain and the Mediterranean. They can also be found in saltwater lakes and large river estuaries. They can be caught in traps or trawled, but the best are line-caught. Wild fish have become very expensive – but sea bass can be farmed.

Other names The French for sea bass is *bar*; due to their ferocity, they are also known as *loup de mer* (sea wolf). In Italian, they are *spigola* or *branzino*; in Spanish, *lubina*.

Buying Sea bass are available all year round, as whole fish or as fillets. They are best in spring and early summer, before they spawn. Line-caught, wild sea bass have the finest texture and flavour, but farmed fish are acceptable and cheaper. Look for bright, silvery skin and clear eyes. Allow about 200g/7oz per serving.

Cooking Sea bass have few small bones and fine, firm flesh that holds its shape well. They have a delicate flavour and can be cooked by almost any method – grilled (broiled), baked, braised, poached, shallow- or stir-fried or steamed.

A whole poached sea bass, skinned and served cold with mayonnaise, makes a great party dish. Plainly cooked sea bass can be served with any number of sauces, from *beurre blanc* to fresh tomato coulis and Oriental sesame dressing. A classic French dish is *bar au fenouil*, grilled sea bass served on a bed of fennel twigs flamed with Pernod. Sea bass are highly prized in China,

SCALING SEA BASS

The skin of sea bass is excellent to eat and it becomes deliciously crisp when grilled (broiled) or pan-fried. It does, however, have very hard scales, so it is essential to scale sea bass before cooking. Ask your fishmonger to do this, or follow the instructions in the section on Buying and Preparing Fish.

where they are braised with fresh root ginger and spring onions (scallions), while the Japanese slice the flesh wafer-thin and use it raw for sashimi.

Alternatives Good substitutes to use in most recipes are grey mullet, sea bream, grouper and John Dory.

Other varieties Speckled bass (*Dicentrus punctatus)* has small black spots on its back and sides. It is found mainly in the southern Mediterranean and is very similar to sea bass. Two other varieties, striped bass and black bass, come from North America and southern seas. Both are excellent fish.

Stone Bass/Wreckfish (*Polyprion americanum*)

This ugly cousin of the sea bass lives in deep Atlantic waters, often amid wrecked ships, which is how it came by its alternative name. This makes it difficult to catch; it can only be line-fished at a depth of more than 150m/500ft, so it is seldom found in shops and markets. Its Italian name is *cernia di fondale* (bass from the deep). It has dark skin and large, bony fins and the end of its tail is straight, not v-shaped like the tails of other types of bass.

Cooking If you do find stone bass for sale, it is likely to be as fillets or steaks, which can be cooked in the same way as any other white fish.

Comber (*Serranus*)

These smaller members of the grouper family have reddish or brownish skin with wide vertical markings. *Serranus scriba* is so called because its markings are said to resemble scribbles.

Cooking Comber have delicious, firm white flesh. The whole fish can be poached, steamed, braised or baked in the oven. Fillets and steaks can be grilled (broiled), pan-fried or steamed.

THE SEA BREAM FAMILY

There are about two hundred species of sea bream, some of which, unusually for seafish, are vegetarian. They have tall, compact bodies and slightly snub noses.

Habitat Sea bream are found in all warm and temperate coastal waters, including the Atlantic, up to the Bay of Biscay.

Gilt-head Bream (*Sparus aurata*)

This beautiful fish has silver scales, a gold spot on each cheek and a golden crescent in the middle of its head from which it takes its name. Its dense, juicy white flesh has been highly prized for thousands of years; the ancient Greeks and Romans considered it a fish fit for feasting. Gilt-head breams are hermaphrodite, starting life as male and becoming female as they mature.

Other names Gilt-heads are also known as royal bream. Sometimes in English they are called daurade (also spelt *dorade*), as in French. The Italian name is *orata*, the Spanish is *dorada*.

Buying Gilt-heads grow to a length of 60cm/24in and can weigh up to 3kg/6½lb. They are sold whole or as fillets. There is a lot of wastage, which makes this quite an expensive fish. Nowadays, gilt-heads are farmed successfully in the Mediterranean, which makes them less costly. Fresh fish should have bright, shiny scales.

Cooking All bream have wide scales that must be removed before cooking. Whole gilt-head bream can be treated like sea bass or sole – baked, grilled (broiled), poached, steamed in seaweed, or braised. The flesh should be scored on both sides before the fish is grilled or baked whole, to ensure even cooking. The dense flesh is robust and can withstand spicy or aromatic flavours.

Gilt-head fillets can be pan-fried, grilled or baked. Extremely fresh fish can be used raw to make sashimi.

Red Bream (*Pagellus bogaraveo*)

This tall, rosy-red fish has a pronounced black spot above the pectoral fin on each shoulder. It grows to about 50cm/20in and is usually sold already filleted. It lives deep in the sea and feeds on crustaceans and molluscs, which make it particularly tasty. Red bream is found in northern European waters, but swims southwards in winter to spawn, and is a much sought after fish in Spain and Portugal.

Other names Young red bream have small blue spots on their backs and are sometimes known as blue-spotted bream. In French, red bream is called *dorade commune* (common bream); the Italians call it *pagro*, *pagello* or *occhialone*, meaning big eye. The Spaniards call it *besugo*.

Cooking Extremely fresh red bream can be eaten raw as *sashimi*. Whole fish and fillets should be cooked in the same way as snapper, bass or red mullet.

Black Bream (*Spondyliosoma cantharus*)

This large bream is sometimes found in the North Sea. It is actually dark grey, with beautiful golden stripes running from head to tail. Unlike the gilt-head, it is unisexual and monogamous. Like gilt-head bream, it can be baked, grilled (broiled), poached, steamed in seaweed, or braised. The flavour and texture are similar, but not as fine.

Ray's Bream (*Brama brama*)

These large, shoaling fish live in depths of 100m/328ft and below, but come up to the surface in summer, sometimes with tragic consequences, as the eponymous John Ray found when he discovered huge quantities of the fish stranded on the coast of Britain in the 17th century. Ray's bream are brownish-grey, with firm flesh and a good flavour. They should be cooked in the same way as other bream.

UNUSUAL SPECIES OF BREAM

Among the many varieties of bream, there are a number whose names describe their decorative appearance. The two-banded bream, which makes very good eating, has two distinct vertical black bands fore and aft. Annular bream, which is the smallest of its group, has a dark ring around its tail, as does saddled bream, while sheepshead bream has an upturned snout. The small varieties of bream, such as annular and saddled, are used for soup. Bream can also be stuffed and grilled (broiled) over a wood fire.

Dentex (*Dentex dentex*)

These relatives of the sea bream are particularly popular in Mediterranean countries, in whose waters they are found. They are also found to a lesser extent in the East Atlantic. Their colour varies with their age; young dentex are grey, changing first to reddish pink, then to a beautiful steel blue with a sprinkling of dark spots.

Other names *Denté* in French; *dentice* in Italian; *dentón* in Spanish.

Cooking Although dentex can grow up to 1m/39in in length, they are best eaten when about 30cm/12in long. Fish this size can be grilled (broiled) whole or baked with herbs. Larger specimens should be cut into steaks and grilled or fried.

Porgy (*Pagrus pagrus*)

The eponymous hero of Porgy and Bess took his name from these rosy-tinted North American relatives of the bass, variations of which are also found in the Atlantic coastal waters around Africa. Porgies grow to a length of up to 75cm/30in and can be cooked whole or as steaks – baked, grilled (broiled), poached, steamed, or braised, using any of the recipes for bream.

THE COD FAMILY

This large family of fish includes haddock, hake, whiting and many other related species of white-fleshed fish. Most come from the Atlantic and other cold northerly waters, although hake is found in the warmer Mediterranean.

Cod (*Gadus morruha*)

Long, torpedo-shaped fish with vibrant yellowish-brown mottled skin and a whitish belly, cod have a large head with a snub nose, a protruding upper jaw and a whiskery barbel on the chin that acts as a sensor as they search for food on the sea bed. They can live to over twenty years and grow to a length of 6m/20ft (weighing up to 50kg/110lb), although such specimens are sadly rare, and most commercially-fished cod weigh 3–8kg/6½–17½lb.

Habitat Cod prefer to live in cold water with a high salt content. They hatch in huge numbers close to the surface of the water, but gravitate down to the sea bed where they feed on crustaceans, molluscs and worms. Large cod feed on smaller fish. Cod can be caught in trawler nets or line-caught.

For years, cod was so plentiful that it was regarded as an inferior fish, fit only to be fried with chips or masked with white sauce. All too often, its succulent, flaky white flesh was overcooked, making it watery or dry. Today, overfishing has depleted stocks so much that now it has become relatively scarce and subsequently more highly appreciated. As the great French chef, Auguste Escoffier, predicted in the 19th century: "If cod were less common, it would be held in as high esteem as salmon"; (at that time, regarded as the king of fish) "for, when it is really fresh and of good quality, the delicacy and delicious flavour of its flesh admit of its ranking among the finest of fish."

Other names In France, fresh cod is called *cabillaud*. In Italy, it is *merluzzo* and in Spain, *bacalao* (which can mean salt cod).

Buying Cod is most commonly trawled or netted, but it can also be line-caught. The first two methods can damage the delicate flesh, so try to buy line-caught fish.

When buying a whole small cod, or codling, the skin should be shiny and clear. There is a lot of wastage in whole cod, which makes these fish very expensive, so they are more usually sold as steaks and fillets. Shoulder steaks have the finest flavour. Buy thick cuts from the shoulder or middle of the fish and always check that the flesh is very white. Never buy cod with discoloured patches. The fresher the fish, the firmer and flakier the flesh will be.

Frozen cod is usually frozen at sea to retain freshness and flavour, but is never as good as fresh fish. It is available as steaks, fillets, breaded cuts and fish fingers.

COD PRODUCTS

Fresh cod can be salted or dried (see Dried and Salted Fish). The roe is often smoked and used to make the Greek spread taramasalata. *The liver produces cod liver oil, which tastes rather unpleasant but is very good for you. Cod liver oil is available in liquid and capsule form.*

Cooking Cod holds its texture well and can be cooked in many different ways, but it is vitally important not to overcook it. The flavour is robust enough to take quite strong and spicy flavours. Whole fish can be poached in a court-bouillon and served cold with mayonnaise or tartar sauce. Cod can also be baked or roasted in the oven or braised in white wine.

Most cooking methods are suitable for cod fillets and steaks, except for grilling (broiling), which can destroy the flaky texture. They can be poached, steamed, braised in tomato sauce or topped with a crust of breadcrumbs and herbs and baked. They are also delicious floured and sautéed, or coated with batter and deep-fried. Cod makes an excellent substitute for more exotic fish in curries. A classic English dish is poached cod with parsley sauce. Fresh and smoked cod fillets can be used to make fish cakes, croquettes, old fashioned fish pies, salads and mousses.

Alternatives Any firm-fleshed white fish can be substituted for cod, including flat fish such as brill, halibut and turbot.

Coley (*Pollachius virens*)

Traditionally regarded as a poor relation of cod, fit only for feeding to the cat, coley has rather unappealing greyish flesh, which is responsible for its low price. Long and slim, the fish has a protruding lower jaw and no barbel. The skin on the back is dark grey, lightening to mottled yellow on the sides and almost white on the belly. Coley generally weigh 5–10kg/11–22lb, but they can be smaller.

Habitat Coley live in huge shoals in both deep waters and near to the surface. They prefer cold, very salty water. They are voracious predators who prey on herring and have cannibalistic tendencies.

Other names Coley are also known as saithe, coalfish and pollock (not to be confused with pollack). In French, they are *lieu noir*, in Italian *merluzzo nero* and in Spanish *abadejo*.

Buying Coley are sometimes sold whole, weighing 1–4kg/2¼–8¾lb, but are more usually sold as steaks, cutlets and fillets. The unattractive grey flesh looks off-putting, but whitens during cooking. It should feel firm to the touch. Coley must be extremely fresh, otherwise there is a risk of the flesh becoming woolly and unpleasant.

WHITENING COLEY

Coley flesh is a rather unappetizing grey colour. To help whiten the flesh, many cooks recommend rubbing it with freshly squeezed lemon juice before cooking, as this tends to reduce its greyish tinge.

Cooking Coley is less fine than cod in texture and flavour. Its grey colour can be masked by coating the fish in batter or using it in a fish pie, casserole or fish cakes. It will withstand robust flavours and can be baked, braised, grilled (broiled) or fried. Smoked coley has an excellent flavour, but is seldom available commercially. It is worth trying if you have a home smoker.

Alternatives Haddock, cod or any firm-fleshed white fish can usually be used in place of coley.

Haddock (*Melanogrammus aeglefinus*)

These fish are generally smaller than cod, growing up to 1m/39in long and weighing 1–2kg/2¼–4½lb. They have dark brownish-grey skin with a black lateral line and a black spot just above the pectoral fin, which is said to be the thumbprint of St Peter. Their eyes are large and prominent. They live close to the sea bed and prefer water with a high salt content.

Habitat Haddock are shoaling fish that live at the bottom of cold northern seas in Europe and North America. They feed on molluscs, worms and other small fish and spawn in the coldest, saltiest water they can find, off the coast of Norway and the Faroes, for example.

Other names In North America, haddock are known as scrod. In French, the fish is called *aiglefin* (from the Latin name). Confusingly, the French name for smoked haddock is *haddock*. In Italian, haddock is *asinello*; in Spanish it is *eglefino*.

Buying Fresh haddock is at its best in winter and early spring, when the cold has firmed up the flesh. You may find whole small haddock (weighing 450g–2kg/1–4½lb) at the fishmonger's, but the fish is usually sold as fillets. Before you buy, prod the flesh to make sure that it is firm.

Cooking Fresh haddock is versatile and can be cooked in the same way as cod. When cooking it whole, leave the skin on to hold the delicate flesh together.

Haddock is the perfect fish for deep-frying and it makes wonderful fish and chips (French fries). It also makes excellent fish lasagne and pie, especially mixed with an equal quantity of smoked haddock.

Alternatives Haddock is often considered to be interchangeable with cod, but its white flesh has a more delicate flavour and a softer, less flaky texture.

Hake (*Merluccius merluccius*)

This most elegant member of the cod family is a long, slim fish with two spiny dorsal fins, bulging eyes and a protruding lower jaw without a barbel. The head and back are steely grey and the belly is silvery white. The inside of the mouth and gills is black. A mature fish can grow up to 1m/39in, but the average length is 30–50cm/12–20in.

Habitat Hake are found in most temperate and cold waters. By day, they live near the sea bed, but at night they move to the surface to hunt oily fish.

Other names The French call hake by several names: *merlu*, *colin* and *merluchon* (small immature fish). The Spanish call it *merluza*. In Italian, it is *nasello*. In North America, hake is known as whiting, though it is far superior to the European whiting.

Buying As a result of overfishing, hake are becoming quite scarce and expensive. Hake can be trawled or caught on long lines. Try to buy line-caught fish, which have a better texture. Hake must be very fresh, or it becomes flabby. The flesh has a pinkish tinge; it will always feel soft to the touch, but should never feel limp. Whole fish should have bright eyes and smell of the sea.

When calculating how much hake to buy, allow for 40 per cent wastage for whole fish. Keep the head, as it makes particularly good soup or fish stock.

Hake is usually sold as cutlets or steaks. Those cut from near the head have the best flavour. The fish has few bones, and these are easy to remove. Avoid buying fillets, as they tend to disintegrate during cooking.

Cooking Whole hake can be poached, baked or braised in wine, lemon juice and fresh herbs. Like all fish, it should never be overcooked. Steaks can be grilled (broiled), coated in egg and breadcrumbs and deep-fried, or sautéed in olive oil and garlic. They can also be layered with potatoes and onions, or with tomatoes and cheese and baked *au gratin*. Light buttery sauces go well with hake, as does piquant caper sauce. Shellfish such as mussels and clams are perfect partners. A popular Spanish hors d'oeuvre is *escabeche*, cold marinated hake.

Alternatives Haddock or cod can be substituted for hake in any recipe.

Other varieties North American silver hake is a small, streamlined fish with an excellent flavour. Varieties of hake are also found in the warmer waters of South America and southern Africa, but do not taste as good as northern hake.

Pollack (*Pollachius pollachius*)

These attractive fish have steely grey backs and greenish-yellow bodies. They have a jutting lower jaw and no barbel. Pollack are smaller than cod (less than 1m/39in long).

Habitat Pollack can live either in shoals near the surface of the sea, where they feed on sprats and herrings, or close to the bottom where they eat deep-sea prawns (shrimp) and sand-eels.

Other names Its yellow colour gives pollack the name of *lieu jaune* in French, *merluzzo giallo* in Italian and *abadejo* in Spanish.

Buying Pollack are at their best in autumn and winter. They are usually sold as fillets, cutlets or steaks. If you need a whole fish, look for a superior line-caught specimen.

Cooking Pollack has a drier texture and less pronounced flavour than cod, so it benefits from a creamy, highly flavoured sauce. It is good for fish pies, soups, baking, braising, deep-frying or sautéeing. It can be used in place of cod, haddock or hake in any recipe.

Pouting (*Trisopterus luscus*)

This is a poor (and cheap) relation of the whiting. It is comparatively small (about 25cm/10in long), with brown papery skin.

Other names It is also known as pout. In French it is *tacaud*, in Italian *merluzzo francese* and in Spanish *faneca*.

Buying Pouting goes off extremely quickly and must be eaten very fresh. If possible, buy a whole fish and ask the fishmonger to fillet it for you.

Cooking As for whiting.

Whiting (*Merlangus merlangus*)

Similar in appearance to haddock, whiting are small fish (about 30–40cm/12–16in long). They have greenish-grey skin, a silvery belly and a black spot at the base of the pectoral fin. The head is pointed, with a protruding upper jaw and no barbel.

Habitat Whiting are found all over the Atlantic, from Iceland to northern Spain. They feed on crustaceans and small fish such as sand-eels and herrings, and are often found near rocky shores.

Other names Whiting's old name was merling. The French call it *merlan*, the Italians *merlano* and the Spanish *merlán*. Do not confuse it with North American whiting, which is actually hake.

Buying Whiting is abundant all year round. It is cheap and tends to be undervalued. However, really fresh whiting is well worth buying. Whole fish should be shiny. Fillets should be pearly white and feel soft but not flabby. Stale whiting may have a woolly texture and unpleasant taste, so make sure that you buy only absolutely fresh fish. Whiting are small, so allow two fillets per serving. They may be boned through the back, leaving the two fillets attached.

Cooking The whiting's meltingly tender flesh makes it an ideal basis for a soup, as it contributes a velvety texture. It is also excellent for quenelles and fish mousses. Whiting is a versatile fish that can be coated in breadcrumbs or batter and fried. It can also be pan-fried, grilled (broiled) or gently poached in wine or court-bouillon and served with a lemony sauce or flavoured butter. Always season whiting well.

Alternatives Plaice, flounder or sole can be used, and all the members of the cod family.

WHITING EN COLÈRE

A once immensely popular dish was merlan en colère *(angry whiting). Whole fish were baked with the skin on, then curled around so that their tails could be stuck through their eye sockets or into their mouths. Presumably the name came from the assumption that the fish was chasing its own tail in anger.*

THE GURNARD FAMILY

Gurnard are rather odd-looking fish with cylindrical bodies, high, armour-plated heads with wide mouths, and strange pectoral fins with the three lowest rays divided into "fingers". They emit a strange grunting, caused by vibrating the swim bladder. Gurnard weigh between 100g/3½oz and 2kg/4½lb. There are several types, which are distinguished by their colour; all have lean, white flesh with a firm texture but rather insipid taste. They are rich in iodine, phosphorus and protein.

Habitat Gurnard are found in the Atlantic and Mediterranean. They live on or near the sea bed, using their "fin fingers" to seek out the crabs, prawns (shrimp) and small fish that live in the sediment.

Other names Sea robin and gurnet. The French name, *grondin*, echoes the fish's grunting sound. In Italian, they are *capone*, meaning large head; in Spanish, *rubios*.

Grey Gurnard (*Eutrigla gurnardus*)

These fish have brownish-grey backs and silvery bellies. They grow to a maximum length of 45cm/18in. The lateral line is scaly and should be removed before cooking.

Red Gurnard (*Aspitrigla cuculus*)

This pinkish-red fish is the most attractive member of the gurnard family. It has bony extensions to the lateral line, which give it the appearance of vertical stripes on its back. It has the finest flavour of all the gurnards and is sometimes substituted for red mullet or snapper.

Tub Gurnard (*Trigla lucerna*)

This larger gurnard is orangey-brown with bright orange pectoral fins. It is an excellent swimmer and sometimes leaps right out of the water, which explains its alternative name of flying gurnard.

Buying Gurnard are bony fish with an unexceptional flavour, so they tend to be cheap. They are usually sold whole – ask the fishmonger to remove the spiny fins and the skin. Beware, especially in France, of buying red gurnard masquerading as red mullet (*rouget*). The latter is vastly superior.

Cooking Small gurnard are best used in soups and stocks. Larger fish can be braised or baked on a bed of vegetables with a little white wine. Take care when eating whole gurnard, as they are very bony. Fillets can be coated in egg and breadcrumbs and fried, or steamed and served with a sauce.

Alternatives Red or grey mullet can be used in any gurnard recipe.

Scorpion Fish (*Scorpaena scrofa, Scorpaena porcus*)

Like gurnard, scorpion fish have huge heads and armour-plated cheeks. Their enormous scaly heads have loose folds of skin above and between the eyes. The dorsal fin is made up of large poisonous spines. The smaller brown scorpion fish has a finer flavour than its larger cousin.

Habitat Scorpion fish are found throughout the Mediterranean and off the coast of North Africa. They also live in Atlantic waters, from the English Channel to Senegal.

Other names The French for scorpion fish is *rascasse* (*chapon* in the south of France). Italians call it *scorfano*; in Spanish it is *cabracho* or *rascacio*.

Buying Scorpion fish are usually sold whole. You should allow for wastage; a 2kg/4½lb fish will only serve four people.

Cooking Scorpion fish is best known as an essential ingredient in bouillabaisse. Whole fish can be baked or braised with fennel; fillets can be cooked *à l'antillaise*, braised with tomatoes, potatoes and red peppers.

Alternatives Monkfish, snapper, John Dory or gurnard can be used at a pinch.

THE MULLET FAMILY

Over a hundred different species of mullet are found in temperate and tropical seas. These belong to two main groups, which are unrelated and very different in both appearance and flavour. They are grey mullet and red mullet.

Grey Mullet (*family Mugilidae*)

Varieties of grey mullet are found all over the world. These beautiful silvery fish resemble sea bass, but have larger scales and small mouths, suited to their diet of seaweed and plankton. They are shoaling fish that live around the sea bed, so they sometimes smell and taste rather muddy. A good grey mullet has lean, slightly soft, creamy white flesh with a pleasant flavour.

Habitat Grey mullet are found in coastal waters and estuaries all over the world.

Varieties The finest is the golden mullet (*Liza aurata*), which has a thin upper lip and gold spots on its head and the front of the body. It is one of the smallest mullets, growing only to about 45cm/18in long. In French, it is known as *mulet doré*. The thick-lipped mullet (*Crenimugil* or *Chelon labrosus*) has, as its name suggests, thick lips and a rounded body. This mullet is sometimes farmed. The thin-lipped mullet (*Liza ramada*) has a golden sheen, a thin upper lip and a pointed snout, which gives it its French name of *mulet porc*.

The largest mullet is the common or striped grey mullet (*Mugil cephalus*), which can grow up to 70cm/28in. This fish has a brown body, silvery back and a large head. Its eyes are covered with a transparent membrane. In French it is called *mulet cabot*. There is also a small Mediterranean mullet whose main claim to fame is its ability to leap out of the water to escape predators. This variety is called the leaping grey mullet (*Liza saliens*).

Buying Except in France, you are unlikely to find differentiation between the varieties of grey mullet at the fishmonger. Try to choose fish that come from the high seas rather than estuaries, as the latter often have a muddy taste and can be flabby. Grey mullet are usually sold whole – ask the fishmonger to scale and skin them. Keep the roes. Larger fish may be sold filleted.

Cooking Grey mullet must be scaled before being cooked. Any muddiness can be eliminated by soaking the fish in several changes of acidulated water. Whole fish are very good stuffed with fennel and grilled (broiled). Slash the sides and add a splash of aniseed-flavoured alcohol before cooking the fish, and serve with a buttery sauce.

GREY MULLET ROE

This is a delicacy and can be eaten fresh, fried in butter or used in a stuffing for a baked fish. When salted and dried, mullet roe is the authentic basis of taramasalata *and* bottarga *or* boutargue.

Red Mullet (*Mullus surmuletus and Mullus barbatus*)

These are among the finest of seafish. They are small (up to 40cm/16in long), with pinkish-red skins streaked with gold. Their Roman-nosed heads have two long barbels on the chin. They have lean, firm flesh, which has a robust and distinctive flavour.

Other varieties *Mullus surmeletus* is more correctly known as *surmullet*; it has rosy red skin and is larger than *Mullus barbatus*, which has three yellowish stripes along each side and grows to a length of 30cm/12in.

Goatfish Types of red mullet known as goatfish because of their long, beard-like barbels are found in the Pacific and Indian Oceans. They are smaller (up to 20cm/8in long) and less colourful than cold-water mullet and have drier, less tasty flesh.

Habitat Red mullet are found in Atlantic and Mediterranean waters. They live on sandy or rocky areas of the sea bed, feeding on small sea creatures.

Other names Red mullet are sometimes known as woodcock of the sea, due to their gamey flavour when cooked complete with their liver. In the US, they are known as goatfish, regardless of size or place of origin. The French for mullet is *rouget*; depending on the variety, it is *rouget barbet*, *rouget de roche* or *rouget de vase* (*Mullus barbatus*). In Italian, red mullet is *triglia*; in Spanish, it is *salmonete de roca* (*Mullus surmuletus*) or *salmonete de fango* (*Mullus barbatus*).

Buying Red mullet has delicate flesh that is highly perishable, so it is essential to buy extremely fresh fish. They should have very bright skin and eyes and feel very firm. The scales should be firmly attached, not flaking off the skin. Because they are small, red mullet are usually sold whole, but large fish are sometimes filleted. The flesh is quite rich, so a 200g/7oz fish will be ample for one person. Ask the fishmonger to scale and gut it for you, and keep the liver.

Cooking The best ways to cook red mullet are grilling (broiling) and pan-frying. Score the sides before grilling a whole fish to ensure even cooking. Red mullet go well with Mediterranean flavours such as olive oil, saffron and tomatoes. They can be cooked *en papillote* with herbs, or made into mousses and soufflés. Very small, bony fish are often used in bouillabaisse.

THE WRASSE FAMILY

This large family of fish is notable for its varied and dazzling colours. Wrasse range from steely blue to green, orange and gold; in some species, the sexes have different colours. All wrasse have thick lips and an array of sharp teeth. They are small, seldom growing to more than 40cm/16in long.

Habitat Wrasse are found in both Atlantic and Mediterranean waters. They live near rocky coasts, feeding on barnacles and small crustaceans.

Varieties The most common type is the ballan wrasse (*Labrus berggylta*), which has greenish or brownish skin, with large scales tipped with gold. Male and female cuckoo wrasse (*Labrus mixtus*) have strikingly different coloration; the males are steely blue with almost black stripes, while the females are orangey-pink with three black spots under the dorsal fin. The five-spotted wrasse (*Symphonus quinquemaculatus*) has only five spots, while rainbow wrasse (*Coris julis*) have spiny dorsal fins and a red or orange band along their body.

Other names In French, wrasse is known as *vielle*, *coquette* and *labre*. In Italian, it is *labridi*; in Spanish *merlo*, *tordo* or *gallano*.

Buying Wrasse are available in spring and summer. Look for sparkling skin and bright eyes. Ask the fishmonger to scale and clean the fish. Allow 400g/14oz per serving.

Cooking Most wrasse are fit only for making soup, but some larger varieties, such as ballan wrasse, can be baked whole. Make a bed of sliced onions, garlic, smoked bacon and potatoes, bake in the oven at 200°C/400°F/Gas 6 until soft, then add the wrasse, moisten with white wine and bake for 10–15 minutes.

Oily Fish

Fish such as herrings, mackerel and sardines have always been popular because they are cheap and nutritious. In recent years they have received an excellent press, due to their natural health-giving properties. They contain protein and vitamins A, B and D, and essential omega-3 fatty acids, which are known to reduce the risk of clogged arteries, blood clots, strokes and even cancer. Most nutritionists recommend that you include at least one serving of oily fish in your diet every week. Oily fish swim near the surface of the sea and live in shoals that can be enormous.

The Herring Family

Clupeiformes, which include herrings and their relatives – sardines, anchovies, sprats and pilchards, are the largest family of oil-rich fish.

Herring (*Clupea harengus*)

There are numerous different varieties of herring, each confined to its own sea area – the North Sea, Baltic, White Sea (an inlet of the Barents sea), the coast of Norway and many other colder coastal areas. Herring are prodigiously fertile fish, which is a good thing as they have been overfished for centuries and are becoming more scarce.

Herring are slender silver fish with a central dorsal fin and large scales. They seldom grow to a length of more than 35cm/14in. Their oily flesh can be cured in many ways: smoking, salting, drying and marinating in vinegar and spices.

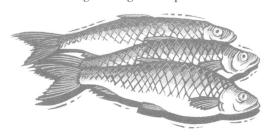

Habitat Herring live in huge shoals in cold northerly waters, where they feed on plankton. They are migratory fish that come inshore to spawn. They sometimes change their habitual route for no apparent reason, so there may be a glut of fish in a particular area for several years, but no herring at all the next year.

Varieties Herring are mostly known by the name of the region where they are located – North Sea, Baltic, for example. Each variety has its own spawning season, which influences the eating qualities of the fish.

Buying Like all oily fish, herring must be absolutely fresh, or they will taste rancid. They are at their best before they spawn. Look for large, firm fish with slippery skins and rounded bellies containing hard or soft roes; hard roes are the female eggs, soft roes the male milt. Soft herring roes are a particular delicacy. By running your hands along the belly of the fish, you will be able to tell whether the roes are hard or soft. If the fishmonger cleans them for you, be sure to keep the roe. Once herring have spawned, they lose condition and weight and their flesh becomes rather dry.

As herrings contain numerous soft bones, ask the fishmonger to bone or fillet them for you. They can be gutted either through the belly or through the gills.

Cooking The oiliness of the flesh makes herrings particularly suitable for grilling (broiling) and barbecuing. Slash whole fish on both sides to ensure even cooking. Herring are good served with a tart or acidic sauce to counteract the richness.

Whole herrings are excellent baked with a stuffing of breadcrumbs, chopped onions and apples. They are also good wrapped in bacon and grilled, or grilled with a mustard sauce. Both whole herrings and fillets are delicious rolled in oatmeal and then pan-fried in bacon fat. Serve with lemon juice.

Herring fillets can be made into fish balls, or cooked in a sweet-and-sour sauce made with tomato ketchup, wine vinegar, honey and Worcestershire sauce. They are also delicious soused in a vinegary marinade.

Fillets are also traditionally made into rollmops or smoked to make kippers – these processes are explored fully in the sections on Pickled and Smoked Fish.

Alternatives Sardines, sprats and mackerel can be cooked in the same way as herrings.

HERRING ROES
Soft roes have a creamy, melting texture. They can be tossed in seasoned flour, gently fried in butter and served as they are, or devilled with a little cayenne pepper and Worcestershire sauce and served on hot toast. They also make a delicious omelette filling. Poached in stock and mashed, they can be used as a spread, in a stuffing for whole baked herrings or added to a sauce or savoury tart filling. Hard roes have a grainy texture, which people tend either to love or loathe. They can be baked or braised under the fish to add extra flavour.

Anchovies (*Engraulis encrasicolus*)
These small, slender fish seldom grow to more than 16cm/6in; the average length is only 8–10cm/3–4in. They have steely blue backs and shimmering silver sides, and the upper jaw protrudes. Most anchovies are sold filleted and preserved in salt or oil, but fresh anchovies are quite delicious.

Habitat Anchovies are pelagic fish and are found in tightly packed shoals throughout the Mediterranean, in the Black Sea (where, sadly, pollution has depleted stocks) and the Atlantic and Pacific Oceans.

Other names In French, anchovy is known as *anchois*; in Italian *acciuga* or *alice*; and in Spanish *boquerón*.

Buying Fresh anchovies should be cooked and eaten as soon as they are caught. The Mediterranean produces the best anchovies, and these are at their peak in early summer. By the time they have been exported, they will have lost much of their delicate flavour. When buying, look for sparkling skins and bright, slightly bulging eyes.

Preparing Your fishmonger is unlikely to clean anchovies for you, but they are easy to prepare at home. To gut, cut off the head and press gently along the body with your thumb to squeeze out the innards. To fillet, run your thumbnail or a stubby blunt knife along the length of the spine from head to tail on both sides and lift off the fillets.

Freezing Since fresh anchovies are hard to come by, it is worth freezing them when there are plentiful supplies. Remove the heads and clean the fish, then pack them head-to-tail in a freezer box, separating the layers with sheets of clear film (plastic wrap). Cover the box with a lid and freeze. Defrost before using.

Cooking Whole anchovies can be grilled (broiled) or fried, or coated lightly in egg and flour and deep-fried. They make an excellent *gratin* when seasoned with olive oil and garlic, topped with breadcrumbs and baked. Fillets can be fried with garlic and parsley, or marinated in olive oil, onion, garlic, bay leaves and crushed peppercorns.

Sardines and Pilchards (*Sardinia pilchardus*)
Pilchards are larger, more mature sardines. The largest pilchards grow to 20cm/8in, while sardines may be only 13–15cm/5–6in long. They are slim fish, with blue-green backs and silvery bellies. They have thirty scales along the mid-line on either side. Their flesh is compact and has a delicious, oily flavour. Canned sardines and pilchards are very popular as a kitchen stand-by.

Habitat Sardines take their name from Sardinia, where they were once abundant. They are pelagic shoaling fish, and are found throughout the Mediterranean and Atlantic. Various related species are also found in other parts of the world.

Other names Sardines are easy to recognize on foreign menus: they are *sardine* in French; *sardina* in Italian and Spanish; and *pilchard* or *sardine* in German. Confusingly, the French use the word *pilchard* when speaking of canned herring.

Buying Sardines are at their best in spring and early summer. They do not travel well, so try to buy from local waters and avoid any damaged or stale-looking fish. Small sardines have the best flavour, but larger fish are better for stuffing. Depending on the size, allow 3–5 sardines per serving.

Cooking Sardines should be scaled and gutted before being cooked. This is easy to do; just cut the head almost through from the backbone and twist, pulling it towards you. The innards will come away with the head. Whole sardines are superb grilled (broiled) or barbecued, which crisps the skin. They can be coated in egg and breadcrumbs, fried and served with fresh tomato sauce, made into fritters or stuffed with capers, salted anchovies or Parmesan cheese and baked. They make an excellent sauce for pasta and are also delicious marinated and served raw.

Alternatives In most recipes, large anchovies, sprats or smelts can be used instead of small sardines.

Sprats (*Sprattus sprattus*)

These small silvery fish look very similar to sardines or immature herrings, but are slightly squatter. Once the sprat was an important fish, but they are seldom sold fresh these days, being mostly smoked or cured, or sold as fishmeal.

Habitat Sprats are abundant in the Baltic, North Sea and the Atlantic and are also found in fjords and estuaries. They are available fresh, smoked or canned in oil.

Other names *Sprat* in French, *papalina* in Italian and *espadin* in Spanish. Smoked sprats are called *brisling* in Norway.

Cooking Sprats can be cooked in the same way as anchovies and small sardines. They have very oily flesh and are delicious when fried in oatmeal or deep-fried in batter. Raw sprats can be marinated in vinaigrette.

Whitebait

This name is given to tiny silver fish – only about 5cm/2in in length – that are caught in summer as they swim up estuaries. The name can refer to immature sprats or herrings, or to a mixture of both fish.

Other names Whitebait are *blanchaille* in French; this name is also used to describe tiny freshwater fish. The Italian name for them is *bianchetti*; the Spanish *aladroch*.

Buying Whitebait do not need to be cleaned. They are available fresh in spring and summer, and frozen all year round. Allow 115g/4oz per person as an appetizer.

Cooking Whitebait are cooked whole. They are delicious deep-fried and served with brown bread and butter. Prepare them for cooking by dunking them in a bowl of milk, then shake them in a plastic bag containing flour seasoned with salt and a little cayenne pepper. Deep-fry until very crisp.

Mackerel (*Scomber scombrus*)

These streamlined fish are easily identified, thanks to their beautiful greenish-blue skin. They have wavy bands of black and green on their backs, while the bellies are silvery. The smooth, pale beigey-pink flesh is meaty, with a distinctive, full flavour.

Habitat Mackerel are pelagic shoaling fish, often found in huge numbers in the North Atlantic, North Sea and Mediterranean. They spend the winter near the bottom of the cold North Sea, not feeding at all.

Other names Larger mackerel are known as *maquereau* in French; small specimens are called *lisette*. In Italian, mackerel is called *sgombro* and in Spanish it is known as *caballa*.

Buying Mackerel are delicious when extremely fresh, but not worth eating when they are past their best. They are in their prime in late spring and early summer, just before spawning. Look for firm fish with iridescent skin and clear, bright eyes. Small mackerel are better than large fish. Larger specimens are sometimes sold filleted, and either sold fresh or smoked. Mackerel is a popular canned fish, and may be canned in either oil or tomato sauce.

Cooking Whole mackerel can be grilled (broiled), barbecued, braised or poached in court-bouillon, white wine or cider. Make slashes on both sides of each fish with a sharp knife before cooking over direct heat. Like herrings, they need a sharp sauce to counteract the oily richness of the flesh; traditional accompaniments include sorrel, gooseberry, horseradish or mustard sauce. Mackerel fillets can can be cooked in the same way as herring – either coated in oatmeal, pan-fried in bacon fat and served with a squeeze of lemon juice, or braised with onions and white wine. Raw mackerel fillets can be marinated in sweet-and-sour vinaigrette to make an appetizer.

OTHER VARIETIES OF MACKEREL

Chub mackerel (Scomber japonicus colias) *are similar to Atlantic mackerel, but are also found in the Mediterranean and Black Sea. They have larger eyes and less bold markings on their backs. Spanish mackerel* (Scomber colias) *have spots below the lateral line. The rarer* Orcynopsis unicolor *is found near the coast of North Africa. It has silvery skin with spots of gold.*

Horse mackerel (Trachurus trachurus) *or scad, and similar fish such as jack mackerel and round robin, resemble herrings and are not, despite their name, true relatives of mackerel. They are edible, but their flesh is rather insipid and they tend to be very bony. They can all be cooked in the same way as mackerel.*

"Blue" Fish

Although they are not related to each other, several species of oily fish are known collectively as "blue" fish (not to be confused with bluefish). All have smooth, taut skin with virtually undetectable scales and firm, meaty flesh. Varieties of "blue" fish are found in most temperate and tropical seas.

Bluefish (*Pomatomus saltatrix*)

Found in the Mediterranean and American Atlantic waters, bluefish are extremely aggressive and are often fished for sport. They often chase shoals of fish into harbour mouths. They have sheeny blue-green backs and masses of very sharp teeth. Bluefish are hugely popular in Turkey, where they are displayed in fish markets with their bright red gills turned inside out like elaborate rosettes to indicate their freshness. The flesh of bluefish is softer and more delicate than that of mackerel, but they can be cooked in the same way.

The Tuna Family

Tuna have been popular for centuries. They were highly prized by the Ancient Greeks, who mapped their migratory patterns in order to fish for them. The Phoenicians preserved tuna by salting and smoking them, and in the Middle Ages tuna were pickled. A shoal of immense tuna fish travelling through the high seas is a truly magnificent sight. These beautiful, torpedo-shaped fish can grow to an enormous size (up to 700kg/1540lb). They have very powerful muscles and firm, dark, meaty flesh. There are many varieties of tuna, but due to centuries of overfishing, only half a dozen varieties are available commercially.

Habitat Tuna are related to mackerel and are found in warmer seas throughout the world, as far north as the Bay of Biscay.

Other names Tuna is also known as tunny fish. In French, it is *thon*; in Italian *tonno*; in Spanish *atun*. In Japan it is called *maguro*.

Buying Tuna is usually sold as steaks. It is a very substantial fish, so allow only about 175g/6oz per serving. Depending on the variety, the flesh may range from pale beigey-pink to dark red. Do not buy steaks with heavy discolorations around the bone, or that are dull-looking and brownish. The flesh should be very firm and compact.

Cooking Tuna becomes greyish and dry when overcooked, so it is essential to cook it only briefly over high heat, or to stew it very gently with moist ingredients. It has become fashionable to sear tuna fleetingly, leaving it almost raw in the middle; if this is not to your taste, cook the tuna for about 2 minutes on each side – no more.

The following cooking methods are suitable for most types of tuna. Steaks can be seared, grilled (broiled), baked or braised. They benefit from being marinated for about 30 minutes before cooking. Tuna marries well with Mediterranean vegetables such as tomatoes, (bell) peppers and onions, as well as olives. Most varieties can be eaten raw as *sashimi*, *sushi* or *tartare*, but they must be absolutely fresh. Very thinly sliced raw tuna can be marinated in vinaigrette or Oriental marinades. Tuna fillets are quite delicious cut into very thin escalopes, dusted lightly with flour and pan-fried like veal *scaloppine* in butter.

Salad Niçoise

Tuna is the essential ingredient in this substantial Provençal salad. Although the salad can be made with drained canned tuna, it is infinitely nicer to use seared or grilled (broiled) fresh fish. Arrange some shredded cos (romaine) lettuce in a salad bowl and add the tuna, some quartered hard-boiled eggs, thickly sliced cooked new potatoes, tomato wedges, crisply-cooked green beans, some pitted black olives and a few anchovy fillets. Just before serving, toss the salad in a little garlic-flavoured vinaigrette dressing.

Albacore (*Thunnus alalunga*)

Also known as longfin, due to its long pectoral fins, this tuna is found in temperate and tropical seas, although only the smaller specimens venture into the North Sea. Albacore has pale, rosy flesh whose colour and texture resemble veal. Once known as "Carthusian veal", it could be eaten by monks when eating meat was not permitted. It is frequently used for canning.

Other names Albacore is also known as "white" tuna. In French it is *thon blanc* or *germon*; in Italian *alalunga* and in Spanish *atun blanco* or *albacora*.

Cooking Because its rosy-white flesh is so akin to veal, albacore is often cooked in similar ways – as pan-fried escalopes or larded with anchovy fillets and pork back fat, and braised.

False Albacore (*Euthynnus alletteratus*)

This comparatively small tuna (weighing about 15kg/33lb) is found only in warmer waters, generally off the coast of Africa. It is sought-after in Japan; it is used for *sashimi*.

Bigeye (*Thunnus obesus*)

This fat relative of the bluefin is found in tropical waters. It has rosy flesh and is substituted for bluefin when that superior tuna is unavailable. It is sometimes known as blackfin tuna. Other languages continue the rather rude reference to its obesity; in French, it is *thon obèse*, in Italian, *tonno obeso* and in Spanish *patudo*.

Bluefin (*Thunnus thynnus*)

Considered by many to be the finest of all tuna, bluefin are also the largest, and can grow to an enormous size (up to 700kg/ 1,540lb), although the average weight is about 120kg/264lb. Bluefin have dark blue backs and silvery bellies. Their oily flesh is deep red and has a more robust flavour than albacore. Bluefin is the classic tuna for *sushi* and *sashimi*.

Habitat Bluefin are found in the Bay of Biscay, the Mediterranean and tropical seas. They are very strong swimmers, and a dense shoal powering its way through the sea is an awesome sight.

Other names In Australia, the fish is known as Southern bluefin. Due to its bright red flesh, bluefin is *thon rouge* in French. In Italian it is merely *tonno*; in Spanish it is known as *atun*.

Buying Bluefin tuna is extremely expensive, largely because the Japanese will pay almost any price for it. It has an almost gamey flavour and is best when it has been kept for a week. Once the flesh has turned from bright red to light brown, however, it should be avoided at all costs – the tuna is past its prime.

Bonito (*Sarda sarda*) and Skipjack (*Katsuwonus pelamis*)

These fish fall somewhere between tuna and mackerel. There are two main types of bonito: Atlantic *(Sarda sarda)* and skipjack or oceanic. The Atlantic bonito is also found in the Mediterranean and Black Sea; skipjack is most commonly found in the Atlantic and Pacific Oceans.

Bonito are inferior to true tuna, with pale flesh which can be dry. Skipjack are usually used for canning. They are popular in Japan, where they are known as *katsuo* and are often made into dried flakes, which is a main ingredient of *dashi* (stock).

Other names Skipjack have dark blue parallel lines along their bellies and are sometimes known as "striped tuna". In French they are *bonite à ventre rayé* (striped belly); in Italian *bonita*; in Spanish *listado*.

Frigate Mackerel (*Auxis rochei*)

Despite its name, this fish is actually a tuna that is found in the Pacific and Indian Oceans. It grows to only about 50cm/20in and has red, coarse flesh. Some are small enough to cook whole.

Yellowfin (*Thunnus albacores*)

These large tuna are fished in tropical and equatorial waters. Weighing up to 250kg/ 550lb, they resemble albacore, but their fins are yellow. They have pale, pinkish flesh and a good flavour.

Other names Confusingly, the French and Italians call yellowfin *albacore* and *tonno albacora* respectively. In Spanish, it is *rabil*.

Buying In Europe, yellowfin are generally sold frozen as steaks. Make sure that they have not begun to thaw before you buy. Frozen yellowfin is available all year round.

Cooking Very fresh yellowfin can be eaten raw as *sashimi* or *sushi*, but is better cooked in any recipe that is suitable for tuna.

FLAT FISH

All flat fish start life as pelagic larvae, with an eye on each side of their head like a round fish. At this stage, they swim upright near the surface of the sea. As they mature, the fish start to swim on one side only and one eye moves over the head. Later, they gravitate to the sea bed and feed on whatever edible creatures pass by. Because they do not have to chase their food, their flesh is always delicate and white. They have a simple bone structure. With the exception of flounder, flat fish are seldom found outside European waters.

Brill (*Scophthalmus rhombus*)

Similar to turbot in appearance and taste, brill has fine softish white flesh with a delicate flavour. It can grow to about 75cm/30in and can weigh up to 3kg/6½lb, but are often smaller. The fish have slender bodies and there are small, smooth scales on the dark grey skin on the top. The underside is creamy or pinkish white.

Habitat Brill live on the bottom of the Atlantic, Baltic Sea and Mediterranean.

Buying Many people prefer turbot to brill; others think that brill is every bit as good. Brill is considerably cheaper than turbot and available almost all year round, as whole fish or fillets. Brill lose condition after spawning and can contain a great deal of roe just before, so avoid buying them at that time. There is a lot of wastage in all flat fish; you will need a 1.5kg/3–3½lb fish for four.

Cooking Brill can hold its own against robust red wine and is often cooked in *matelote* or red wine sauce. Small fish (up to 2kg/4½lb) are best cooked whole; they can be baked, braised, poached, steamed, pan-fried or grilled (broiled). Whole poached brill is good garnished with shellfish. Fillets of brill *à l'anglaise* are coated in egg and breadcrumbs, then pan-fried in butter.

Other names In French, brill is *barbue*, in Italian *rombo liscio*, "smooth turbot"; its Spanish name is *rémol*.

Alternatives Any halibut, sole or turbot recipe is suitable for brill.

Halibut (*Hippoglossus hippoglossus*)

These are the largest of all the flat fish, sometimes growing up to 2m/6½ft and weighing well over 200kg/440lb, although they normally weigh between 3kg/6½lb and 15kg/33lb. Halibut have elegant, elongated greenish-brown bodies, a pointed head with the eyes on the right-hand side, and pearly white undersides. The flesh is delicious with a fine, meaty texture.

Habitat Halibut live in very cold, deep waters off the coasts of Scotland, Norway, Iceland and Newfoundland. They migrate to shallower waters to spawn. A warm-water variety is found in the Pacific. These fish are voracious predators, which will eat almost any type of fish or crustacean, and will even devour birds' eggs that roll off cliffs and into the sea.

Other names Halibut is called *flétan* in French and *halibut* in Italian and Spanish.

Buying: Young halibut, called chicken halibut, weigh 1.5–2kg/3¼–4½lb, and one will amply serve four. Larger fish are almost always sold as steaks or fillets. Go for steaks cut from the middle rather than from the thin tail end, and allow for 175–200g/6–7oz per serving. Fresh raw halibut is a good choice for *ceviche*, *sashimi* and *sushi*.

BEWARE OF POOR ALTERNATIVES
*The Greenland halibut (*Reinhardtius hippoglossoides*) is vastly inferior to true halibut. It is a much smaller fish, growing to only 1m/39in long. It is known as turbot in Canada; and black halibut in Germany and France.*

Cooking Chicken halibut can be baked, braised, poached or cooked with shallots, mushrooms and white wine. The flesh of large halibut can be dry, so should be braised or baked with wine or stock.

Alternatives Brill can be substituted for halibut in any recipe. Turbot or John Dory can also be used.

Flounder (*Platichthys flesus*)

This is another large family of fish, which can be found around the world, from Europe to New Zealand. The mottled grey-brown skin has orange spots and is rough. Flounders can grow to 50cm/20in, but they usually only measure 25–30cm/10–12in.

They sometimes hybridize with plaice, which they resemble, having a similar soft texture and undistinguished flavour.

Habitat Flounders live close to the shore and are sometimes found in estuaries. They spend their days on the sea bed, not feeding, but become active at night.

Other names Many types of flounder are found in America, where they are known as summer, winter and sand flounders. Other varieties have such descriptive names as arrowtooth, black, greenback and yellow-belly. In France, they are called *flet*, in Italy, *passera pianuzza*, in Spain, *platija*.

Buying Flounders must be extremely fresh. Make sure they have glossy skins and a fresh smell, or buy them when still alive.

Cooking As for brill or plaice.

Plaice (*Pleuronectes platessa*)

These fish have smooth, grey-brown skin with orange spots. The underside is pearly white. The eyes are on the right-hand side; a ridge of bony knobs runs from behind them to the dorsal fin. Plaice can live for up to 50 years and weigh up to 7kg/15½lb – the average is 400g–1kg/14oz–2¼lb. They have soft, rather bland white flesh.

Habitat Plaice are found in the Atlantic and other northerly waters, and also in the Mediterranean. They are bottom-feeding fish, which are most active at night.

Other names In France, plaice are *plie* or *carrelet*; in Italy, *passera* or *pianuzza*; in Spain, *solla*.

Buying Plaice must be very fresh, or the flesh tends to take on the texture of cotton wool. These fish are available throughout the year, whole or as fillets, but are best avoided in the summer months, when the flesh is flaccid and tasteless. In fresh plaice, the orange spots on the dark skin will be bright and distinctive. Dark-skinned plaice fillets are cheaper than white-skinned, but there is no difference in flavour. There is a lot of wastage on plaice, so you should allow a whole 350–450g/12–16oz fish per serving, or 175g/6oz fillet.

Cooking Any sole or brill recipe is suitable for plaice. Deep-fried in batter, plaice is a classic fish to serve as fish and chips. Whole plaice or fillets can be coated in beaten egg and fine breadcrumbs, then pan-fried in melted butter. Steamed or poached plaice is very easy to digest and makes good invalid food. For plaice *à la florentine*, bake a whole fish or white-skinned fillets in fish stock and white wine, lay the fish on a bed of lightly-cooked spinach, cover with a creamy cheese sauce and grill (broil) until bubbling and golden brown.

Alternatives Flounder, sole and brill can all be substituted for plaice.

Sole/Dover Sole (*Solea solea*)

Arguably the finest fish of all, Dover sole have a firm, delicate flesh, which has a superb flavour. Their oval bodies are well proportioned, with grey or light brown skin that is sometimes spotted with black. The eyes are on the right-hand side. The nasal openings on the underside of the fish are small and widely separated, which helps to distinguish these sole from lesser varieties. Dover sole can weigh up to 3kg/6½lb, but the average is 200–600g/7oz–1lb 6oz.

The ancient Romans adored sole and called them *solea Jovi* (Jupiter's sandal) after their chief god. The firm flesh was often preserved. During the reign of Louis XIV of France, sole was regarded as truly fit for a king, and the great chefs of the time created extravagant dishes with this tasty fish. During the earlier part of the 20th century, it was the mainstay of English fish cookery.

Habitat Dover sole are found in the English Channel and the Atlantic Ocean and also in the Baltic, Mediterranean and North Seas. They come inshore to spawn in spring and summer. For the most part, they spend their days buried in the sand on the sea bed and hunt for food at night.

Other names In French Dover sole is *sole*; in Italian, *sogliola*; in Spanish, *lenguado*.

Buying Sole are at their best three days after being caught, so if you are sure that you are buying fish straight from the sea, keep them for a couple of days before cooking. The skin should be sticky and the underside very white. Whole sole are graded by weight; a 225g/8oz fish will serve one person. If you want to serve two, buy a fish weighing at least 675–800g/1½–1¾lb, which will yield four decent-size fillets, but could prove costly. It is best to buy a whole fish; if you ask the fishmonger to fillet it for you, keep the bones and trimmings to make fish stock (and help to justify the cost).

MISTAKEN IDENTITIES

*Sand or partridge sole (*Pegusa lascaris*) are very similar in appearance to Dover sole and are sometimes sold as "Dovers", although they are smaller and inferior fish. Their key distinguishing feature is a much larger nasal opening on the underside. Another species, known as tongues, (*Dicologlossa cuneata*) are smaller (only 7.5–10cm/3–4in in length). In France, these fish are sometimes sold as baby Dover sole, when they are known as* séteaux *(or* cétaux*) or* langues d'avocat *(lawyers' tongues).*

Cooking There are many, many recipes for sole, but a plain lightly grilled (broiled) fish served with a drizzle of melted butter and lemon juice is hard to beat. Skin both sides before cooking. Small sole can be coated in egg and breadcrumbs and pan-fried or deep-fried; larger specimens can be poached, steamed or cooked in butter *à la meunière*. Fillets can be fried, poached in wine or served with an elaborate sauce, or given an Asian twist with soy sauce, lemon grass and fresh root ginger. They can be steamed and rolled up around a stuffing or used to line a mould, which is then filled with shellfish mousse.

Alternatives Nothing tastes quite like Dover sole, but lemon sole, plaice and other flat fish can be cooked in the same way.

Lemon Sole (*Microstomus kitt*)

Despite the name, lemon sole is related to dab, plaice and flounder. They are oval in shape, with the widest part well towards the head. They have smooth, reddish brown skin with irregular marbling and a straight lateral line, very small heads and bulging eyes. The flesh is soft and white, similar to that of plaice but slightly superior.

Habitat Lemon sole are found in the North Sea and Atlantic Ocean and around the coast of New Zealand. They lead largely stationary lives on the stony or rocky sea bed and vary enormously in size depending on local conditions.

Other names In the US, lemon sole are known as yellowtail flounder. In France, they are *limande-sole*; in Italy *sogliola limanda*; in Spain, *mendo limón*.

Buying Lemon sole are available all year round and are sold whole or as fillets. They must be very fresh and should still have a tang of the sea.

Cooking Lemon sole are at their best when cooked simply; use them in any plaice or Dover sole recipe.

Turbot (*Psetta maxima*)

What turbot lacks in looks, it makes up for in texture and taste. Highly prized since ancient times, it was called *le roi de carême* (the king of Lent) in the Middle Ages. The great chefs of the time created sumptuous recipes, marrying turbot with langoustines, truffles, lobster sauce and beef marrow.

Turbot have tiny heads and large, almost circular bodies with tough, warty, brown skin similar to a toad's. Unusually, the white underside is sometimes pigmented with grey. They can grow to 1m/39in in length and can weigh as much as 12kg/26lb. The flesh is creamy white, with a firm, dense texture and a superb sweet flavour.

Habitat Turbot live on the sea bottom in the Atlantic, Mediterranean and Black Seas, and have been introduced to the coastal waters around New Zealand. They can be farmed successfully, and this has improved both the quality and the size of the fish.

Other names They are *turbot* in French; *rombo chiodato* in Italian; *rodaballo* in Spanish. Small young turbot, weighing up to 2kg/4½lb, are called chicken turbot.

Buying Turbot is an extremely expensive fish, especially wild specimens. Farmed fish are cheaper, but they can be fatty. Turbot should have creamy white flesh; do not buy fish that have a blue tinge. It is available all year round, sold whole, as steaks and fillets. A chicken turbot, which weighs about 1.5kg/3–3½lb, will feed four people. There is a lot of wastage, so if your fishmonger fillets a whole turbot for you, ask for the bones and trimmings; they will make a superb stock.

Cooking It is neither practical nor is it economical to cook a whole turbot that weighs more than about 1.5kg/3–3½lb in a domestic kitchen. To cook a chicken turbot, grill (broil) it or poach in white wine and fish stock, using a large frying or roasting pan. Traditionally, turbot was poached in milk to keep the flesh white, then served with hollandaise sauce. Almost any cooking method is suitable for turbot, except deep-frying, which would be a waste; it is essential not to overcook it. Creamy sauces such as lobster, parsley and mushroom go well with plainly-cooked turbot. Chunks of poached turbot dressed with a piquant vinaigrette, make a delicious salad.

Alternatives Nothing quite equals turbot, but brill, halibut, John Dory and fillets of sole make good substitutes.

TURBOT KETTLES

In the days of affordable luxury, a whole huge turbot might be steamed in a huge, diamond-shaped copper turbot kettle with handles on the points and a grid for lifting out the cooked fish.

Nowadays you will only find one of these kettles in the kitchen of a stately home or a fine restaurant. Modern turbot kettles are usually made of stainless steel or aluminium.

Migratory Fish

Certain species of fish undertake an annual mass migration from one area to another to spawn or feed. They follow a specific route, although how they know which route to take remains a mystery. Each year salmon and sea trout migrate from the sea to spawn in the fresh water of the river; having spawned, they return to the sea, and so the pattern continues. Eels, on the other hand, travel from rivers and lakes to spawn in salt sea water, entailing a very long journey of thousands of miles.

Eels (*Anguillidae*)

There are more than twenty members of the eel family. All are slim, snake-like fish with smooth, slippery skin and spineless fins. Most have microscopic scales that cannot be seen by the naked eye. The *Anguillidae* family are freshwater fish, but other species, such as conger, moray and snake eels, are marine fish. Eels have fatty white flesh with a rich flavour and firm texture.

Eels have been a popular food since Roman times, and were highly prized in the Middle Ages. Their mysterious life cycle gave rise to all sorts of improbable myths; one popular belief was that they were loose horsehairs that came to life when they touched the water. The less fanciful truth was discovered by a Danish scientist as recently as at the end of the 19th century.

Habitat Freshwater eels are born in the Sargasso Sea. Each female eel lays up to 20 million eggs and both she and her male partner die immediately after the eggs have been laid and fertilized. The eggs hatch into minuscule larvae, which are carried on the ocean currents to the coasts of Europe and America, then back to the rivers where their ancestors matured. This journey takes a year for American eels and between two and three years for European eels. No one has yet fathomed how the babies know which direction to take. When the baby elvers enter the estuaries in huge flotillas, they are tiny transparent creatures not more than 8cm/3¼in long. As they mature, their skin colour changes to yellow, then to green and finally to silver. At this stage, the eels begin the journey back to the Sargasso Sea, where they spawn and immediately die.

Varieties Tiny elvers are known as glass eels (*civelles* or *piballes* in French). Adult European eels (*Anguilla anguilla*) and the American eels (*Anguilla rostrata*) are known as *anguille* in French, *anguilla* in Italian and *anguila* in Spanish. Both Japanese eels (*Anguilla japonica*) and Australian eels (*Anguilla australis*) are known as short-finned eels, while *Anguilla dieffenbachii* is the long-finned eel.

Skinning an Eel

You will probably prefer to ask your fishmonger to kill and skin your eel, but if this is not possible, it is not difficult to do it yourself.

1 Grip the eel in a cloth and bang its head sharply on a hard surface to kill it. Put a string noose around the base of the head and hang it firmly on a sturdy hook or door handle.

2 Slit the skin all round the head just below the noose. Pull away the top of the skin, turn it back to make a "cuff", then grip with a cloth or two pairs of pliers and pull the skin down firmly towards the tail. Cut off the head and tail.

3 Alternatively, kill the eel and chop it into sections, leaving the skin on. Grill (broil) the pieces, skin-up, turning frequently until the skin has puffed up on all sides. When cool enough to handle, peel off the skin.

Buying You may find tiny elvers for sale in the spring – these are a great delicacy and are extremely expensive. One kilo consists of up to two thousand tiny elvers.

Adult eels are at their plumpest and best in autumn when they have turned silver with almost black backs. Females weigh three times as much as males, so a female silver eel is highly prized. Farmed eels are available all year round. Eels should be bought alive, as they tend to go off very quickly once dead. Ask the fishmonger to skin them for you and to chop them into 5cm/2in lengths.

Cooking Tiny elvers can be tossed in seasoned flour and deep-fried; soak them first in acidulated water to remove the mud. Eel is an extremely versatile fish; it can be fried and served with parsley sauce and is also good poached or braised in red wine. If you grill (broil) it, marinate it first, then wrap it in streaky (fatty) bacon to keep it moist. Eel is excellent in soups and casseroles, such as *matelote*, and the rich, robust flesh marries well with strong, aromatic Oriental flavours. Two classic English eel recipes are jellied eels and eel pie with mashed potatoes and green "liquor". Eels are also delicious smoked.

Conger Eel (*Conger conger*)

These marine eels can grow to an enormous size – sometimes up to 3m/9ft 9in, although the usual length is 60–150cm/2–5ft. They are ferocious carnivores with long, thick scaleless bodies and very bony firm white flesh, which is quite good to eat.

Habitat Conger eels are found in temperate and tropical seas, living in wrecks and rocky crevices. Many live in deep water, but some prefer to lurk in shallow inshore waters, causing panic among unfortunate swimmers who may inadvertently disturb a rather large specimen.

Other names In French conger eel is *congre*, in Italian *grongo*, and in Spanish *congrio*.

Buying Conger eel has the merit of being cheap. It is available from early spring to autumn and is usually sold cut into chunks or steaks. Ask for a middle cut from near the head end; the tail end is extremely bony. If you are offered a whole conger, ask the fishmonger to fillet it, and keep the head and bones for soup or stock.

Cooking Conger is best used for soups or hearty casseroles. Its dense flesh makes it good for terrines. Thick middle cuts can be roasted, poached or braised and served with a *salsa verde*.

Moray Eel (*Muraena helena*)

These eels are even more fearsome than the conger eel. They grow to only about 2m/6ft 6in, but are extremely vicious and will not hesitate to bite. Moray eels have long, flattened bodies and thick, greenish leathery skin with a pattern of light spots and no scales. The white flesh is rather tasteless and extremely bony.

Habitat Most species of moray eel are found in tropical and sub-tropical waters, but some occur in the Atlantic and Mediterranean. These eels typically anchor the tail end of their bodies in rock crevices and corals and wait with their mouths agape for catching any unlucky prey that comes too close.

Buying Morays are mostly fished for sport and are seldom found in fishmongers. When they are available, they are sold in chunks rather than whole.

Cooking Morays are really fit only for soup, and are often used in the traditional *bouillabaisse*. They can be cooked gently in cider, then the flesh removed from the bone and used in fish pies or fish cakes. The tail end is full of sharp bones. Avoid it, unless you are making stock.

THE SALMON FAMILY

Known as the king of fish, salmon is probably the most important of all fish, prized by sportsmen and gastronomes alike. Various species are found throughout the world, but the finest by far is the Atlantic salmon. All salmon spawn in fresh water. Some species spend their lives in landlocked waters, but after two years, most salmon migrate upstream to the sea to feed before returning to spawn in the rivers where they were born. This long trek makes them sleek and muscular, providing their luxurious flesh. Once they return to fresh water, salmon stop feeding, only starting again when they go back to the sea.

Salmon have suffered from over-fishing and environmental disturbance, and wild fish have become rare and expensive. Once, it was possible to land salmon weighing 20kg/44lb or more, but such magnificent fish have now disappeared. Fortunately, salmon are now being farmed successfully, although early salmon farms produced fish with flabby, bland flesh, which was often riddled with sea lice, which attacked and further decimated the wild stocks. Lessons have been learned, and it is now possible to buy healthy, well-flavoured farmed salmon at a reasonable price.

Atlantic Salmon (*Salmo salar*)

These magnificent fish have silvery-blue backs, silver sides and white bellies. In comparison to their large, powerful bodies, their heads are quite small. The heads and backs are marked with tiny black crosses. Salmon's fine fatty flesh is deep pink and firm with a superb, rich flavour.

Habitat Atlantic salmon can be found in all the cold northern waters of Europe and America. They are spawned in rivers, then undertake the exhausting journey back to the sea, returning to the river to spawn.

When young salmon, which are 10–20cm/4–8in long, first migrate to the sea, they are called smolts. After a year or two of eager feeding, salmon reach a weight of 1–2kg/2¼–4½lb and make their first spawning run; these young fish are called grilse. The males develop elongated hooked jaws that help them to fight against the strong currents. Some fish may spawn only once or twice in their lifetimes; others may spawn up to four times.

Salmon were a very popular food in the Middle Ages, when they were braised with spices, potted or salted, or made into pies and pâtés. Once they became rarer, they were regarded as a luxury and chefs vied to marry them with extravagant ingredients such as lobster, crayfish and cream.

Other names In French, they are *saumon*; in Italian *salmone*; in Spanish *salmón*.

LANDLOCKED SALMON

The deep, cold lakes of Canada and North America are home to landlocked salmon; these are variously known as ouananiche, lake salmon and sebago.

Buying Salmon are sold whole, as steaks, cutlets, fillets and large middle and tail cuts. The best (and most expensive) salmon are wild fish. Wild salmon are sleeker, with firmer, lustrous skin and deep pink flesh. They are available from spring to late summer. Late-spawning fish, which return to the sea in autumn, are known as kelts; they have not eaten for many months and are thin and in poor condition and are not worth buying. Grilse – young salmon with an average weight of about 1.4kg/3lb – are cheaper than large wild fish and will serve two generously. Scottish and Irish wild salmon are the finest of all; Atlantic salmon from Greenland and Scandinavia is less highly regarded but are still tasty.

The quality of farmed salmon can be variable. The flesh should be firm and dark pink with creamy marbling and not too much fat, not flabby, pale or grey. Salmon heads are surprisingly heavy, so if you buy whole salmon allow 350–400g/12–14oz per serving. If buying steaks or cutlets you will only need 200g/7oz per person. If removed, ask for the head to make stock.

Cooking There is almost no limit to the ways in which you can prepare salmon. It can be eaten raw as salmon *tartare*, *sashimi* or in *sushi*. It can be marinated in oil, lemon juice and herbs or salted and marinated to make *gravad lax*. It can be poached, pan-fried, seared, grilled (broiled), baked or braised, or wrapped in pastry as *saumon en croûte*. Poached salmon is delicious hot or cold; a whole fish poached in court-bouillon makes a superb festive dish served with plain or green mayonnaise and cucumber. It is also excellent with a spicy salsa.

Hot poached salmon cries out for hollandaise or a rich seafood sauce or *beurre blanc*. If you do not have a fish kettle large enough for a whole salmon, wrap the fish in foil, moisten with white wine, then bake.

Salmon fillets can be thinly sliced into escalopes and flash-fried, or sandwiched together with fish or shellfish mousse or vegetable purée and baked or braised. They are delicious made into fish cakes, kedgeree, pâté and mousse. Try them potted in butter flavoured with mace, or as *rillettes*. Steaks can be cooked in red wine, poached, baked *en papillote* with white wine and herbs or Oriental flavourings, grilled (broiled), pan-fried or barbecued. Salmon is also delicious cold- or hot-smoked. It can be cured in salt and is one of the most popular canned fish to be found in the world.

Alternatives Sea trout and good-quality brown or rainbow trout can be used instead of salmon.

Pacific Salmon (*Onorhynchus*)

Five species of Pacific salmon are found around the Pacific coast from California to Alaska, and another is found in northern Japan. Even the largest, the Chinook or king salmon, is smaller and slimmer than its Atlantic counterpart. Other Pacific salmon include the sockeye or red salmon, chum or dog salmon and pink salmon. None is as fine as Atlantic salmon and all types are frequently sold canned. Canned salmon makes a good kitchen standby.

Sea Trout (*Salmo trutta*)

Although they are closely related to the brown trout, sea trout differ from other trout species in that they migrate to the sea like salmon. They closely resemble salmon, but have smaller, less pointed heads and squarer tails. Sea trout seldom grow to more than 3kg/6½lb, which makes them much more manageable for cooking. They have very fine, dark pink flesh, which is beautifully succulent and has a delicate, mellow flavour for you to savour.

Other names Sea trout are also known as salmon trout or sewin. In French, they are *truite de mer*; in Italian *trota di mare*; and in Spanish *trucha marina*.

Buying Sea trout are always wild, but they do not cost as much as wild salmon. They are sold whole and you will find that a 2kg/4½lb fish will serve 4–6 people. They should be bright and silvery with an almost golden sheen.

Cooking As for salmon.

EXOTIC FISH

Thanks to modern transportation, exotic fish from tropical seas all over the world are now available in European and North American markets. Warm-water fish never have quite as good a flavour as those from colder climes, but they add variety to a fish diet and are often very beautiful. Do not be alarmed about cooking unfamiliar fish; they can be cooked in the same way as other species and go well with exotic flavourings.

Barracouta/Snoek (*Thyrsites atun*)

This long, thin fish has smooth, blue-grey skin with silver sides and belly, a flat dorsal fin running almost the length of the body and spines near the tail. They can grow to 2m/6½ft long, but are generally 60–90cm/24–36in in length. The lower jaw protrudes and there is a single lateral line. The dryish flesh is dark, but whitens on cooking. Barracouta have long, irregular bones.

Habitat Barracouta are found in temperate regions of the southern hemisphere.

Other names In Australia and New Zealand, barracouta is often shortened to couta. In South Africa, they are snoek.

Buying Barracouta are not sold fresh in the northern hemisphere, but you may find them canned or smoked.

Cooking Barracouta can be fried, grilled (broiled) or baked. They are often pickled in vinegar and spices, and marry well with Oriental flavours. It is delicious smoked.

Barracuda (*Sphyraena barracuda*)

These fearsome-looking game fish have long slender bodies, forked tails and sharp teeth capable of delivering a vicious bite. They strike fear into the hearts of divers, who often encounter these fish on coral reefs. There are about twenty species. The largest is the great barracuda, which has dark bars and scattered black blotches on its greenish skin. This fish can grow to over 1m/39in in length. Other species include the yellowtail and small Pacific and Mexican barracudas. All have meaty, rich, oily flesh, which has the reputation of being toxic. Play safe by not eating raw fish.

Habitat Barracuda are found in warm waters, mainly in the Pacific and Caribbean, but sometimes in warmer Atlantic seas. Young fish travel in schools, but older specimens are solitary. Barracuda will often follow divers around the reefs, or even walkers along the shore, which gives them the probably undeserved reputation of being predatory.

Other names In French, it is known as *brochet de mer*, because it resembles pike. Italians call barracuda *luccio marina*, while in Spain it is *espeton*.

Buying Small barracuda (up to 3kg/6½lb) are best. Ask the fishmonger to scale and fillet them. Larger fish are often sold filleted. It is available all year round.

Cooking The rich flesh of barracuda lends itself well to Oriental and exotic spices and flavourings. It is oily, so avoid cooking with butter, cream or too much oil. Small whole fish can be grilled (broiled), barbecued or baked. Fillets and steaks can be marinated in spices and grilled or baked or curried.

Alternatives Any firm-fleshed oily fish, such as tuna or bonito.

Barramundi (*Lates calcifer*)

This beautiful giant perch has an elongated silver body with a dark grey back, a curved lateral line and a protruding lower jaw. Barramundi can grow to an enormous size, often weighing more than 20kg/44lb; the record catch so far weighed 250kg/550lb. The best size for eating is about 10kg/22lb, although whole baby barramundi (barra) are popular in Australia. The chunky white flesh has a delicate flavour.

Habitat Barramundi are found in Indo-Pacific waters, from Japan to the East Indies. They often swim close to the shore and are sometimes found in estuaries and brackish water.

Other names Giant perch.

Buying You are unlikely to find barramundi outside the Antipodes and Asia. Small fish are sold whole and larger specimens are sold as steaks or fillets. Look for bright skin and white flesh.

Cooking Whole fish can be grilled (broiled), barbecued, braised, baked or fried. Cook fillets and steaks in the same way as bream, snapper, grouper and mullet.

Flying Fish (*Exocoetidae*)

These are the fish that gave their name to the Exocet missile, because of their habit of gliding (not flying) astounding distances through the air at about 60kph/40mph. They are supported by a disproportionately large, highly-developed, wing-like, spineless pectoral fin. Flying fish begin their flight below the water, at high speed, bursting through the surface into the air. Only then do they expand their pectoral fins, which allow them to glide for about 30 seconds before dropping, tail-first, back into the sea. Flying fish may look spectacular, but their flavour is less exciting.

Habitat Various species of flying fish are found in the Caribbean, Pacific and warm Atlantic waters. They are attracted by bright lights, and fishermen encourage the fish to fly into their nets by hanging a lamp over the side of the boat.

Other names The French call flying fish *exocet*; the Italians *pesce volante*; and the Spanish *pez voador*.

Buying Flying fish are usually displayed whole so that customers can admire their exotic shape. Large fish are sometimes filleted. They do not travel well, so are best eaten near the shores where they are caught.

Cooking Whole fish or fillets can be dusted in seasoned flour and deep-fried, baked *au gratin* or braised with vegetables.

Grouper (*Epinephelus*)

These fish are members of the extensive sea bass family. Dozens of species of these non-shoaling carnivorous fish are found in all the warm seas of the world; all have firm white flesh and make good eating. They look extremely gloomy, with upturned protruding lower lips, giving them the appearance of permanently sulky teenagers. They have beautiful colouring, often with mottled skin. One of the largest is the spotted jewfish or giant grouper, which can weigh more than 300kg/660lb; even larger is the Queensland grouper, which can weigh over half a ton, and has been known to attack and terrorize divers. Smaller species include the red, black, yellowmouth and Malabar groupers.

Habitat Warm-water groupers inhabit all warm seas, from Africa to the Caribbean. Most inhabit rocky shores, but many live on deepwater reefs.

Other names In Australia, grouper are called rock or reef cod. In France, *merou*; in Italy, *cernia*; in Spain, *mero*.

Varieties There are two types of grouper: red groupers have reddish-brown skin with yellowish markings; black groupers range from pale to very dark grey.

Buying Grouper are available throughout the year. Fish weighing up to 5kg/11lb are sold whole, or may be filleted or cut into steaks. You are unlikely to find any distinction made between the different varieties of grouper. All taste very similar and are interchangeable.

Cooking Grouper can be cooked in all the same ways as sea bass. It goes well with spices and Caribbean flavourings.

Alternatives Sea bass and bream can be substituted for grouper.

Mahi Mahi/Dolphinfish (*Coryphaena hippurus*)

These strange and beautiful fish have long, tapering streamlined bodies, with a high ridge of fin running down the body from the head to the forked, swallow-like tail. They are among the fastest swimmers, with a top speed of 80kph/50mph per hour. Their skin changes colour as they swim, from green and gold to silver and grey, with gold and blue spots. The average weight is 2.5kg/5½lb, but fish have been known to grow to ten times that weight. The flesh is firm and white, with a sweet flavour.

Habitat Mahi mahi are found in almost all the warm seas. They are very inquisitive fish, which are easy to catch, since they are drawn to objects floating on the water.

Other names Mahi mahi is the Hawaiian name for these fish, which are also known as dorade or dolphinfish, though they are not actually related to dolphins. In French, they are *coryphene*; in Italian *lampuga*; and in Spanish *llampuga*.

Buying Available from spring through to autumn, mahi mahi is sold as steaks or fillets. Do not buy frozen fish, as it is completely lacking in flavour.

Cooking The Hawaiians usually eat mahi mahi raw, but it is best grilled (broiled) or fried. It marries well with spicy flavours and is delicious served with a piquant salsa.

Alternatives Monkfish, John Dory, cod or any firm-fleshed fish can be substituted.

Parrot Fish (*Scarus* spp)

Perfectly adapted to living in proximity to coral reefs, parrot fish have hard, parrot-like beaks with which they nibble the coral. There are almost a hundred species of parrot fish. All have compact, brightly coloured bodies and large scales. They come in a variety of vibrant hues – green, blue, red and multi-coloured. The largest is the rainbow parrot fish, which can grow up to 1m/3½ft, but most are only 30cm/12in long. Like many types of exotic fish, parrot fish look much better than they taste.

Habitat Parrot fish are found in tropical and sub-tropical seas. They live in large numbers around coral reefs, crushing the coral to reach the soft sea creatures inside, or scraping algae from surrounding rocks.

Other names In French, they are *perroquet*; in Italian *pesce pappagallo;* in Spanish *vieja*.

Buying Many supermarkets now stock parrot fish. Make sure that the colours are clear and bright; avoid fish that look faded. A larger 800g–1kg/1¾–2¼lb fish will serve two. These are sometimes sold filleted, or can be filleted on request.

Cooking Parrot fish can be rather bland, so spice them up with tropical flavours, such as coconut milk, garlic, chilli and lemon grass. Whole fish can be baked or braised; they taste good with a spicy salsa.

Alternatives Red snapper, bream and John Dory can all be used instead of parrot fish.

Pomfret (*Stromateus* spp)

These small, silvery fish are almost circular with very pointed dorsal and anal fins and curved forked tails, not unlike those of flat fish. They have almost no scales and their white flesh is soft, with a mild flavour.

Habitat A variety of pomfret is found in the Mediterranean, but the best-flavoured fish come from the Indian and Pacific oceans. Butterfish are found off the north-west coast of America.

Other names Pomfret from the north-west Atlantic are known as butterfish, and in America also go by the names of dollar fish, and pumpkinseed fish, due to their shape, which in Europe is likened to that of the chestnut. In France, they are *castagnole du Pacifique*; in Italy *pesce castagna*; and in Spain *castagneta*.

Buying Pomfret are available most of the year, either fresh or frozen. A small whole fish weighing about 400g/14oz will feed one person. Fillets from small pomfret are rather thin, so if possible, buy a larger fish and ask the fishmonger to fillet it for you.

Cooking Whole pomfret can be grilled (broiled), fried, baked, poached or steamed. This fish goes well with spices and Oriental flavours such as coconut, lemon grass and tamarind. Beloved of Indian chefs, pomfret makes excellent curries and is often cooked in a tandoor. Because the fillets are thin and the flesh is soft, pomfret fillets should be cooked only briefly.

Alternatives Trout can be used instead of pomfret, as can any flat fish.

Pompano (*Alectis ciliaris*) and Jack (*Seriola*)

This large family of fish comprises more than two hundred species. All are oily fish, similar to mackerel, but with a stronger flavour. The dark flesh becomes lighter on cooking. Jacks vary enormously in size and shape, but all have forked tails and virtually scaleless iridescent skin. Among the most common jacks and pompanos are the small leatherjacket, the yellowtail, the amberjack and crevalle jack. The best of all for culinary purposes is the Florida pompano, which has white, meaty flesh, while the strangest-looking pomfret is the lookdown, a small glum-looking fish with a flat, thin body and a high domed forehead.

Habitat Pompano and jacks are found in warm seas all over the world. They travel in schools, either around coral reefs or, like Florida pompano, close to the shore.

Other names Both in Australia and New Zealand, yellowtail jack are known as kingfish. In French, jack is called *carangue*; in Italian *carango*; and in Spanish *caballa*. Pompano is *palomine* in French; *leccia stella* in Italian and *palometa blanca* in Spanish.

Buying Pompano and jack are available all year round. They are usually sold whole, but may be filleted. Outside Florida, you are likely to find only farmed pompano, but this is of excellent quality.

Cooking Jack can be cooked in the same way as mackerel. The robust flesh lends itself to spicy Oriental flavours such as chilli, ginger and coriander. Pompano and jack can be stuffed with breadcrumbs or crab meat and baked, barbecued or grilled (broiled). They can be cooked *en papillote*, steamed or poached in stock flavoured with Oriental ingredients such as soy sauce or Thai fish sauce and fresh ginger. The Japanese use the fillets raw as *sashimi*.

Snapper (*Lutjanidae*)

More than 250 species of snapper are found in warm seas throughout the world. The finest to eat is the American red snapper (*Lutjanus campechanus*), which is bright red all over, including the eyes and fins. The silk snapper is similar, but has a yellow tail. Other species include the pink snapper, or *opakapaka*, mutton snapper, which is usually olive green with vertical bars (but can change colour), the yellowtail snapper and the African and Indo-Pacific. All have domed heads with large mouths with canine-like teeth that can snap quite vigourously, and big eyes that are set high on the head. Most snappers weigh between 1.5 and 2.5kg/3¼ and 5½lb, although the large mutton snappers can weigh up to 10kg/22lb, while yellowtails average only 250g/9oz. Snappers have firm, slightly flaky well-flavoured white flesh and make very good eating.

Habitat Red snapper come from deep waters around Florida and Central and South America. Other varieties are found in warm waters from the Atlantic to the Caribbean and Indo-Pacific.

Other names Snapper from the Indian Ocean and Arabian Sea are known as job or jobfish. In French, *vivaneau*; in Italian, *lutianido*; in Spanish, *pargo*.

Buying Snapper are available all year round. Many fish sold as red snapper are a different, inferior species; true American red snapper have red eyes. A whole fish weighing about 1kg/2¼lb will feed two people, while a 2kg/4½lb fish makes a good meal for four.

Cooking Snapper can be baked, grilled (broiled), poached, steamed and pan-fried. It lends itself to exotic and Caribbean flavours, such as chilli, mango and coconut.

Alternatives Grey mullet, bream, John Dory and sea bass can be substituted.

Tilapia (*Tilapia*)

Members of the enormous *Cichlids* family, tilapia have only one nostril on either side of their heads. The female is considerably smaller than the male and carries her fertilized eggs in her mouth. Scientists have successfully bred tilapia that produce offspring that are almost exclusively male. Tilapia are freshwater fish, but they can also live in salt water and are found in tropical seas. There are many different varieties of tilapia, with colours ranging from grey to bright red. Their flesh is white and moist, with a pleasant, sweet flavour.

Habitat Tilapia are native to the Nile but can also be found in warm tropical waters, both fresh and salt. They are farmed all over the world.

Other names In Egypt and Israel, tilapia are sometimes marketed as St Peter's fish (not to be confused with John Dory).

Buying Tilapia are available all year round. Small fish are sold whole, but larger fish are filleted. A small whole fish (weighing about 350g/12oz) will serve one person; a 675g/1½lb fish serves two.

Cooking Whole tilapia can be stuffed and baked, grilled (broiled) or barbecued. The rather bland flesh benefits greatly from the addition of Chinese flavourings and spices, such as chilli, ginger and coriander. Fillets can be coated in egg and breadcrumbs or batter and deep-fried.

Alternatives Carp, bream and zander can be used instead of tilapia.

CARTILAGINOUS FISH

These fish have no bones; their skeletons are made entirely of cartilage. They do not have swim bladders to control buoyancy, but have developed very large livers, whose high oil content helps the fish to float. This oil is often extracted and used medicinally.

Almost all cartilaginous fish have long snouts and mouths set well back on the underside of the head. They have several rows of teeth. As one row wears away, they use the next. They have stiff, fleshy fins and no scales, but their bodies are covered with backward-facing denticles, which give them a rough texture.

THE SHARK FAMILY

This family ranges in size from the small dogfish to the huge basking shark, which can weigh up to 4000kg/8800lb. Shark flesh is firm, meaty and slightly sweet.

Buying Shark is sold as steaks, loin or fillets. The flesh has a faint smell of ammonia, which disappears during cooking only if the shark is very fresh.

Cooking Shark meat is a match for robust and aromatic flavours. Steaks can be grilled (broiled), pan-fried or barbecued. They can be dry, so marinate them in olive oil and lemon juice, or lard them with pork fat.

Steaks can also be braised or baked *au gratin* in a mornay sauce. Shark can be added to fish soups or stews and is good cold in salads. It is ideal for home-smoking.

Alternatives Any meaty fish.

Blue Shark (*Prionace glauca*)

This migratory shark has sharp teeth, a sleek indigo-blue back, shading to bright blue on the sides and a snow-white belly. It seldom grows to more than 4m/13ft long. The fins are used to make shark's fin soup.

Other names In French, it is *peau bleu*; in Italian *verdesca*; in Spanish *tintorera*.

Dogfish (*Scyliorhinus caniculus*)

Three species are eaten: the lesser spotted dogfish, the spur-dog or spiny dogfish and the larger nursehound. The first has grey-brown skin with numerous brown spots, the second has grey skin, while the nursehound's skin is reddish. The thick, rough skin is usually removed before sale. Lesser spotted dogfish grow to about 80cm/32in, spur-dogs to 1.2m/4ft and nurse-hounds to 1.5m/4ft 9in; the fish you find in the market are usually half that size. The flesh is white or pinkish with a firm texture and a good flavour.

Habitat Different varieties are found in cool temperate waters all around the world.

Other names Dogfish are variously known as huss, flake, rigg and rock salmon. Spur-dogs are also known as spiky dogs or spinebacks. In French, they are *petite* or *grande roussette*, or *saumonette*. In Italian they are *gattopardo*; in Spanish *pata-roxa*.

Buying Dogfish are sold skinned, often as fillets. They are available all year round. They must be very fresh, so sniff them to make sure they do not smell of ammonia.

FILLETING DOGFISH

The central cartilage in dogfish is very easy to remove, and there are no small bones. It is usually sold as a whole skinned fish, To fillet it, use a sharp knife with a long blade to cut down through the flesh on either side of the cartilage, using the full length of the blade and keeping it as close to the cartilage as possible. The fillets with fall away.

Cooking Dogfish has good firm flesh and can be cooked as monkfish and skate. It is good in stews and soups and is perfect for fish and chips. It can also be grilled (broiled) or barbecued, or cooked and flaked and used in salads. Dogfish is delicious smoked.

Porbeagle (*Lamna nasus*)

These stocky, dark mole-grey sharks are closely related to the great white shark. They are surface swimmers, found in cold and temperate seas. Porbeagles are widely regarded as the finest sharks for eating, with meaty, pink flesh which is sometimes likened to veal. It is usually sold as loin or fillets.

Other names In French, porbeagle is known as *taupe* or *veau de mer*; in Italian it is *smeriglio*; in Spanish *cailón*.

Cooking Porbeagle can be sliced into thin escalopes, dipped in egg and breadcrumbs and pan-fried or used in other shark recipes.

Tope (*Galeorhinus galeus*)

These small grey sharks have pointed, upward-tilting noses and triangular teeth. They are best cut into chunks and used in mixed fish soups and stews. In France it is *milandre*; in Italy *cagnesca*; in Spain *cazón*.

Ray and Skate (*Raja*)

It is virtually impossible to distinguish between ray and skate on the fishmonger's slab, since only the "wings" are sold. These fish have large, kite-shaped bodies with long, thin tails and enlarged flattened pectoral fins (the wings). The skin is greyish-brown and smooth, knobbly or even thorny. Both ray and skate have short snouts and large mouths on the underside with sharp, slashing teeth. They can be differentiated by the shape of the snout; in skate, this is pointed. The largest rays can grow to 2.5m/8ft and weigh up to 100kg/220lb.

The thornback ray (*Raja clavata*) is considered to have the best flavour, but there is little between the edible skates and rays. They have moist, meaty pinkish flesh with a fine texture and flavour. Usually, only the wings are eaten, but the cheeks are regarded as a delicacy, as are the small medallions from the tail.

Habitat Rays and skates are found in cold and temperate waters. They are lazy, bottom-living fish that hide on the sea bed waiting for their prey to pass by. They have evolved a way of breathing without opening their mouths. Most rays lay eggs, each enclosed in a four-horned black sac known as a "mermaid's purse".

Other names The common skate (*raie* in French; *razza* in Italian; *raya* in Spanish), thornback ray or roker, rough skate and butterfly skate.

Buying Skate is available most of the year, but is best in autumn and winter. Smaller wings are sold whole; if you want a larger piece, ask for a middle cut. The wings are covered with a clear slime, which regenerates itself even after death. To test for freshness, gently rub off the slime and make sure that it reappears. Even fresh skate smells faintly of ammonia. This is normal, and will disappear during cooking.

SKINNING COOKED SKATE

If the skin is still on when you buy skate, it is best to leave it on and scrape it off once it has been cooked.

1 Lay the cooked skate wing on a board. With a blunt knife, scrape off the skin from the thicker part towards the edge.

2 Discard the skin. Scrape the flesh off the cartilage in the same way.

Cooking Before cooking skate, wash it well in cold water to eliminate the ammoniac smell. The classic skate dish is *raie au beurre noir* (with black butter). Skate can also be grilled (broiled), deep-fried in batter or curried, and makes a delicious salad. Its gelatinous quality makes it good for soups and fish terrines and mousses.

Alternatives Fillets of brill, sole, John Dory or turbot can be used instead.

DEEP SEA AND GAME FISH

Throughout the world's oceans, there are several varieties of deep-sea fish that never come close to the shore. Many are unusual shapes and vibrant colours, which are rarely seen by consumers, since the fish are filleted on board the boats that travel far out to sea to trawl the fish. Most edible deep-sea fish are found around the coasts of New Zealand, South Africa and South America. The Caribbean is home to huge game fish, such as marlin, and keen fishermen will pay vast sums for a day's sport.

Antarctic Sea Bass (*Dissostichus eleginoides*)

Not a true sea bass, this fish is also known as toothfish, icefish and Chilean sea bass. It has only recently been fished commercially and little is known about it. The white flesh has a good texture and a pleasant flavour.

Habitat Antarctic sea bass inhabits the southern oceans from Antarctica to the Falklands and Chile.

Buying Available all year round as fillets. Prod the flesh to make sure that it is firm. When buying Antarctic sea bass, make sure that you are not paying for real sea bass.

Cooking Cook Antarctic sea bass in the same way as cod or any round white fish. It will benefit from a well-flavoured sauce.

Grenadier/Rattail (*family Macrouridae*)

There are about fifty species of these odd-looking shoaling fish. They may be the most abundant of all fish, but as they live at depths of 200–6000m/656–19,700ft, it is hard to be sure. Grenadiers have large, pointed heads that contain sensors to help them navigate in the dark ocean depths, and bodies that taper into filament-like tails. Their swim bladders vibrate to produce a grunting sound. Grenadiers have white flesh with a delicate, fairly moist texture.

Habitat They can be found throughout the world and live at great depths, feeding on luminous creatures.

Buying Fillets are available all year round. You may find fresh fish, but in the northen hemisphere they are usually frozen.

Cooking Fillets can be deep- or pan-fried or grilled (broiled). They benefit from a cream sauce and are good baked *au gratin*.

Alternatives Cod, hake, hoki or any other fairly firm white fish can be used instead.

Hoki (*Macruronus novaezelandiae*)

Although hoki resemble grenadiers, they are related to hake and have the same white flesh and flaky texture. They have blue-green backs with silvery sides and bellies, and their bodies taper to a point. Their average length is 60cm–1m/24–39in.

Habitat Hoki occur in fairly large numbers around the coasts of Southern Australia and New Zealand; a similar species is found around South America. They live at depths of 500–800m/1640–2626ft.

Other names In Australia, hoki are called blue grenadier. In New Zealand, they are sometimes called whiptail or blue hake.

Buying Hoki is available all year round, as fillets, loins and other cuts. It is frequently used to make fish fingers or ocean sticks.

Cooking Hoki is suitable for most cooking methods. It is best served with a robust tomato-based sauce or a creamy sauce. It can be cubed for kebabs, or smoked.

Alternatives Hake, monkfish and huss can be substituted for hoki.

Marlin (*family Istiophoridae*)

These magnificent-looking billfish, so called because of their elongated upper jaw, are renowned for their speed and endurance and are usually fished for sport. They have beautiful slender bodies with smooth iridescent skin and a high dorsal fin, which they fold down when speeding through the water.

There are several species of marlin, the best-known being blue, black (the largest), white (the smallest) and striped. All can attain huge weights (up to 300kg/660lb) but the average is 160–200kg/352–440lb. The deep pink flesh is high in fat and has a firm texture with a disappointing flavour.

Habitat Marlin are found in warm seas throughout the world. They have no teeth, but use their bill to spear schooling fish.

Other names In French, marlin are *makaire*; in Italian *pesce lancia*; in Spanish *aguja*.

Buying Marlin are available in summer usually as loins and steaks. Try to buy cuts from smaller fish. In the US, marlin is usually sold smoked rather than fresh.

Cooking Cook as swordfish, or cut into cubes and marinate to make *ceviche*.

Alternatives Swordfish, shark, and tuna.

Sailfish (*Istiophorus spp*)

The sailfish resembles marlin, but looks even more spectacular. It has a beautiful streamlined body with a golden back spotted with blue, and a high, wavy blue dorsal fin, which it unfurls like a sail to travel through the water at up to 96kph/60mph. Sailfish are tremendous fighters and will perform amazing aerial acrobatics when hooked by fishermen.

Habitat As for marlin.

Other names Sailfish are *voilier* in French; *pesce vela* in Italian; and *pez vela* in Spanish.

Buying Available in summer as loins and steaks. Buy cuts from smaller fish.

Cooking As for marlin.

Orange Roughy (*Hoplosthetus atlanticus*)

These ugly fish have orange bodies and fins and massive heads with conspicuous bony ridges and cavities. Although they are not large (about 1.5kg/3½lb), they are always cleaned and filleted at sea. The pearly white flesh is similar in texture to that of cod, but has a sweet shellfish flavour.

Habitat For many years, it was thought that orange roughy only inhabited Icelandic waters, but, in the 1970s, large numbers were found in the deep waters around New Zealand and most of the world's stocks now come from there.

Other names In Australia orange roughy is sometimes known as sea perch. In French it is called *hopostète orange*; in Italian *pesce specchio* (mirror fish); and in Spanish *reloj*.

Buying Orange roughy is available all year round, usually as fillets. Most is usually frozen at sea.

Cooking Orange roughy holds together well when cooked, and its crab-like flavour marries well with other seafood. It can be used for soups and stews, and is good poached, pan-fried, roasted or steamed. It can also be dipped in batter or egg and breadcrumbs and fried.

Alternatives Cod, haddock or any firm white fish can be substituted.

Redfish/Ocean Perch (*Sebastes marinus*)

These beautiful red fish were once the most important deep-sea fish, with vast catches landed every year. As new varieties of fish have become available, redfish have become less popular. Redfish can grow to 5kg/11lb. The white flesh is moist and sweet.

Habitat Redfish inhabit the cold, deep waters of the Atlantic and Arctic Oceans. Related species *(Helicolenus spp)* are found in the Pacific.

Other names Ocean perch or Norway haddock. In French, they are *rascasse* (not to be confused with their relative, the scorpion fish); in Italian, *scorfano* (ditto); in Spanish, *gallineta nórdica*.

Buying Redfish are available all year round, sold whole or as steaks and fillets. A whole fish weighing 400–600g/14oz–1lb 6oz will feed one person; a 1–1.5kg/2¼–3½lb fish will feed two.

Cooking Redfish is well suited to all cooking methods. Try it with rich Mediterranean flavours and spices such as tomatoes, garlic and batter, or baked in a creamy sauce.

Alternatives Hake or cod can be used instead of redfish.

Swordfish *(family Xiphiidae)*

Famous as both a culinary and game fish, swordfish differs from other billfish in having neither scales nor teeth. In all other respects, it is dramatic and graceful to look at as it powers through the water with only the curve of its dorsal fin visible above the surface. Its long "sword" represents up to one-third of its total length. It appears to be a powerful weapon, but no one is certain whether it is actually used to kill its prey, or merely to stun small fish. Swordfish can grow to an enormous size, weighing up to 600kg/1320lb. Their excellent white, meaty flesh is very low in fat and tends to dryness, so it needs careful cooking.

Habitat Swordfish are migratory fish that are widely distributed in warm, deep waters around the world. They may migrate into northern European seas, but are more common in the Mediterranean.

Other names In French, swordfish is *espadon*; in Italian it is *pesce spada*; in Spanish, *pez espada*.

Buying Fresh swordfish is available all year round, usually sold as steaks. Frozen fish is also available, but is best avoided. Because swordfish is so meaty and substantial, 150–165g/5–5½oz will provide an ample portion for one person. Try to buy fairly thick steaks, as thinner ones are more apt to dry out during cooking.

Cooking It is essential not to let swordfish dry out during cooking, so baste it frequently with olive oil when grilling (broiling) or barbecuing and serve with a drizzle of extra virgin olive oil or some herb butter. Swordfish makes excellent kebabs and can withstand a robust or spicy sauce. It is delicious marinated in a mixture of olive oil and lemon juice that has been flavoured with garlic and fresh herbs, then seared in a very hot pan or chargrilled. Swordfish can also be braised with Mediterranean vegetables such as (bell) peppers, tomatoes, courgettes (zucchini) and aubergines (eggplant). Grilled or barbecued swordfish are good served with a spicy, fresh tomato salsa made using fresh coriander (cilantro).

Alternatives Shark and tuna can be used instead of swordfish.

MISCELLANEOUS FISH

A few fish do not slot neatly into any obvious category. Their only connection is that they are all exceptionally good to eat and are a strange-looking collection.

John Dory (family Zeidae)

These fish are so slim that they look almost like upright flat fish. Dories have extremely ugly faces and spiny dorsal fins trailing long filaments. Their most distinguishing feature is a large black spot ringed with yellow right in the middle of their bodies; this is said to be the thumbprint of St Peter. Despite its unattractive appearance, John Dory is one of the most delicious of all fish, with firm, succulent white flesh.

Habitat Dories are found in the Atlantic; those from American coastal waters are American dories *(Zenopsis ocellata)*, while fish from the eastern Atlantic, from Britain and Norway to Africa, and from the Mediterranean are European dories *(Zeus faber)*. Another species, from the southern hemisphere *(Zeus japonica)*, inhabits the Indo-Pacific oceans.

Other names The name John Dory is said to come from the French *jaune doré* (golden yellow), which describes the golden sheen of very fresh dories. Another theory is that it comes from the Italian *janitore* (janitor). John Dory is also known as St Peter's fish. Indeed, most countries celebrate the St Peter legend in describing the fish. The French call it *St Pierre*; the Italians *San Pietro*; the Spanish *pez de San Pedro*.

Buying Thanks to its large head, almost two-thirds of a dory's weight is wastage, which makes it very expensive. Small dories weighing 1–2kg/2¼–4½lb are sold whole; a 1kg/2¼lb fish will feed two people. For fillets, buy the largest fish you can afford, otherwise the fillets will be too thin. Allow 150–200g/5–7oz per serving.

BOUILLABAISSE

This Provençal fish soup is really more of a stew than a soup and was originally cooked on the beach by fishermen, using those fish that had little market value. It can contain monkfish, weaver fish, John Dory and other Mediterranean fish, plus small crabs and other shellfish, all cooked together with tomatoes, potatoes and onions and flavoured with garlic, olive oil and saffron. Sometimes the cooking liquid is served on its own as soup, accompanied by garlicky croûtons, with the fish served as a separate course.

Cooking Whole fish can be grilled (broiled), braised, baked, steamed or poached. It goes well with Mediterranean flavours. Fillets can be cooked in the same way as sole, brill and turbot. They are superb served with a red wine, white wine or creamy sauce. Small fillets can be used in soups, or with other fish in a mixed grill or *panaché*.

Alternatives Brill, sole, halibut and turbot can be used instead of John Dory.

Monkfish/Anglerfish (*Lophius piscatorius*)

This very ugly fish has an enormous head, a huge mouth fringed with sharp teeth and a dangling "rod" on its nose, which gives monkfish its alternative name of anglerfish. Its comparatively small body has brown, scaleless skin. On the fishmonger's slab, the only part of a monkfish you are likely to see is the tail. The head is usually removed because of its weight, ugliness and the fact that only the cheeks are worth eating. The tail, on the other hand, has a superb firm texture and a delicious sweetness, rather like lobster. The only bone the tail contains is the backbone, which makes it especially easy to prepare and very pleasant to eat. Monkfish liver is a great delicacy.

Habitat Monkfish are found in the Atlantic and Mediterranean. They lurk on the sea bottom dangling their rods to lure passing fish. They are extremely predacious and will swim to the surface to prey on small birds.

Varieties The best monkfish are *Lophius piscatorius* and the similar *L. budegassa*, which is highly prized in Spain. American monkfish or goosefish *(L. americanus)* is considered inferior, while New Zealand monkfish *(Kathetostoma giganteum)* really is a poor relation.

Other names Monkfish is also known as monk or angler. In French, it is *lotte* or *baudroie*, *crapaud* or *diable de mer* ("sea toad" or "devil"); in Italian *coda di rospo* or *rana pescatrice* ("fishing frog"); and in Spanish, *rape*.

Buying Monkfish is available all year, but is at its best in spring and summer before spawning. It is sold as whole tails, fillets or medallions. Generally speaking, the larger the tail, the better the quality; avoid thin, scraggy tails. For tails with the bone in, allow 200g/7oz per person. A 1.5kg/3¼lb tail will serve four to six people. Ask the fishmonger to skin the tail.

PREPARING MONKFISH TAILS

The tails are the best bit of the monkfish. Because of their high water content, fillets should be cooked with very little liquid. They are easy to prepare.

1 Grasp the thick end of the tail firmly with one hand and peel off the skin with the other, working from the thick to the thin end. Carefully pull off the thin, dark or pinkish membrane.

2 Fillet the tail by cutting through the flesh on either side of the backbone with a sharp knife (there are no small bones). The bone can be used to make stock.

Cooking One of the best ways to cook a whole monkfish tail is to make *gigot de mer* – tie it up with string, stud with slivers of garlic and thyme or rosemary leaves, anoint with olive oil and roast in a hot oven. Monkfish is also very good grilled (broiled), made into kebabs, pan-fried, poached and served cold with garlicky mayonnaise, or braised with white wine, saffron and cream or Mediterranean vegetables. It goes very well with other seafood such as salmon, red mullet and shellfish, and is used in *bouillabaisse*. Thin escalopes are delicious marinated in olive oil and lemon juice, then coated with flour and sautéed in butter.

Alternatives Nothing has quite the same nice firm texture as monkfish, but conger eel, John Dory, shark or cod can all be used.

Opah (*Lampris regius*)

Variously known as moonfish, sunfish or mariposa, this slim, oval fish has a steel blue back shading into a rose-pink belly, with silver spots all over. It has red fins, jaws and tail, and, unusually, is the only member of its family. It is toothless and scaleless, and can grow to a huge size. Some specimens weigh over 200kg/440lb and measure more than 2m/6¼ft, though the average weight is about 20kg/44lb. The flesh is salmon pink, with a flavour similar to tuna.

Habitat Opah are found in warm waters throughout the world, but so far only solitary specimens have been caught, and little is known about them.

Other names In French, opah is *poisson lune*; in Italian, *lampride* or *pesce rè*; in Spanish, *luna real*.

Buying If you can find opah, ask your fishmonger to cut it into steaks or escalopes.

Cooking Treat opah in the same way as salmon or tuna. Do not overcook. Serve with a creamy sauce or mayonnaise.

Alternatives Tuna, shark or salmon.

FRESHWATER FISH

Nothing can beat the really fresh taste of a freshwater fish. Sadly, pollution has depleted nature's supply and so many of the freshwater fish we buy are farmed. Apart from trout and zander, you will find few of the fish in this chapter on the fishmonger's slab; most are eaten by the anglers who catch them for sport. If you are lucky enough to be given a freshly caught fish, relish it.

Carp (*Cyprinus carpio*)

These members of the minnow family are among the hardiest of all fish and can live for hundreds of years. Although they can grow to over 35kg/77lb, most of the carp caught weigh only about 2kg/4½lb. There are three main varieties of carp: the very scaly common carp; the scaleless leather carp and the mirror carp, which has only a few large irregularly spaced scales that can easily be removed with a fingernail. All carp have compact, meaty flesh.

Originally natives of Asia, carp were highly prized by Chinese emperors as ornamental pets and as food; they frequently featured on festive banquets. Travellers along the Silk Routes brought them to Europe, where they proliferated in unpolluted fresh water and became a staple food of Eastern European Jews who lived far from the sea, but could cultivate carp in ponds. The tongues were regarded as a delicacy. Carp are still immensely popular in Chinese cuisine; the lips are considered the finest part and they command high prices.

Habitat In their natural state, carp like living in muddy and polluted waters, which they seem to prefer to clean streams and lakes. Nowadays, they are extensively farmed in clean ponds. In the wild, they are considered the most difficult freshwater fish to catch; despite being toothless, they are very powerful fighters, and can demolish fishing tackle.

Other names In French, carp is called *carpe*, and in Italian and Spanish *carpa*.

Buying Most commercially available carp are farmed and weigh 1–2kg/2½–4½lb. A 2kg/4½lb fish will amply serve four. Look for a plump fish, preferably containing roe or milt, which are considered a delicacy. A classic dish is *tourte de laitances* (soft roe or milt), which combines puréed carp and pike with soft carp roes; the mixture is then baked in a puff-pastry tart. You may find live carp for sale; if so, ask the fishmonger to prepare the fish, gutting it and removing the bitter gall bladder from the base of the throat. If you buy a common carp, ask your supplier to scale it for you.

Preparing If you have to scale carp yourself, pour boiling water over the fish to loosen the scales before scraping them off.

Cooking Carp is an incredibly versatile fish, which can be delicious if prepared with interesting flavourings. It can be stuffed with fish mousse or stuffing and baked, and is also extremely good braised, opened out flat and grilled (broiled) or deep-fried, or poached in a tasty sweet-and-sour sauce. A traditional German or Polish Christmas Eve dish is carp cooked in beer or white wine. Carp marries very well with many Oriental flavours such as fresh root ginger, soy sauce and rice wine, and is good added to fish casseroles and soups that have been well flavoured with plenty of ripe tomatoes, fresh herbs and garlic.

Carp can be cooked *au bleu*, or stewed with red wine and mushrooms to make a *meurette*. A classic dish is *carpe à la Juive*, a sweet-and-sour cold dish made with whole or thickly-sliced carp braised with onions, garlic, vinegar, raisins and almonds. When cooked, the whole fish (or the slices re-formed into the original shape), is left to cool in the sauce, which turns to jelly.

Alternatives Catfish, perch and zander can be substituted for carp.

CARP ROE

This roe has a delicate texture and flavour and is much sought after in France, where it is poached and served in pastry cases or ramekins, or made into fritters, omelettes and soufflés. A classic dish is tourte de laitances, *which combines puréed carp and pike with soft carp roes; the mixture is then baked in a puff-pastry tart.*

Catfish (*Ictalurus* spp)

These fish take their name from the long whiskery barbels that help them to locate their prey in the muddy waters where they live. There are dozens of species, ranging from tiny fish to gigantic specimens, which can weigh several hundredweight. Catfish are extremely hardy and can live out of water for a considerable time. These fish are found all over the world, but the best fish for eating are the American species known as bullheads, which have firm, meaty, rather fatty white flesh and very few bones.

Habitat These bottom-living fish feed on live and dead prey. They inhabit muddy waters around the world and are farmed in America and Canada.

Other names In French, catfish is *silure*; in Italian *pesce gatto*; in Spanish *siluro*.

Buying Catfish is sold skinned and usually filleted. Its chunky flesh is filling, so 175g/6oz is ample for one person. Sniff the fish before you buy to make sure that it smells fresh and sweet. Avoid fillets from very large fish, which can be rather coarse.

Cooking The classic southern American cooking method for catfish is to coat it in cornmeal, deep-fry it and serve with tartar sauce. It can also be grilled (broiled) or pan-fried in butter, baked, or cooked like eel, whose flesh it resembles. The tough skin must be removed before cooking. Catfish makes a good addition to fish soups and stews with hearty flavourings such as garlic and tomatoes, or Caribbean spices.

Alternatives Any trout or perch recipe is also suitable for catfish.

Char (*Salvelinus alpinus*)

These trout-like fish are members of the salmon family. They have silvery-green sides dotted with pale spots, and pink bellies. The white flesh is firm and succulent, with a delicate flavour. Char, which used to be abundant in cold lake waters, are becoming increasingly rare in the wild, but they can be farmed. The most common varieties are Arctic char, char, brook trout and lake trout. They can be distinguished from trout by their smaller scales and rounder bodies.

Habitat Arctic char are found in cold-water lakes in North America, Canada, Britain and Iceland. Other species inhabit the lakes of northern France and the Swiss Alps. Brook and lake trout (which are actually char) live in the lakes of North America; Dolly Varden is found from Western North America to the Asian coast.

Other names Char is *omble chevalier* in French, *salmerino* in Italian, and *salvelino* in Spanish.

Buying If you are lucky, you may find wild char in summer and early autumn. Farmed Arctic char from Iceland and America are available all year round. Small fish are sold whole; larger char may be cut into steaks.

Cooking Char can be cooked like trout and salmon trout. It can be poached, braised, fried, grilled (broiled) or barbecued.

POTTED CHAR

In the 18th and 19th centuries, when char proliferated in England's Lake District, this dish became a popular delicacy.

1 Flake leftover cooked char, removing the skin and bones. Weigh the boned fish, then place the fish is a bowl. Melt an equal weight of butter in a pan. Flavour with nutmeg or mace and season, then pour over the flaked fish.

2 Put the fish and butter in ramekins and cover with clear film (plastic wrap), then chill until firm. Seal with a thin layer of clarified butter and cover again; it will keep in the refrigerator for a week.

Grayling (*Thymallus arcticus*)

A relative of trout, grayling is a silvery fish with a small mouth and a long, high dorsal fin spotted with gold. These small fish (rarely weighing more than 1.2kg/2½lb) have firm white flesh with a delicate trout-like flavour; they are said to smell of thyme when first caught. They should be eaten within hours of being caught.

Habitat Grayling are found in lakes from Europe to North America and the northern coasts of Asia, but as these become more polluted, their numbers are declining.

Other names In France, it is called *ombre*; in Italy *temolo*; in Spain *salvelino* or *timalo*.

Cooking Grayling must be scaled before cooking. Pour boiling water over the fish and scrape off the scales with a blunt knife. These fish are excellent brushed with melted butter and grilled (broiled) or pan-fried. To enhance the faint aroma of thyme, put a few fresh thyme leaves inside the fish. Grayling can also be baked and potted like char.

Gudgeon (*Gobio gobio*)

These small fish have large heads, thick lips and delicious, delicate flesh. They live at the bottom of European lakes and rivers.

Other names Gudgeon are called *goujon* in French.

Cooking Gudgeon must be gutted and wiped clean before cooking. Coat them in flour or very light batter and deep-fry until very crisp and golden. Sprinkle with salt and serve with lemon wedges.

Roach (*Rutilis rutilis*)

These members of the minnow family have greenish-grey skin and golden eyes and can weigh up to 1.75kg/4–4½lb. Their white flesh is firm and has quite a good flavour. Their greenish roe, which turns red when cooked, is excellent to eat. Roach contain lots of bones. Use tweezers to remove as many as possible before cooking.

Habitat Roach inhabit sluggish waters in Europe and North America. Unusually for the minnow family, they are also sometimes found in brackish coastal waters.

Other names In French, roach is *gardon*, in Italian *triotto*; in Spanish *bermejuela*.

Cooking Small roach can be fried with other tiny fish to make a *friture*. If you don't mind the bones, larger fish can be grilled (broiled), fried, or baked in white wine.

Pike-Perch/Zander (*Stizostedion lucioperca*)

Zander (sometimes sander) look like a cross between perch and pike, but have a much more delicate and appealing flavour. They have greenish-grey backs with dark bands, and hard, spiny dorsal fins and gills. Zander can grow quite large, sometimes weighing up to 5kg/11lb, and their fillets are delicious and meaty. American pike-perch are known as walleye. Zander can be farmed, and are cooked in the same way as perch.

Perch (*Perca fluviatilis*)

These fish have greenish-gold skins and coral fins. Their humped backs have a spiky dorsal fin. Perch are highly prized for their firm, delicate white flesh. They grow slowly and can reach a weight of 3kg/6½lb, but the average weight is only about 500g/1¼lb.

Habitat Perch are found in sluggish streams, ponds and lakes throughout Europe and North America, and as far north as Siberia.

Other names The American yellow perch is similar to the common perch and is often simply called perch. In French, it is *perche*; in Italian *pesce persico*; in Spanish, *perca*.

Cooking Perch must be scaled the moment they are caught. If they are not, plunge the fish into boiling acidulated water for a few moments, then peel off the entire skin. Small perch can be pan-fried or deep-fried in oil. Fillets can be pan-fried and served with a buttery sauce. Larger fish can be baked, poached, grilled (broiled), or stuffed with breadcrumbs and braised in wine.

Pike (*Esox lucius*)

These fearsome fish have rather elongated, upturned noses and hundreds of sharp teeth. Pike can grow up to 1.5m/5ft, but fish this size are not good to eat, as the flesh is dry and tough. Pike have soft white flesh that is full of sharp bones. During the spawning season, pike roes can become toxic, so they should never be eaten.

Habitat Pike are solitary, aggressive fish who can be found in the streams and ponds of Eastern Europe, Britain and France. The muskellunge and pickerel, which are close relations of pike, are found in America and Canada.

Other names The large American pike, muskellunge is also known as musky. In France, pike is called *brochet* (pickerel is *brocheton*); in Italy, *luccio (luccio giovane)*; in Spain *lucio (lucio joven)*.

Buying Pike are at their best in autumn and early winter. The best fish to buy are small whole fish weighing 1.2–1.7kg/2½–4½lb, which will feed four to six people. Large pike are sold as steaks; these can be tough.

Cooking Scale pike before cooking. Pour over a little boiling water – not too much, as the natural slime on the fish keeps it tender. Whole fish can be stuffed and baked or braised. Small pike are good cooked *au bleu*, or poached in a court-bouillon. Pike can also be cooked *à la Juive*, like carp. Fillets and steaks are best marinated for several hours before cooking to offset any dryness. They can then be pan-fried, braised or baked with white wine and served with a creamy shellfish sauce. They can be made into mousses, terrines and fish cakes.

PIKE QUENELLES

These featherlight oval dumplings are the most famous pike dish and are delicious served with a creamy sauce.

1 Purée 450g/1lb skinned pike fillets in a food processor or blender until smooth, adding 4 egg whites, one at a time, until completely amalgamated. Chill.

2 Whip 475ml/16fl oz/2 cups double (heavy) cream until stiff, then fold it into the fish mousse. Season with salt, white pepper and nutmeg and chill for an hour.

3 To cook, bring a pan of fish stock or water to a bare simmer. Shape the fish mousse into ovals using two tablespoons and drop them into the trembling, not boiling, liquid, a few at a time.

4 Poach for about 10 minutes until the quenelles are cooked through, but still creamy in the centre. Lift the cooked quenelles out of the water with a slotted spoon and drain on kitchen paper.

Shad (*Alosa*)

The largest member of the herring family, shad is a migratory fish that spawns in fresh water. It resembles a fat silvery-green herring and can weigh up to 5kg/11lb. The main species of shad are the allis, thwaite and American. Although the white flesh has a fine, rich flavour, it is full of fine bones.

Habitat Allis and thwaite shad are caught in the Loire and Garonne rivers in France. American shad is found all along the North American coast from Canada to Florida. In the 19th century, American shad were introduced to the Pacific and are now fished from Alaska to southern California.

Other names In French, shad is *alose*; in Italian *alosa*; in Spanish *sábalo*.

Buying Shad are at their best in spring. They are usually sold whole. A 1.5kg/3–3½lb fish will serve four. Ask the fishmonger to clean, scale and bone the fish. Make sure you keep the roe, which is good to eat.

Cooking Once the fish is cooked, make a series of incisions about 10cm/4in apart along its length and pull out as many bones as possible with your fingers. Whole shad can be stuffed with fish mousse, spinach or sorrel and baked, or poached and served on a bed of sorrel with *beurre blanc*. Fillets and steaks are good grilled (broiled), deep-fried or pan-fried and served with tomato sauce; check for small bones before serving.

SHAD ROES

The large-grained roe is the best part of the shad. It has the wonderfully crunchy texture of caviar and is said by some to have aphrodisiac qualities. Shad roes are delicious poached, then creamed with butter, cooked finely chopped shallots, cream, egg yolks and lemon juice. Serve them on toast as an appetizer, or use to garnish cooked shad.

Sturgeon (*family Acipenseridae*)

This fish is part of a family of fish that were abundant in prehistoric times. Their long, thin bodies are armour-plated with several rows of bony scales. They have long, shovel-shaped snouts, with four whiskery barbels that are used for detecting food. Sturgeons can live for more than 150 years, growing to a length of 9m/29½ft and weighing up to 1400kg/3080lb. There are about two dozen species, among them European, beluga, sevruga, oscietra and the sterlet. They have firm, white flesh with a rich texture. Sturgeon can, however, be dry and somewhat indigestible. The fish is often sold smoked, but its real glory is its roe – caviar (see Dried and Salted Fish). In Russia, the bone marrow (*vésiga*) of the fish is dried and used in *coulibiac*.

Habitat Sturgeon are migratory fish that live in the sea but swim into rivers to spawn. They were once plentiful in European and American rivers, but are now found mainly in the rivers that feed the Black and Caspian Seas. They are farmed in France and California.

Other names In French, sturgeon is called *esturgeon*; in Italian it is *storione*; and in Spanish, *esturión*.

Buying Wild sturgeon is at its best in spring and early summer. Farmed fish is available all year round, sold as steaks or large cuts.

Cooking Sturgeon needs careful cooking to make it palatable, and should be marinated or barded with canned anchovy fillets to keep it moist. Its texture is similar to veal and it is often cooked in the same ways, as breaded escalopes or braised steaks. It can be poached in white wine, or baked in a creamy sauce. In Russia, sturgeon is poached with vegetables and served hot with tomato sauce, or cold with a garnish of lemon, gherkins, olives, mushrooms, langoustines, and horseradish. It can be home-smoked.

Tench (*Tinca tinca*)

This fat-bodied relative of the minnow has a coppery-green body covered with small scales and a thick coating of slime. Tench are hardy, fighting fish. They live in sluggish streams and tend to taste muddy, but they make a good addition to a fish stew. They can also be baked or fried, and should be served with a robustly flavoured sauce to enliven the rather bland flesh. They must be scaled and thoroughly cleaned before cooking; scalding them with boiling water helps to remove the scales.

Trout (*family Salmonidae*)

The best known of all freshwater fish, trout are popular with gourmets and fishermen alike. The two main species are brown trout *(salmo trutta)* and rainbow trout *(salmo gairdneri)*. Rainbow trout are extensively farmed. They have silvery-green bodies with dark spots and a pinkish band along the sides. Wild fish have moist white flesh with a sweet flavour; farmed rainbow trout are often fed on a special diet to give the flesh a more appealing pink tinge.

Brown trout come from cold mountain streams and lakes. They have coppery-brown skin dotted with red or orange and brown spots. Their flesh is a delicate pink and their flavour exquisite, but sadly they are seldom found in shops.

Golden trout and coral trout are farmed hybrid trout, with vibrantly coloured skin. Their pinkish flesh is more like that of rainbow trout and tastes very similar.

Habitat Rainbow trout are native to America, but have been introduced to many other parts of the world. Brown trout are natives of Europe; they have also been introduced to America. Golden trout are not found naturally in the wild.

Other names In French, trout is *truite*; in Italian *trota*; in Spanish *trucha*.

Buying Trout are available all year round, usually farmed. Unlike many other fish, they freeze well. For fresh trout, look for a good coating of slime, bright clear eyes and red gills. Trout are usually sold whole with the head on. They are inexpensive; allow one fish per person, unless very large.

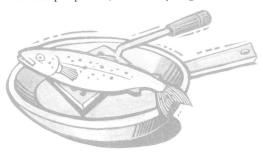

Cooking Trout are very versatile. They are easy to eat, as the flesh falls away from the bone once cooked. The best way to cook a freshly-caught trout is *à la meunière*; dust it with flour, fry in clarified butter until golden brown. Live trout can be cooked *au bleu*. Other cooking methods include poaching, baking, braising, frying, grilling (broiling) and barbecuing. Trout go well with many flavours, such as bacon, onions, garlic and nuts. In Normandy, they are often baked *en papillote* with apples, cider and cream. They are also excellent for home-smoking and make delicious mousses and terrines. If you find roes in your trout, these can be puréed, mixed with seasoned breadcrumbs and used as a stuffing for the fish.

Alternatives Almost any freshwater fish can be used instead of trout.

Whitefish (*family Salmonidae*)

These members of the salmon family are silvery white and resemble trout. Whitefish live in cold, clear lakes in northern Europe and America. In Britain they are sometimes called vendace or powan. They have a pleasant texture and flavour, somewhere between trout and grayling.

DRIED & SALTED FISH

Since prehistoric times, the dehydrating effects of sun and wind have been used as a means of preserving fish. Even today, in remote communities, fish hung out to dry like washing are a common sight. Any fish can be dried in this way; before the days of frozen fish, fishermen would salt and dry whatever they caught in their nets – cod, haddock, herring, mackerel, eel, pike, salmon and sturgeon.

Dried/Salt Cod and Stockfish

The most commonly available dried fish is cod and its relatives (haddock, ling and pollack). Dried cod is variously known as *baccalà* (Italy), *bacalhau* (Portugal) and stockfish (Scandinavia, northern Europe, the Caribbean and Africa). Stockfish is not salted before being dried. Dried cod must be soaked for many hours in fresh, cold water – sometimes for up to a couple of weeks – before it becomes palatable. Stockfish needs to be beaten with a rolling pin to tenderize it, and you may need a saw to cut it.

Buying Make sure you buy the best quality fish, or no amount of soaking will restore its texture. Thick middle cuts are best. Stored in a dry place, it will keep for months.

Preparing Salt cod needs less soaking than stockfish, but it still needs to be left to soften in a bowl of cold water for at least 24 hours. The best way is to leave the tap (faucet) trickling into the bowl; if this is not practical, change the water every 8–12 hours. Taste the fish before cooking to check that it is not too salty; if it is, continue to soak it.

Cooking Dried and salt cod can be poached or baked. Never boil it, as it will toughen. It is a classic ingredient of Provençal aioli. In Spain and Portugal, salt cod is often cooked with tomatoes, peppers, olives, onions and garlic. It also marries well with potatoes and split peas, in a stew or on top of a mound of creamy mash. It makes wonderful fish cakes, fritters and mousses.

Bombay Duck

None knows quite why this dried fish from the Indian sub-continent is called Bombay duck; it may be a corruption *bommaloe macchli* – the Bombay name of the fish. As soon as the fish is caught, it is filleted and hung on cane frames to dry. Bombay duck looks and tastes similar to pork scratchings. It is served as an appetizer or used as a garnish for rice and curry dishes. Uncooked Bombay duck has an unpleasant, pungent smell that fades a little when it is grilled (broiled), but is intensified when it is deep-fried. Keep the heat low when grilling – it is ready when it is crisp and curls at the edges. When cold, serve with drinks or crumble over curries or rice.

Mojama

Known as *mojama*, *mosciame* or *missama*, these salted, sun-dried tuna fillets are very popular in Spain, Sicily and other countries with Arabic influence. Mojama is eaten as a nibble with a glass of fino sherry, or served on slices of baguette that have been rubbed with garlic and drizzled with olive oil.

Shark's Fin

Dried shark's fin is highly prized in China. The fins are sun-dried and preserved in lime. In its dried state, shark's fin looks like a very bushy beard, but after long soaking it becomes a gelatinous, viscous mass. It is highly nutritious and is eaten as a tonic.

SALTED FISH ROE

The best-known is caviar, the eggs of the sturgeon. Others include grey mullet, cod, lumpfish and salmon. In Sweden, bleak roe is compressed into a form of caviar paste called *løjrom* or *kaviar*. It tastes rather sweet, and is an acquired taste.

Caviar

Made from sturgeon roe lightly cured with salt and borax, caviar is the most expensive luxury food in the world. It has a unique texture and an incomparable flavour. The three main types of caviar take their names from the species of sturgeon from which the eggs come. The rarest and most expensive is beluga. The dark grey eggs are large and well separated. Osciotra is golden brown, with smaller grains and an oily texture. Sevruga is the cheapest caviar. It comes from the smallest and most prolific fish and has small, pale greenish-grey grains with a salty flavour. Arguably the best caviar of all comes from Iran; the finest is marketed as Imperial caviar and each tin contains only the eggs from a single fish. The best caviar is harvested from fish that are just about to spawn; the eggs are pale and full of flavour.

Each type of caviar is graded. The finest, malassol, is slightly salted. Second grade caviar is saltier and may be made from a mixture of roes. Inferior quality sevruga roe is pressed into a solid mass (pressed caviar), which squashes the eggs. It has a strong, salty taste and can be oily. It is fine for cooking and is cheaper. The best caviar is always fresh.

Despite its high price, caviar is so sought-after that the world's population of sturgeon is endangered almost to the point of extinction. Sturgeon are now found almost exclusively in the Caspian Sea. Recently, however, the fish have been farmed successfully in France.

Buying Never buy caviar that seems cheap. Caviar should be kept in the refrigerator at 0–3°C/32–37°F. Once a jar or can of caviar is opened, it should be eaten within a week. **Serving** Caviar should be served chilled. Never serve or eat it with a silver spoon, as this will react with the caviar and give it a metallic taste. A proper caviar spoon is made of bone. Traditionally, caviar is served with blinis and soured cream. Chopped hard-boiled (hard-cooked) egg and onions make it go further. It is also delicious served with toast and unsalted butter. Allow about 25g/1oz caviar per person as a first course.

Grey Mullet Roe/Bottarga/Tarama

Dried grey mullet roe is regarded as a great delicacy. The orange roe is salted, then dried, pressed and packed in a sausage shape inside a thin skin. Wrapped in clear film (plastic wrap), it will keep for several months. Grey mullet roe is the traditional ingredient of *taramasalata*.

Salmon Caviar/Keta

This is made from orange-pink salmon roe. The eggs are much larger than sturgeon caviar and have a pleasant, mild flavour and an excellent texture. They can be used to garnish pâtés and mousses, or can be eaten like caviar with soured cream and blinis. A squeeze of lemon enhances the flavour. The name *keta* comes from the Russian for chum salmon. Salmon caviar is sold in jars.

PICKLED FISH

As well as salting or drying fish to preserve them, you can pickle them in vinegar or brine. Before the days of frozen fish, this was another way of making your catch last longer. Many countries have their own pickled fish, such as Dutch *maatjes* herring, German soused herring and Swedish *gravad lax*. Fish particularly suited to pickling are oily ones such as herrings.

Baltic/Bismarck Herring
The herrings are split like kippers and marinated in white wine vinegar and spices, ranging from red (bell) peppers to juniper berries. The fillets are layered with onion rings and carrot rounds for about 24 hours. These are delicious with sour cream.

Maatjes Herring
Fat young female herrings (the name means maiden or virgin in Dutch) are skinned and filleted before being lightly cured in salt, sugar, spices and saltpetre, which turns the flesh a brownish-pink colour. In Holland and Belgium they are eaten with chopped raw onion. The Scandinavian equivalent is *matjes*. These have a stronger flavour and are generally eaten with some sour cream and chopped hard-boiled egg.

Pickled Herring
Herring fillets are marinated in vinegar and spices, then coated in a sour cream sauce. Pickled herring are also sometimes known as marinated herring.

Soused Herring and Bratheringe
These marinated herrings are simple to prepare at home. In the German version, *bratheringe*, herring fillets are lightly floured and fried until golden, then steeped in a boiled marinade of vinegar, pickling spice and herbs. Soused herring are not fried before being marinated.

Rollmops
Herring fillets are rolled up, skin-side out, around peppercorns and onions, secured with wooden toothpicks (cocktail sticks) and packed in a marinade. Serve with rye bread, or a cucumber salad dressed with a sour cream and dill sauce.

Gravad lax/Gravlax
This Swedish speciality cures fresh raw salmon fillet with dill, sugar, salt and coarse peppercorns. *Gravad lax* is often packed with a dill-flavoured mustard sauce.

Jellied Eels
These are made by boiling pieces of eel in a marinade of white wine vinegar and herbs, then leaving them in the liquid with lots of chopped parsley until the mixture sets to a light jelly. Jellied eels are becoming rare, but are available frozen and in cans. Serve with thick slices of bread and butter.

CANNED FISH

This is a very useful store-cupboard (pantry) ingredient and a broad choice, from tiny anchovy fillets to larger fish such as salmon and tuna, is readily available in supermarkets. While canned fish never has the subtle texture and flavour of fresh fish, it can be delicious in its own right and is invaluable for salads and sandwiches.

Anchovies

Fillets of this fish are canned or bottled in oil. They are a staple ingredient of *salade niçoise* and *tapenade* and are used as a topping for pizzas and *crostini*. They can be mashed into butter as a topping for grilled (broiled) fish, or added to tomato sauces. Anchovies enhance the flavour of many non-fish dishes without making them taste fishy. Once opened, anchovies perish quickly, so use at once.

Pilchards

These fish are large, older sardines. They lack the subtle flavour of sardines, so are usually canned in tomato sauce.

Salmon

Canned salmon is a useful kitchen standby. It is available in several grades, from the cheapest pink chum salmon to the best-quality wild red Alaskan fish. Canned salmon is good for making mousses, soufflés and fish cakes.

Sardines

These were the first fish to be canned. The finest sardines are fried in olive oil before canning. Most sardines are beheaded and gutted before being packed raw, complete with backbones, in groundnut (peanut) or olive oil. Inferior or damaged fish are packed in tomato sauce. Sardines in olive oil are the best; the more expensive varieties are left to mature for at least a year before being sold, to soften the bones and mature the flavour. Serve them whole on hot toast or mash them with lemon juice and cayenne pepper to make a pâté, stuff them into hard-boiled eggs or make them into sandwiches.

Tuna

In recent years, canned tuna has received a bad press because dolphins were often caught in the tuna nets and slaughtered unnecessarily. Nowadays, most tuna is line-caught. The best canned tuna is the pale albacore, which is usually canned in one solid piece. Cheaper varieties of tuna such as skipjack and yellowfin are often sold as chunks or flaky broken pieces. Tuna comes packed in olive oil (the best), vegetable oil or brine, which is healthier and lighter.

Serve it with pasta, in sandwiches and salads, or make into a pâté or fish loaf. It is used in the classic Italian dish *vitello tonnato*, which comprises loin of veal coated in a thick tuna-flavoured mayonnaise.

SMOKED FISH

Today smoking is used less for preserving and more for imparting a unique flavour. There are two methods of smoking fish, cold and hot, which give very different results. For both methods, the fish must first be salted in dry salt or brine. They are then smoked over different types of wood, which impart a distinctive flavour. Every smokery produces fish with a different taste and texture.

COLD-SMOKED FISH

A high degree of skill is required when cold smoking to get the flavour and texture just right. The process is done at a temperature of 30–35°C/86–95°F, which cures but does not cook the fish. Some cold-smoked fish are eaten raw; others are cooked.

Smoked Salmon

This is made by brining the fish, then dry curing it in sugar with flavourings such as molasses or whisky, and smoking it over wood chips. Depending on the strength of the cure, the type of wood used and the smoking time, smoked salmon can vary in colour from pale pink to brownish-red.

Buying Smoked salmon is usually sold ready-sliced, with the slices separated by sheets of transparent paper. Whole sides are sliced, then reassembled to restore the original shape of the fillet. The thinner the salmon is sliced the better. Whole sides are sometimes sold unsliced and are cheaper. The most expensive smoked salmon is made from wild fish, but good-quality farmed fish give excellent results.

Freshly-sliced smoked salmon is best, but vacuum packs are better value and perfectly acceptable. Frozen smoked salmon is also available. Smoked salmon trimmings are much cheaper than slices and are perfect for mousses, pâtés and omelettes. In Jewish delicatessens, you will find *lox*, a heavily-cured salmon with a reddish-gold colour.

Serving Top-quality smoked salmon should be eaten just as it is, served with very thinly sliced brown bread and butter. Cheaper smoked salmon can be served in traditional Jewish style with cream cheese and thinly sliced raw onion as a topping for bagels, or in sandwiches. Smoked salmon makes a delicious salad. Scraps can be stirred into omelettes, mixed into pasta and puréed to make mousses. If you are slicing smoked salmon yourself, slice thinly across the grain, working from head to tail.

Cold-smoked Trout

A cheaper alternative to smoked salmon is cold-smoked trout, which looks similar to smoked salmon, but has a much more delicate flavour. It can be eaten in the same way as smoked salmon.

Smoked Halibut

Sold thinly sliced, smoked halibut has translucent white flesh and a very delicate flavour. It makes an excellent addition to a plate of assorted smoked fish, or can be used like smoked haddock. Try it with a mild, creamy horseradish sauce.

Smoked Sturgeon

This luxury smoked fish has pale pinkish flesh with a rich flavour and a succulent texture. It should be thinly sliced across the grain. Eat it with very thinly sliced brown bread and butter.

Smoked Haddock

There are many types of smoked haddock, from fluorescent dyed yellow fillets to pale, naturally cured fillets and finnan haddock or haddie, which are split and look like pale-golden kippers. They are named after the Scottish village of Findon where the special smoking process originated. Use it in any smoked haddock recipe, but it must be boned and skinned after cooking. Glasgow pales are lightly brined and smoked, resulting in a very delicate flavour.

Buying If possible, avoid artificially dyed smoked haddock and opt for more natural pale beige fillets.

Cooking Smoked haddock is succulent and delicious. It is usually eaten hot, but fillets can be thinly sliced and marinated and eaten raw as a starter. Smoked haddock can be grilled (broiled) like kippers or poached in milk or water. Serve it with butter or topped with a lightly poached egg, or *à la florentine* on a bed of creamed spinach. A classic Scottish dish is ham 'n' haddie, in which finnan haddock is pan-fried in ham fat and topped with slices of fried ham. It makes excellent mousse or pâté, and also features in kedgeree and omelette Arnold Bennett: a sumptuous omelette oozing with cheese, cream and smoked haddock.

Smoked Herrings or Kippers

These are made by brining split herrings, then hanging them up in pairs and smoking over oak fires for 4–18 hours. Dye is often added to the brine, resulting in reddish-brown kippers, but the best are undyed and therefore paler. Kippers can be unpopular because they have so many bones.

Buying Look for the plumpest kippers you can find. Always try to buy undyed kippers. Frozen, boil-in-the-bag kipper fillets can be convenient, but tend to have a flabby texture and insipid flavour.

Cooking Many people are nervous about cooking kippers because of the smell. To avoid any unpleasant odour, put them head-down into a tall jug, pour over boiling water and leave to stand for 10 minutes, by which time the kippers will be cooked. If you serve kippers often, it is better to keep a jug especially for cooking them. Kippers can also be microwaved and are good grilled (broiled), skin-side up, or shallow fried in butter. Raw kippers can be marinated and served as a starter.

BONING COOKED KIPPERS
To bone cooked kippers, lay the kipper on a plate, skin-side up. Run a knife point around the edge to lift up the skin. Run the knife point down the backbone and eat the flesh that lies on top of the bones.

Bloaters

These are herrings that are left ungutted before being briefly salted, then smoked for 12 hours. The guts impart a slightly gamey flavour and the enzymes they contain cause the herring to become slightly bloated in appearance during smoking. Because they have not been gutted, bloaters do not keep as well as other smoked herring and should be eaten within a few days. Always gut them before serving.

Other varieties *Harengs saurs* are a great speciality of Boulogne in France; they are even more bloated than English bloaters. Most bloated of all are the Swedish *surströmming*. Like *harengs saurs,* they are traditionally eaten with potatoes.

Cooking Bloaters can be eaten as they are in salads and sandwiches. They can also be mashed into a paste with lemon juice and cayenne pepper or grilled (broiled) and served with butter. To skin bloaters, pour boiling water over and leave for 2 minutes, then peel off the skin.

Hot-smoked Fish

Fish that are smoked at a temperature of 80–85°C/176–185°F, which simultaneously cures and cooks them, need no additional cooking. Trout, mackerel, eel and herrings can all be hot-smoked. Recently it has become fashionable to hot-smoke salmon, producing a different flavour and texture from cold-smoked salmon.

Arbroath Smokies

These hot-smoked haddock are beheaded and gutted but left whole. They have deep golden skin and soft pale-gold flesh with a more delicate flavour than cold-smoked haddock. In their native Scotland, they are a popular breakfast or supper dish. Smokies are sold whole, so ask the fishmonger to split them open for you. Grill (broil) and serve with butter. They make a good pâté mashed with butter and lemon juice.

Smoked Eel

This fish has a very rich, dense texture and can only be eaten in small quantities. The skin, which is easily removed, is black and shiny and the flesh has a pinkish tinge. The eel can be served as an hors d'oeuvre, with horseradish or mustard sauce, or made into a salad or pâté. It is particularly good served on a bed of celeriac *rémoulade*. Smoked eel also makes a good addition to a platter of mixed smoked fish. When buying smoked eel, check that the skin is shiny and has not dried out. For an ample serving for one, you will need about 90g/3½oz.

Brisling, Sild and Sprats

These small hot-smoked herring with rich oily flesh are usually skinned and filleted and served cold as a starter with brown bread and butter. They can also be brushed with melted butter and lightly grilled (broiled), then served hot with toast.

Buckling

These large, ungutted hot-smoked herrings have a rich flavour. They are best eaten cold with brown bread and butter, but can be mashed into a paste or grilled (broiled) and served with scrambled eggs.

Smoked Mackerel

This has a rich flavour and a succulent velvety-smooth texture. The fillets are sold loose or pre-packed. They are sometimes coated in a thick layer of finely crushed peppercorns. Smoked mackerel is delicious eaten cold in a salad, or with horseradish sauce and a generous squeeze of lemon juice. It makes an excellent pâté and can be flaked and added to an omelette or quiche. Try it instead of smoked haddock in a kedgeree. Allow one fillet per person.

Skinning Smoked Mackerel
To skin smoked mackerel, lay the fish on a board, skin-side up. Starting at the tail end, peel back the skin towards the head. Pull away any fins and bones.

Smoked Trout

Among the finest of all hot-smoked fish, smoked trout should be plump and moist, with a beautiful golden-pink colour. The flesh has a delicate flavour and is less rich than smoked herring or mackerel. The best smoked trout is first brined, then gutted and hot-smoked over birch with the addition of a little peat for a smokier flavour. Smoked trout is usually sold as skinned fillets, but you may occasionally find them whole, with the head on. Skin them like smoked mackerel. Smoked trout is delicious served on its own with dill or horseradish sauce. It can be made into mousses or pâté and is also good in salads, omelettes and flans. Allow one fillet per person as a starter; two as a main course.

Fish Sauces & Pastes

For centuries, man has produced fish sauces made by fermenting whole fish or various parts, including the entrails, into a savoury, salty liquid to flavour and enhance fish dishes. Do not be confused by the term sauce – these are not to be served on their own but should be used as flavourings or condiments. Numerous sauces and pastes are made all over the world from Europe to the Far East.

Anchovy Essence

Salted anchovies are processed into a thick, rich pinkish-brown sauce with an intensely salty flavour. A few drops will enhance the flavour of almost any savoury dish, but anchovy essence must be used sparingly, or it will overpower the other ingredients.

Nam Pla/Thai Fish Sauce

This pungent, salty sauce is produced by packing small fish such as anchovies in brine in barrels and leaving them to ferment in the hot sun for several months. Curiously, the resulting sauce does not taste of fish but more like a very intense soy sauce.

Almost unheard of in the West a few years ago, *nam pla* is now an essential ingredient in every adventurous cook's store cupboard. It is a staple ingredient in all Far Eastern cooking; in Vietnam, it is called *nuoc cham*. It can be added to any savoury dishes, or mixed with flavourings such as garlic, lime juice and chilli to make a dipping sauce, or can be used to add flavour to salad dressings. *Nam pla* is an essential ingredient in Thai green curry paste, a spicy mixture containing shallots, garlic, hot green chillies, lemon grass, fresh root ginger, coriander (cilantro), lime leaves, coriander seeds and cumin seeds, groundnut (peanut) oil, light brown sugar and salt and pepper.

When buying, *nam pla* should be a clear amber colour; if it is dark brown it will have a very fishy taste.

Shrimp Paste

This speciality of Malaysia and Indonesia is made from salted, fermented shrimps. The powerful-smelling paste, which is also called *blachan, terasi* or *belacan*, is sold in blocks and is mixed with other ingredients to make a flavouring for stir-fries, soups and other savoury dishes.

Worcestershire Sauce

This rather spicy sauce contains anchovies, although you would never guess. Originally produced in India, the precise ingredients of Worcestershire sauce remain a closely guarded secret, but they include malt and spirit vinegar, molasses, tamarind, garlic, onions and spices as well as anchovies.

Worcestershire sauce gives a lift to any savoury dish and can be used sparingly to enliven a marinade. It is also an essential ingredient in a Bloody Mary cocktail. The original and genuine Worcestershire sauce, made by Lea and Perrins, is vastly superior to all its imitators.

CRUSTACEANS

These creatures belong to the enormous family of decapods, ten-limbed creatures that are believed to be descendants of invertebrates that lived on the earth over 200 million years ago. These curious-looking creatures with their hard carapaces and spidery limbs hardly look like the most appealing of foods, but the sweet flesh concealed within the shell is delicious.

CRABS AND LOBSTERS

These crustaceans may require considerable effort both to prepare, cook and eat, but they are well worth it.

CRABS

There are dozens of varieties of crab, ranging from hefty common crabs to tiny shore crabs. They travel hundreds of miles in a year from feeding to spawning grounds and are often caught in baited pots sited on the sea bed far from the shore. As their bodies grow, crabs shed their shells and grow a new carapace. At first the new shells are soft. These "soft-shell" crabs are a delicacy and can be eaten whole, shell and all. Female crabs are known as hens. They have sweeter flesh than the males, but are smaller and their claws contain less flesh.
Other names In French, crab is *crabe*, *tourteau* or *araignée*. In Italian, *granchio* or *granseola*; in Spanish; *cangrejo* or *centolla*.

Blue Crab (*Callinectes sapidus*)

These crabs have steely-grey bodies and bright, electric-blue legs and claws. They are found in American waters and are prized for their white meat.
Soft-shell crabs are blue crabs that have shed their hard carapaces and are tender, with sweet, creamy flesh. They are delicate and do not keep or travel well, so they are generally sold frozen, although you may find fresh ones in the US in the summer.

Common Edible Crab/Brown Crab (*Cancer pagarus*)

These large brown-red crabs can measure well over 20cm/8in. They have powerful claws that can deliver an extremely nasty nip, but they contain plenty of tasty meat. Common edible crabs are found on Atlantic coasts and parts of the Mediterranean.
Cooking These are the perfect crabs for boiling to serve cold with mayonnaise. The claws contain plenty of firm meat. After cooking, this can be removed from the shell in one piece, marinated in a Worcestershire sauce and Tabasco dressing and served as a cocktail snack. The claw meat is delicious deep-fried. The liver and roe of these crabs are also very good.

Dungeness/California Crab (*Cancer magister*)

These trapezium-shaped crabs are found all along the Pacific coast. They are similar to common edible crabs and can be cooked in exactly the same way.

King Crab (*Paralithodes camtschiatica*)

Looking like huge spiny spiders, king crabs are hideous, but very good to eat. Their size is awe-inspiring; a mature male king crab can weigh up to 12kg/26lb and measure 1m/39in across. Their triangular bodies are bright red, with a creamy underside. Every part tastes good, from the body meat to that from the narrow claws and long legs.

Buying Only male king crabs are sold; they are larger and meatier than the females. Cooked legs are available frozen, and king types of crab meat is frequently canned. Unlike most crab meat, canned king crab is of excellent quality and highly prized. The best comes from Alaska, Japan and Russia, where it is sold as kamchatka crab.

Snow Crab (*Chionoetes* spp)
Also known as queen crabs, these crabs from the north Pacific have roundish pink-brown bodies and exceptionally long legs. The delicious, sweet flesh is difficult to remove from the body, but the claw meat is more accessible. Snow crab meat is usually sold frozen or canned.

Spider Crab (*Maia squinado*)
These alarming-looking crabs have spiny shells and long, slender legs, which give them the appearance of enormous reddish-pink spiders; hence their alternative name of sea spider. Those found along the Atlantic coasts measure about 20cm/8in across, but the giant species, found in the waters around Japan, measures up to 40cm/16in, with a claw span of almost 3m/9¾ft – a truly terrifying sight.

Stone Crab (*family Lithodidae*)
Similar in appearance to king crabs, stone crabs live at great depths. They have a superb flavour, but are usually sold frozen or canned rather than fresh.

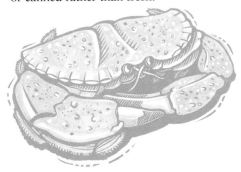

Swimming Crab (*family Portunidae*)
The main distinguishing feature of these crabs is their extra pair of legs, shaped like paddles. Among the species of swimming crabs are mud or mangrove, shore and velvet crabs. Shore crabs are eaten in Italy in their soft-shelled state; they also make great soup. Mud crabs, with their excellent claw meat, are popular in Australia and South-east Asia.

Cooking Crab can be cooked in a multitude of ways. The sweet, succulent meat is rich and filling, so it needs a light touch when cooking. Picking it out of the shell is hard work, but the result is well worth the effort. Recipes for crab meat include devilled crab (where the meat is removed from the shell and cooked with mustard, horseradish, spices and breadcrumbs); crab mornay, in which the meat is combined with a Gruyère cheese sauce enriched with sherry and mushrooms, and potted crab. The flesh marries well with clean Oriental flavours such as lime juice, coriander (cilantro) and chilli; combined with these, it makes the perfect summer salad. Crab meat is perfect for fish cakes such as Thai crab cakes. It also makes excellent soup; a classic Scottish dish is *partan bree*, a creamy crab soup made with fish stock, milk and rice.

In the shell, crab can be boiled and served with mayonnaise, steamed with aromatics or baked with ginger and spring onions.

Soft-shell crabs are usually lightly coated in flour and deep-fried. *Molecchie fritte* is a Venetian speciality: the crabs are soaked in beaten egg before being fried. In China, soft-shell crabs are served with a spicy garnish of chilli or fresh root ginger. Soft-shell crabs can also be sautéed in butter and sprinkled with lightly toasted almonds, or brushed with melted butter and fresh lemon juice, then tossed lightly in flour before grilling (broiling).

LOBSTER

These crustaceans are the ultimate luxury seafood. Their uniquely firm, sweet flesh has a delicious flavour and many people regard them as the finest crustaceans of all. The best lobsters live in cold waters, scavenging for food on the rocky sea bed. Like crabs, they cast off their outgrown shells every couple of years. Their colour varies according to their habitat, from steely blue to greenish-brown to reddish-purple; all turn brick red when cooked. Lobsters grow very slowly, only reaching maturity at six years old, by which time they are about 18cm/7in long. If you find a 1kg/2¼lb lobster, it will be about ten years old.

Lobsters must be bought live or freshly boiled. The powerful pincers, which the creature uses for catching and crushing its prey, can be dangerous. If you buy a live lobster, make sure that the pincers are secured with a stout elastic (rubber) band.

Other names In French, lobster is called *homard*; in Italian, it is *astice*; and in Spanish, *bogavante*.

Canadian/American Lobster (*Homarus americanus*)

The hardiest species of lobster, these are found in large numbers in the waters around Canada and the North American Atlantic. They resemble the European lobster, but are greener in colour and the claws are slightly rounder and fleshier. Although they make excellent eating, their flavour does not quite match up to that of the European lobster. The best-known American lobster is the Maine lobster. Canadian and Maine lobsters are air-freighted live to European markets and shops to meet the demand for these crustaceans. Even taking into account the freight costs, they are considerably cheaper than their European counterparts.

European Lobster (*Homarus gammarus*)

These lobsters, which come from England, Scotland, Ireland, Norway and Brittany, are regarded as having the finest flavour of all. They have distinctive blue-black colouring, and are sometimes speckled with bright blue. European lobsters are becoming increasingly rare and expensive. If they are caught in reasonable numbers during the summer months, they are often held as live stock in vivariums, massive holding tanks built into the sea.

Unfortunately, lobsters do not eat while they are in captivity, so although holding them in the vivariums ensures that they are available throughout the year, the quality of the lobsters deteriorates greatly as the season progresses and so by early spring, the lobsters tend to be undernourished and thin and do not make good eating.

Slipper/Squat Lobster (*Scyllarus arctus*)

There are over fifty species of these warm-water lobsters that are found in temperate waters all over the world. They have wide, flattened bodies, spindly clawed legs and shovel-shaped feelers at the front. The various different species vary in colour and size. The best known squat lobsters are the Australian "bugs"; the best known of these lobsters are the Balmain and Moreton Bay bugs. The Moreton Bay bug is said to have a better flavour than the Balmain. The comparatively small tails of these lobsters

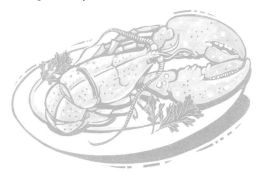

contain wonderfully sweet, tender flesh. Squat lobsters are seldom sold in Europe, but can occasionally be found in France, where they are called *cigales* (grasshoppers) because of the cricket-like noises they make in the water. Italians call them *cicala di mare* and in Spain they are called *cigarra*.

Cooking Lobster

All types of lobster are best cooked very simply to allow the delicate flavour to speak for itself. They can be boiled in salted water or court-bouillon and served hot with melted butter or cold with mayonnaise, plainly grilled (broiled) or fried in the shell with oil and butter. A plain boiled lobster can be the crowning glory of a *plateau de fruits de mer* (seafood platter).

Classical French cookery has a plethora of rich and delicious lobster recipes that reflect the luxurious quality of these crustaceans. These dishes, which are usually served with plain boiled rice to offset the richness, include *lobster cardinale*, with mushrooms and truffles in a velvety sauce; *lobster newburg*, with a cognac and sherry-flavoured cream sauce; *lobster bretonne*, with prawns (shrimp) and mushrooms in a white wine sauce, and the world-famous *lobster thermidor*, with its rich brandy and mustard-flavoured sauce. There are also a number of modern recipes that combine lobster with Oriental flavours such as fresh root ginger and star anise, but these spices should always be used in moderation to avoid overpowering the deliciously delicate flavour of the lobster.

Lobster is superb with fresh pasta. Use it as a filling for ravioli or toss it into tagliolini with plenty of lemon juice and butter. Cold boiled lobster can be diced and made into a lobster cocktail or added to a salad. When cooking lobster, keep the shells to use in a shellfish stock or soup.

PREPARING A COOKED LOBSTER

Whether you buy a ready-cooked lobster or a live one that you cook yourself, they are very easy to prepare. You will need a large, heavy knife or cleaver, a mallet or rolling pin, and a lobster pick to remove the meat from the legs.

1 Hold the body of the lobster firmly in one hand and twist off the claws.

2 Hold the lobster the right way up on a chopping board. Insert a large sharp knife at right angles to the seam between the body and head and press down firmly to split the body and tail lengthways.

3 Turn the lobster round to face the other way and cut firmly through the head. Separate the lobster into two halves and discard the stomach sac.

4 Twist off the legs and then flatten them lightly with the back of the knife. Use a lobster pick to remove the flesh.

5 To remove the meat from the claws, first break up the claws into sections. Hold the larger section of the claw, curved-side down, and sharply pull off the smaller pincer. Twist off the lower section of the claw at the joint.

6 Gently crack the claw shell with a mallet or the end of a rolling pin and remove the flesh.

7 The lobster can be grilled (broiled) in the shell with butter, or the flesh can be diced and used in sauces.

The tomalley, the lobster's green-coloured liver, is considered a great delicacy as is the coral (eggs), which is found in the female (hen) lobster. Both tomalley and coral can be eaten on their own or added to sauces, which can be served with other seafood.

Crawfish (*Palinurus vulgaris*)

These are similar to lobsters, except that they have spiny shells and no claws. They are variously known as spiny lobsters, rock lobsters, langouste and crayfish (but must not be confused with freshwater crayfish). Crawfish are found on the rocky sea bed in many parts of the world. The colour of their shells varies according to where they come from: Atlantic crawfish are dark reddish-brown; those from the Florida coast are brown with quite pale spots; warm-water varieties can be pink or bluish-green. All turn pink or red when cooked. Crawfish have dense, very white flesh, similar to that of lobster, but with a milder flavour. Those from the Atlantic are the finest and sweetest. Crawfish from warmer waters tend to be a little coarse.

Other names In France, crawfish are called *langouste*; in Italy they are *aragosta*; and in Spain *langosta*.

Buying Crawfish are generally sold cooked. Females have a better flavour than males, so always look for the egg sac underneath the thorax. Because there is no claw meat in crawfish, allow one 450g/1lb crawfish per person. Florida crawfish are often sold frozen as "lobster" tails.

Cooking Crawfish can be cooked in the same way as lobster. However, they benefit from spicy seasonings and are excellent in Oriental recipes.

Crayfish (*Astacus astacus*) and Yabby (*Cherax*)

Crayfish are miniature freshwater lobsters, which grow to a maximum length of 10cm/4in. The exception is a species found in Tasmania, which can weigh up to 6kg/13lb. Crayfish have a wonderful flavour and, whatever their colour when alive, turn a glorious deep scarlet when cooked. Over three hundred species are found in well-

SHELLING COOKED CRAYFISH

These miniature freshwater lobsters are easy to shell and taste delicous. Only the meat from their bodies and claws is eaten. Their heads may be used as a garnish.

1 Hold the crayfish between your finger and thumb and gently twist off the tail.

2 Hold the tail shell between your thumb and index finger, twist and pull off the flat end; the thread-like intestinal tract will come away easily. Peel the tail.

3 Hold the head and thorax in one hand. Use the other index finger to prise off the whole underside, including the gills and innards, and discard these. Finally, twist off the claws and discard the head.

oxygenated streams throughout Europe, America and Australia, although most of the European species have been wiped out, largely through pollution and disease. Luckily, crayfish can be farmed successfully. However, the most prolific variety, the voracious American signal crayfish, are prone to a killer disease, which they often pass on to wild native crayfish, resulting in their near-extinction.

Other names The most commonly available crayfish are the European, the red-claw, the American signal, the red Louisiana swamp, the greenish Turkish crayfish, the Australian yabby and the large marron, which is a deep purplish-grey colour. In France, crayfish are called *écrevisse*; in Italy, they are called *gambero di fiume*; in Spain, they are known as *cangrejo de rio*.

Buying Fresh crayfish should be bought alive. There is a lot of wastage, so allow 8–12 crayfish per serving. Keep the shells to make stock, soup or sauces. Frozen crayfish are also available, but are not worth eating on their own.

Cooking Crayfish feature in a great many luxurious dishes, including bisque (a rich creamy soup), sauces and mousses. They are superb poached in a court-bouillon for about 5 minutes and served cold with mayonnaise or hot with lemony melted butter. Only the tail and claw meat is eaten; the head is often used as a garnish. The cleaned heads and shells can be used to make a shellfish stock or soup.

Langoustines/Dublin Bay Prawns/Scampi (*Nephrops norvegicus*)

Smaller relatives of lobsters, langoustines have smooth-shelled narrow bodies with long thin, knobbly claws. They are salmon-pink in colour. The largest can measure up to 23cm/9in, but the average length is about 12cm/4½in. Langoustines were originally found in Norway, hence their Latin name, and they are still sometimes known as Norway lobsters. Nowadays, they are caught all along the Atlantic coast, in the Adriatic and western Mediterranean. The colder the water in which langoustines live, the better the flavour.

Other names The French know them as *langoustine*; the Italians call them *scampo*; while in Spain they are called *cigala* or *langostina*.

Buying Once caught, fresh langoustines deteriorate very rapidly so are often cooked and frozen at sea. Live langoustines are therefore something of a rarity in British and US fish markets, although you will often find them in Europe. If you are lucky enough to find live langoustines, and can be certain of cooking them soon after purchase, they will be an excellent buy. It is important to check that they are still moving; if they have died, they will have an unpleasant woolly texture. Unlike other crustaceans, langoustines do not change colour when cooked, so make sure you know what you are buying. Langoustines are graded by size; larger specimens are better value, as they contain more meat. They are also available frozen, often as scampi (extra large shrimp) tails. If they have been shelled, allow about 115g/4oz per person; you will need twice this quantity if the langoustines are in the shell as there is a lot of wastage.

Cooking Most people probably have encountered tasteless, badly cooked scampi at some time in their lives. However, when langoustines are properly cooked they have a delicate and delicious flavour. They must be cooked very briefly. Roast in oil and garlic in a hot oven for 3–5 minutes; split them and grill (broil) or barbecue for about 2 minutes on each side; or poach in a court-bouillon and serve hot with melted butter. Remember that most langoustines on sale are already cooked, so they should be subjected to as little heat as possible. Whole langoustines are delicious served cold with mayonnaise. They make a wonderful addition to a *plateau de fruits de mer* (seafood platter). Langoustine tails can be baked *au gratin* in a creamy béchamel sauce with mushrooms and Gruyère cheese, or served Scottish-style in a whisky-flavoured sauce. They can also be deep-fried and served with lemon wedges, but take care not to overcook them.

Prawns & Shrimps

These are the world's most popular crustaceans and are eaten in huge quantities around the globe. In the UK, shrimps are simply small prawns. In the US, however, all prawns and shrimps are known collectively as shrimp. Most prawns (or shrimp) have narrow, tapering bodies, curled over at the tail, and long antennae. Their colour varies from species to species.

Cold-water Prawns

These come from northern waters around Europe, Norway and the North Atlantic. As with other crustaceans, prawns from colder waters have a better flavour than those from warm waters.

Common Prawn/Pink Shrimp (*Palaemon serratus*)

These translucent, brownish prawns can grow up to 10cm/4in in length. They are found in deep waters in the Atlantic Ocean and Mediterranean Sea, but related species are found throughout the world. They have an exceptionally good flavour and turn a glorious red colour when cooked. They also command enormously high prices.
Other names Sword shrimp or Algerian shrimp. In France, they are called *crevette rose* or *bouquet*; in Italy, *gamberello*; in Spain, *camarón* or *quisquilla*.

Deep-sea Prawn (*Pandalus borealis*)

Sometimes sold as large shrimps, these cold-water prawns live at great depths in the North Sea. They are hermaphrodite. All begin life as males, but become female halfway through their lifespan. Deep-sea prawns have translucent pink bodies, which turn pale salmon-pink on cooking. They have a delicate, juicy flavour and are almost always sold cooked.
Other names In France, they are *crevette*; in Italy, *gambero*; in Spain, *camarón*.

Mediterranean Prawn (*Aristeus antennatus*)

These very large prawns can measure up to 10cm/4in. The colour varies – the heads can be anything from blood-red to deep coral pink – but once cooked, they turn a brilliant red colour. The flesh is delicious and very succulent. Mediterranean prawns are sold cooked and should be served as they are, with home-made mayonnaise or aioli and French bread. Served in this way, they make a wonderful appetizer; allow 3–4 prawns per person.
Other names Mediterranean prawns are also known as blue or red shrimp. They are called *crevette rouge* in France; *gambero rosso* in Italy; and *carabinero* in Spain and *gamba* in Spanish restaurants.

Butterflied Prawns

Prawns look very attractive when they are split and butterflied. Large butterflied prawns are particularly good grilled (broiled) or barbecued.

1 The easiest way to butterfly prawns is to deepen the incision made to remove the black vein (intestinal tract), cutting nearly but not quite through to the belly.

2 Open the prawn out flat. If the prawns are very large, make the incision right through the belly to give a slightly more pronounced shape.

Common/Brown Shrimp (*Crangon crangon*)

These small shrimps have translucent grey bodies and measure only about 5cm/2in. They live in soft sand in shallow waters, emerging at night in darker camouflage to hunt for their prey. When cooked, they turn brownish-grey. Their small size makes them difficult to peel, but they can be eaten whole and their flavour is incomparable, with a wonderful tang of the sea. They are used to make potted shrimps.

Other names The French call these shrimps *crevette grise* or *boucaud*, the Italians know them as *gamberetto grigio*, while the Spanish call them *quisquilla*.

Warm-water Prawns

These are fished from warmer Asian waters as well as Mexican and Mediterranean seas.

Gulf Shrimp (*Hymenopenaeus robustus*)

These warm-water prawns from the Gulf of Mexico are usually bright red, but may sometimes be greyish-pink in colour. Gulf shrimps can grow very large, each can be up to 40g/1½oz in weight, and have very succulent, juicy flesh.

Kuruma/Japanese Prawn (*Penaeus japonicus*)

These large prawns can grow to a length of 23cm/9in. They have yellowish tails flecked with black. Kuruma are found throughout the Indo-Pacific region and in the Red Sea; some have migrated through the Suez Canal to the eastern Mediterranean.

Tiger/King Prawn (*Penaeus monodon*)

These huge prawns are found throughout the Indo-Pacific. They can grow up to 33cm/13in in length and are ideal for barbecuing. In their raw state, they are a translucent greenish-grey. Although their flavour is not as good as that of cold-water prawns, tiger prawns have succulent, firm flesh. In Europe, they are seldom sold fresh, but they freeze well and are available peeled or in the shell. Peeled tiger prawns usually have the end of the tail left on so that they can be eaten with the fingers.

Cooking The cardinal rule with any prawns or shrimp is not to overcook them. Ready-cooked prawns should preferably be eaten without further cooking. Serve them simply, with lemon and brown bread and butter, or in a salad. If you must cook them, use them in a dish such as pasta where they need only be heated through. They add extra flavour and texture to other fish dishes, such as fish pies, terrines and flans, and combine well with other shellfish. Small prawns and shrimp make an excellent, tasty filling for omelettes, vol-au-vents (patty shells) or little individual tartlets.

Raw prawns can be boiled briefly in salt water or court-bouillon and are delicious grilled (broiled), barbecued or deep-fried in batter. Combined with squid and other fish, deep-fried prawns are a vital ingredient of an Italian *fritto misto* (mixed fried fish). Warm-water prawns can be used for stir-fries, curries or kebabs.

GASTROPODS

Also known as univalves, gastropods are single-shelled creatures belonging to the snail family. Most marine gastropods have the familiar snail shape, with a single spiral shell, but some look more like bivalves and others have no shell at all. All gastropods have a single foot. Edible gastropods vary in size from tiny winkles to conches measuring up to 30cm/12in.

Abalone/Ormer/Sea Ear (*Haliotis tuberculata*)

These can look like bivalves, since their ear-shaped shells give them the appearance of large mussels. Like all gastropods, they have a large, muscled foot that they use to cling to rocks and cliffs. This immensely strong foot can withstand strains up to four thousand times the weight of the abalone, which makes it very difficult to prise them from the rocks, and helps to explain why they are so expensive. Another reason for their cost is that they feed exclusively on seaweed, and pollution is rendering them increasingly rare. In some countries abalone have become a protected species. They are highly prized not only for their flesh, but also for their beautiful shells. These are lined with iridescent mother-of-pearl. There are over a hundred species of abalone living in warm waters throughout the world. Most can grow to about 20cm/8in in length, but the shell of the red abalone *(Haliotis rufescens)*, found in the American Pacific, grows up to 30cm/12in. Their firm flesh, which must be tenderized before it can be eaten, has a subtle flavour of iodine.

Other names In the Channel Islands, one of the few places in Europe where abalone are still found, they are known as ormers. In South Africa, they are known as *perlemoen* or Venus's ear. The French call them *oreilles de St Pierre* or *ormeau*; the Italians, *orecchia marina*; the Spanish, *oreja de mar.*

Buying In Europe, there is a closed season for abalone, and they are limited to only a few days in spring. You are more likely to find fresh abalone in America, Australia and the Far East, often sold sliced and tenderized ready for cooking. Abalone is also available canned, frozen and dried.

Preparing and Cooking Before cooking, the intestinal sac and dark membrane and skirt must be removed. To remove the white flesh, run a sharp knife between it and the shell. The flesh must be beaten vigorously with a wooden mallet to tenderize it. In Japan, it is sliced thinly and eaten raw as *sashimi*. If it is cooked, it must be cooked very briefly, or given long, slow cooking. Thin slices can be sautéed in hot butter, or cut into strips and deep-fried in batter. In China, it is braised with dried mushrooms; in France, it is stewed with dry white wine and shallots. In the Channel Islands, ormers are casseroled with bacon and potatoes.

Conch (*Strombus gigas*)

This large relative of the whelk has a spiral shell. As with all such gastropods, the opening is protected by a hard operculum, which must be removed for access to the flesh inside. Conch (pronounced conk) are native to Florida, the Pacific coast and the Caribbean. The shells are sought after as ornaments and musical instruments. The pinkish flesh is tasty and chewy, and must be beaten to tenderize it before eating.

Buying In their native countries, conches are available all year round. The best are young specimens, known as thin-lipped conches; older conches are described as thick-lipped. They are generally sold out of the shell.

Cooking After tenderizing, conch meat can be marinated and eaten raw, or cooked in a chowder. Some conches can cause stomach upsets; boil the conch in two changes of water to avoid this.

Limpets (*Patella vulgata*)

These gastropods have conical shells. They are found throughout the world, clinging tightly to rocks. When the tide goes out, they nestle into holes in the sand, emerging at night to crawl in a 1m/39in circle around their hole in search of food. Limpets have quite a good flavour, but the small amount of flesh they contain can be very tough. It takes a great deal of effort to prise them off the rocks, so only the larger varieties, which yield more flesh, are eaten. Limpets are not available commercially.

Cooking Wash the limpets and boil them in sea water or heavily-salted water for about 5 minutes, or cook the flesh in fish dishes.

Whelks (*Buccinum undatum*)

Smaller relatives of the conch, whelks have pretty spiral shells measuring up to 10cm/4in. They have rubbery, pinkish flesh with a good flavour, largely because they are scavengers and will bore through the shell of other shellfish to eat their flesh.

Other names There are many varieties of whelk, including the common, the dog, the spiral and the knobbled or giant American whelk, which can grow to 20cm/8in in length. In French, they are variously known as *bulot*, *buccin* and *escargot de mer* (sea snail); in Italian, *buccina*; in Spanish, as *bocina* or *caracola*.

Buying Whelks should be bought alive; check that the operculum is tightly closed. You can buy them boiled and removed from the shell, but these can be rather dry. You will also find whelks pickled in vinegar, or cooked and bottled in brine.

Cooking The best way to cook whelks is to boil them in sea water or heavily salted water for about 5 minutes. Use a cocktail stick (toothpick) to prise the flesh out of the shell. The flesh of large whelks can be sautéed after boiling, or deep-fried in batter. It can be used instead of clams in a chowder, or added to cooked shellfish dishes.

Winkles/Periwinkles (*Littorina littorea*)

These marine snails have thick greenish-brown or black shells, with a pointed end. Most grow no larger than about 4cm/1½in.

Other names In France, they are called *bigourneau* or *littorine*; in Italy, *chiocciola di mare*; in Spain, *bigaro*.

Buying Fresh winkles should be bought alive; check that the operculum is tightly closed. They are also available cooked and bottled in vinegar.

Cooking Like whelks, winkles need only brief cooking. Serve as an appetizer with vinegar or mayonnaise.

COOKING AND PICKING WINKLES AND WHELKS

These little shellfish are delicious and eating them can be great fun.

1 Bring a large pan of well-salted water to the boil. Drop in the winkles or whelks. Simmer winkles for 5 minutes; whelks for 10 minutes. Drain.

2 If the operculum is still covering the opening of the shell, remove it with a pin. Insert the pin into the opening and pull out the cooked flesh.

MOLLUSCS

The mollusc family is divided into bivalves such as mussels and oysters, which have a hinged external shell, and gastropods such as whelks and winkles, which have a single external shell. Cephalopods (squid, cuttlefish and octopus) are yet another group; unlike gastropods and bivalves, they have relatively small internal shells rather than the protective outer shells of other molluscs.

BIVALVES

These molluscs have an attractive, hinged shell that houses soft, delicate flesh inside.

CLAMS

There are hundreds of species of clam, ranging from the aptly-named giant clam which can grow to a length of 1.3m/4¼ft, to tiny pebble-like venus and littleneck clams measuring 5cm/2in. Americans are passionate about clams and eat them in all sizes and forms. Their enthusiasm has spread to Europe, where clams are now farmed. Large species have very thick warty shells; small varieties have smooth shells marked with fine circular striations. Clams have a fine, sweet flavour and firm texture, and are delicious cooked or raw.

Cherrystone/Littleneck Clam (*Mercenaria mercenaria*)

These small clams have a brown-and-white shell. The smallest are the baby littlenecks, with 4–5cm/1½–2in shells. The slightly larger ones (about 7.5cm/3in), named after Cherrystone Creek in Virginia, are about five years old. Both are served raw on the half shell; cooked, they make good pasta sauces. The larger quahogs are unsuitable for eating raw and are known as steamer clams. They have a strong flavour and are often used in clam chowder or pasta sauces.
Other names In France they are *palourde*; in Italy, *vongola dura*; in Spain, *almeja*.

Geoduck Clam (*Panopea generosa*)

These enormous clams are the largest of all American Pacific shellfish and can weigh up to 4kg/8¾lb. Half this weight is made up of two long siphons, which can be extended to more than 1.3m/4¼ft to take in and expel water. Geoduck clams cannot retract these siphons into the shell, and they are often sold separately. These large clams can bury themselves up to 1.2m/4ft deep in sand and it takes two people to prise them out. The siphons and flesh are sliced before cooking.

Palourde/Carpetshell Clam (*Venerupis decussata*)

These small (4–7.5cm/1½–3in) clams have attractive, grooved brown shells with a yellow lattice-like pattern. The flesh is exceptionally tender, so they can be eaten raw, but are also good grilled (broiled).
Other names In French they are called *palourde*; in Italian, they are *vongola verace*; and in Spanish, *almeja fina*.

CLAMBAKES

This American pastime is a beach picnic in which soft-shell or hard-shell clams are steamed over seaweed laid on hot rocks. A pit is dug in the sand, rocks are placed inside and heated, then draped with wet seaweed. Corn on the cob, sweet potatoes and, sometimes, lobsters or soft-shell crabs are also steamed.

Praire/Warty Venus Clam (*Venus verrucosa*)

The unattractively named warty venus is a smallish clam measuring 2.5–7.5cm/1–3in. The thick shell has concentric stripes, some of which end in warty protuberances. These clams are widely found on sandy coasts, from Africa to Europe. They are often eaten raw on the half shell, but are also excellent cooked. The Italians dignify them with the name of sea truffles.

Other names Sometimes known as baby clams, the word *praire* comes from the French, who also call these molluscs *coque rayé*. In Italy they are *verrucosa* or *tartufo di mare*; in Spain *almeja vieja*.

Razorshell/Razor Clam (*Solen marginatus*)

Resembling an old-fashioned cut-throat razor, these clams have tubular shells that are striped gold and brown. Their flesh looks slightly obscene but tastes delicious. Razorshells are often served raw, but can be cooked like any other clam. They can often be found on sandy beaches at low tide, but as they can burrow into the sand at great speed to conceal themselves, you will need to act fast if you want to catch them.

Other names Razorshells are sometimes known as jack-knife clams. The French call them *couteau*; the Italians, *cannolicchio* or *cappa lunga*; their Spanish name is *navaja* or *longuerión*.

Soft-shell/Long-neck Clam (*family Myidae*)

The shells of these wide oval clams gape slightly at the posterior end, giving them their nickname of gapers. They burrow deep into sand and silt, so have a long tube for taking in and expelling water. This siphon can be eaten raw, or made into chowder or creamed dishes.

Other names In French they are *mye*; in Italian, *vongola molle*; in Spanish, they are *almeja de rio*.

Cooking Small clams and razorshells can be eaten raw, steamed or cooked in soups and sauces. Larger clams can be stuffed and baked or grilled (broiled) like mussels, cut into strips and deep-fried in batter, or stewed with white wine or onions and tomatoes. Steamed clams can be added to salads or sauces or used as a garnish. Never throw away the juices that clams contain; these are extremely nutritious and delicious, and can be used for drinks such as *clamata*, shellfish stock or soup.

Cockles (*family Cardium*)

Although traditionally thought of as a typically British food, varieties of cockle (*Cardium edule*) are found all over the world. Their two equal heart-shaped shells of cockles are 2.5–4cm/1–1½in long and have 26 defined ribs. Inside lies a morsel of delicate flesh and its coral.

Other names In America, cockles are known as heart clams. In France, they are *coque*; in Italy, *cuore*; in Spain, *berberecho*.

Buying Fresh cockles are sold by volume. Those with paler flesh are said to taste better than those with dark flesh. The colour of the shell is a good indication of the colour of the flesh, so choose cockles with pale shells. Shelled cockles are available frozen and bottled in brine or vinegar.

Cooking Cockles are full of sand, so must be soaked in salted cold water for several hours before eating. They can be eaten raw or boiled and served with vinegar and brown bread and butter. They are excellent steamed, stewed with tomatoes and onions or made into soup. Cockles can be added to risotto, pasta and other seafood dishes or served cold as an hors d'oeuvre or salad.

Dog Cockle (*Glycymeridae*)

These tropical and warm-water bivalves have large, flat striated shells and resemble scallops. There are four known species: the true dog cockle, bittersweet cockle, violet bittersweet and the giant bittersweet. All are good to eat, but have a much coarser texture and flavour than true cockles. They can be cooked as cockles and mussels.

Other names In French they are *amande*; in Italian, *pié d'asino* (ass's foot); in Spanish, *almendra de mar*.

Mussels (*Mytilus edulis*)

These bivalves have elongated blue-black shells. Unlike most other bivalves, they do not use a muscly foot to anchor themselves to rocks and poles, but with a byssus or "beard", a wiry substance produced by a gland at the base of the foot. Clumps of mussels grow wild on sea shores around the world. The waters they come from must be unpolluted. Their sweet, tender flesh is very nutritious and versatile. Nowadays, most commercial mussels are farmed.

There are many varieties of mussel. The best and most succulent are the blue or European mussels from cold British waters, which can grow to a length of 10cm/4in, although the average size is nearer 5cm/2in. They are large, with sweet-flavoured flesh, which in the female is a beautiful orange; males have paler, cream-coloured flesh. The largest are the New Zealand greenshell or green-lipped mussels *(Perna canaliculus)*, which have a distinctive green lip around the internal border of the shell. These can grow to over 23cm/9in and are very meaty. They are ideal for stuffing, but their flavour is not as good as that of blue mussels.

Other names In French it is *moule*; in Italian, *cozza*; in Spanish, *mejillón*.

Buying Most mussels are farmed and are usually cleaned. They are available all year round and are cheap; 1kg/2¼lb will provide a generous meal for two people. Shelled mussels are available frozen, smoked and bottled in brine or vinegar.

Cooking Mussels are enormously versatile. They can be eaten raw or steamed with Mediterranean or Oriental flavours. Large mussels can be stuffed and baked or grilled (broiled) with flavoured butter, bacon or pesto. They can be wrapped in bacon, then threaded on to skewers and grilled; cooked in cream, wine or cider, deep-fried, or used in omelettes, soufflés, hot or cold soups, curries, pasta sauces, rice dishes or salads. Belgium's national dish, *moules frites*, is fried mussels with chips (fries). For a rather unusual hors d'oeuvre, serve cold steamed mussels *à la ravigote*, with a vinaigrette flavoured with chopped hard-boiled egg, fresh herbs and gherkins.

OYSTERS

Considered one of life's luxuries, people tend either to love or loathe oysters. Their unique, salty, iodised flavour and slippery texture may not appeal to everyone, but their reputation as an aphrodisiac has contributed to their popularity, and they are highly prized all over the world. However, it was not always so; for centuries, oysters were regarded as food for the poor. It was with their growing scarcity resulting from overfishing, that their popularity increased.

Over 100 different varieties of oyster live in the temperate and warm waters of the world. All have thick, irregular, greyish shells, one flat, the other hollow. The flesh is pinkish-grey with a darker mantle and a slippery texture. The reproductive life of oysters is highly unusual. Some change sex from male to female in alternate years, while others are hermaphrodites.

Oysters have been eaten for thousands of years. They were enjoyed by the Celts and Ancient Greeks, but it was the Romans who discovered the secret of oyster cultivation. By the 19th century, European oyster beds had been so comprehensively overfished and stocks were so low that Napoleon III ordered that shipments of oysters be brought from abroad. In 1868, a ship carrying quantities of Portuguese oysters was forced to take shelter from a storm in the Gironde estuary. Fearing that his cargo of oysters was going bad, the captain flung them overboard. They bred prolifically, rapidly replenishing the native stocks, and managed to survive a catastrophic epidemic in 1921 that wiped out the native oysters. In 1967, however, they too were totally decimated by the deadly bonamia virus. Oyster cultivation on a massive scale was the only answer; nowadays, oysters are commercially produced throughout the industrialized world.

Eastern/Atlantic Oyster (*Crassostrea virginica*)

These oysters have rounded shells similar to those of the native oyster. However, they actually belong to the Portuguese oyster family and have a very similar texture and flavour. In North America, they are named after their place of origin; the best known is the Blue Point.

Native Oyster (*Ostrea edulis*)

Considered the finest of all oysters, natives are slow-growers, taking about three years to reach their full size of 5–12cm/2–4½in. Their round shells vary in colour from greyish-green to beige, depending on their habitat, and they have a wonderful flavour. native oysters are named after their place of origin. Among the best known native oysters are the French Belon, the English Whitstable, Colchester and Helford, the Irish Galway and the Belgian Ostendes. Native oysters are the most expensive of all oysters but are well worth the money.

Other names The French call these oysters *huitre plate* or *belon*, to the Italians they are known as *ostrica*, while in Spain, they are called *ostra plana*.

Pacific/Gigas Oyster (*Crassostrea gigas*)

These large cupped bivalves with their craggy shells are the most widely farmed oysters in the world. They are resistant to disease and can grow up to 15cm/6in in the space of just four years, which makes them more economical to produce. Their texture is not nearly as fine as that of native oysters, but their large size means that they are more suitable for cooking than many other types of oyster.

Other names The Pacific oyster is also known as the rock or Japanese oyster. In French, it is *creuse* (hollow); in Italian, *ostrica*; in Spanish *ostión*.

Portuguese Cupped Oyster (*Crassostrea angulata*)

These oysters are natives of Portugal (and Spain and Morocco). They have scaly, grey-brown shells, one of which is slightly concave. They are considered finer than gigas oysters, but not as good as natives. They can grow up to 17cm/6½in. Their flesh is rather coarse and they are declining in popularity. In France, where these oysters are cultivated on a very large scale, they are known as *fines de claires* after the fattening beds where they are farmed. Fatter, tastier (and, of course, rather more expensive) specimens are called *spéciales claires*.

Sydney Rock Oyster (*Crassostrea commercialis*)

This cupped oyster changes its sex from male to female and is extremely fertile. It is farmed in huge numbers on the coast of New South Wales in Australia. It grows very quickly and has a good flavour, but is rather hard to open.

Buying The age-old rule that oysters should not be bought when there is no "r" in the month still holds good throughout the northern hemisphere, not because they are poisonous as was once supposed, but because their flesh becomes unpleasantly soft and milky during the summer breeding season, which runs from May to August. Smoked oysters are available and it is also possible to find frozen oysters.

Cooking Oysters are best eaten raw with just a squeeze of lemon juice or a dash of peppery Tabasco sauce. If you prefer to cook them, do so very briefly. They are good poached or steamed and served with a *beurre blanc* or Champagne sauce, stuffed and grilled (broiled), deep-fried in cornmeal batter, or as a luxurious addition to steak and kidney pie. Classic oyster dishes include oysters Rockefeller and oysters *bienville*.

OYSTER CULTIVATION

Centuries of overfishing and disease have decimated the world's natural stocks of oysters, a sad state of affairs that has been somewhat alleviated in recent years by oyster farming.

Oysters have been successfully farmed since Roman times, but cultivation has now become a highly lucrative business, despite being labour-intensive and very slow. Oysters need constant cosseting and attention from the moment of hatching. A single oyster produces up to a hundred million eggs every breeding season, of which only ten oysters will survive long enough to end up on your plate. It takes at least three years to produce an oyster of marketable size; natives take up to seven years and the giant royals take ten years to mature. The minuscule spats must first be caught and encouraged to settle on lime-soaked tiles or slates.

After about nine months, the growing oysters are transferred to oyster parks, where they are enclosed in wire grills and carefully nurtured while they feed on microscopic plankton. After being left to grow for two or three years, they are placed in nets and fattened for about a year in shallow beds or claires. The final stage of the lengthy cultivation process involves placing the oysters in clean beds for several days under stringent hygiene conditions to expel any impurities. Small wonder that they are so expensive.

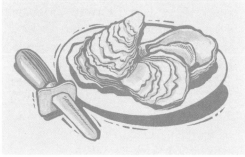

Scallops *(Peeten maximus)*

These very attractive shellfish have two fan-shaped shells, one flat and the other curved, with grooves radiating out from the hinge to the outside edge. They can be found on sandy seabeds in many parts of the world. Unlike many bivalves, they do not burrow into the sand, but swim above the sea bed by opening and closing their shells, which makes them look as though they are leaping through the water. There are about three hundred species of scallop throughout the world, with shells ranging in colour from beige to brown, salmon pink, yellow and orange. The most common species is the common or great scallop, whose reddish-brown shell grows up to 5–6cm/2–2½in. Scallop shells contain a nugget of sweet, firm white flesh joined to the vibrant orange crescent-shaped roe or coral.

Scallops have long been associated with beauty. Botticelli painted the goddess Venus as she was born from a scallop shell; her Greek counterpart, Aphrodite, rode across the sea in a scallop shell pulled by six sea horses. Thanks to a miracle involving St James, scallop shells became the symbol of Christianity and the emblem of medieval pilgrims visiting the shrine at Santiago de Compostela in Spain.

Other names Sometimes known as pilgrim shells, scallops are *coquille St Jacques* in French; *pettine* in Italian; *viera* in Spanish.

Buying Scallops are available almost all year round, but are best in winter when the roes are full and firm. The finest are hand-caught by divers; they are also the most expensive. Allow 4–5 large scallops per person as a main course, three times this number if they are small. Scallops are also available shelled. Always try to buy scallops with their delicious coral, although this is not always possible. Avoid frozen scallops, which have little or no taste.

Cooking The beard and all dark-coloured parts of the scallop must be removed before they are cooked and eaten. Scallops can be thinly sliced and eaten raw with a little lemon juice and olive oil. They need only brief cooking to preserve their deliciously firm yet tender texture. Scallops can be poached for a few minutes in court-bouillon and served warm or cold in a salad with a tomato and basil vinaigrette or mayonnaise.

Whole scallops in the shell can be baked: seal the shells with a flour-and-water paste. They are delicious wrapped in strips of bacon and grilled (broiled), coated in bread-crumbs and deep-fried, pan-fried for about 30 seconds on each side; stir-fried with vegetables or steamed with ginger and soy sauce. They make good pâtés and mousses. *Coquilles St Jacques* is a classic dish in which poached scallops and corals are sliced, returned to the half shell and coated with Mornay (cheese) sauce, then grilled or baked.

Queen Scallop (*Chlamys opercularis*)

These miniature scallops measure about 3cm/1¼in across. Their cream-coloured shells are marked with brown ridges and contain a small nugget of white flesh and a tiny pointed coral. They are cheaper than larger scallops, but have the same sweet flavour. They are often sold out of the shell; allow at least 12 per person. Queenies, as they are sometimes known, are farmed commercially. They are popular in Asia and in Chinese cooking.

CEPHALOPODS

Despite their appearance, cephalopods, are marine molluscs without a shell and they are more closely related to snails than to fish. They are highly developed creatures with three-dimensional vision, memory and the ability to swim at high speeds. They can also change colour according to the outside environment. Their name derives from the Greek for head with feet. The bulbous head contains the mouth, which has two jaws, like a parrot's beak. This is surrounded by tentacles covered with suckers, which are used for crawling and seizing their prey. The sack-shaped body houses the stomach, gills and sex organs.

Most cephalopods have an internal shell, rather than an external one, made from spongy material, which they can inflate to make themselves buoyant. The cuttlebone, from the cuttlefish, is the most familiar of these. Cuttlebones can often be found on beaches, and are used by bird-owners to provide calcium for budgerigars. In Roman times, wealthy ladies ground up cuttlebones and used the powder on their faces and to clean their teeth and their jewellery.

Most cephalopods also contain an ink sac, which emits a blackish fluid designed to repel predators. This fluid, or ink, can be used for cooking. Cephalopods are found in almost all the world's oceans. Unlike many sea creatures, they have not yet suffered from overfishing and are still a sustainable food source.

Cuttlefish

The common cuttlefish *(Sepia officinalis)* has a flattened oval head with brownish camouflage stripes on the back and light coloration on the underside. It has eight stubby tentacles and two long tentacles for catching its prey. These are kept rolled up and hidden in openings near its mouth.

Cuttlefish are comparatively small in size, with bodies of 25cm/10in. When unfurled, the catching tentacles double the cuttlefish's length. As with all cephalopods, the smaller the cuttlefish, the more tender the flesh. The smallest variety is the Mediterranean little or dwarf cuttlefish *(sepiola)*, which grows to only 3–6cm/1¼–2½in. They taste delicious, but are very time-consuming to prepare, as the small cuttlebones must be removed from each one before cooking.

Other names The common cuttlefish is *seiche* in French; *seppia* in Italian; *sepia* in Spanish. Dwarf cuttlefish are *supion* or *chipiron* in French; *seppiolina* in Italian; and *chipirón* in Spanish.

Cooking Tiny cuttlefish are good left whole and sautéed quickly in olive oil and garlic, deep-fried, or cooked in their own ink. They make a good addition to rice dishes. Larger specimens can be cooked like squid.

Squid (*Loliginidae*)

These cephalopods have elongated heads and slender, torpedo-shaped bodies, which end in a kite-shaped fin. Their internal shell is a transparent quill, which looks like a piece of clear acetate. They have ten tentacles, two of which are very long. Squid range from tiny creatures only 7.5cm/3in long to the giant squid that weighs several tons and can grow to a length of 17m/55ft. The most common is the calamary or long-finned squid *(Loligo vulgaris)*, which is found throughout Europe. It has smooth, sandy-red spotted skin and weighs up to 2kg/4½lb. The so-called flying squid does not actually fly, but propels itself out of the water and glides through the air like a guided missile. Squid has firm, lean, white flesh that can be tender and delicious.

Other names In French squid is *encornet* or *calmar*; in Italian it is *calamaro*; in Spanish it is *calamar* or *puntilla*.

Buying Whole squid are sold fresh or frozen and are available all year round. Make sure that they contain their ink sac. Some fishmongers and supermarkets also sell squid ink separately. Squid is also available ready-cleaned, which is very labour-saving. Whole tentacles and rings are available frozen, sometimes as part of a mixed *fruits de mer*. You can also buy ready-battered squid rings for deep-frying, but these are best avoided. Allow 200g/7oz per person.

Cooking The cardinal rule with squid is to cook it either very briefly or for a long time; anything in between and it becomes tough and rubbery. The bodies can be stuffed and baked in tomato sauce, or braised with onions and tomatoes. Squid rings can be coated in batter and deep-fried, or boiled briefly and used for a salad. Tiny squid are delicious chargrilled, sautéed, or coated with egg and breadcrumbs and deep-fried. Squid can be added to pasta sauces and rice dishes such as paella. It goes well with such unlikely ingredients as chorizo sausage and black pudding. Squid is frequently used in Oriental recipes and lends itself well to flavourings such as ginger, chilli and lime. The ink can be used to colour and flavour home-made pasta and risotto.

Octopuses (*Octopus vulgaris*)

Unlike cuttlefish and squid, the octopus has no internal shell, nor does it possess catching tentacles or fins. Octopuses spend their lives lurking in clefts in the rocks on the sea bed, blocking the entrance to their hidey-holes with shellfish and stones. Their eight equal-size tentacles each have two rows of suckers and can grow to a length of 5m/16¼ft. The larger an octopus grows, the tougher it becomes, so smaller specimens make the best eating. Octopus ink is contained in the liver and has a much stronger flavour than cuttlefish or squid ink.

Other names Octopus is called *poulpe* or *pieuvre* in French; *polpo* in Italian; and in Spanish it is *pulpo*.

Buying Octopus is usually sold ready-prepared and frozen, although you may find whole fresh octopus in Mediterranean fish markets. Look for specimens with two rows of suckers on the tentacles; those with only a single row of suckers are the inferior curled octopus.

Cooking Octopus needs to be cooked slowly for a long time. Before including it in a recipe, it is usually a good idea to blanch or marinate it. If the octopus has not been prepared already, cut off the tentacles and press out the beak from the head. Discard the head, turn the body inside out and discard the entrails. Rinse it thoroughly under cold running water, then pound the body and tentacles with a wooden mallet to tenderize them before cutting them into strips. Simmer the octopus in fish stock or salted water for at least 1 hour, until tender. Octopus is also very good stewed with Mediterranean vegetables or robust red wine, or stuffed and baked slowly. Small specimens can be cut into rings and sautéed gently in olive oil. Octopus is best served warm as a salad, dressed with a simple olive oil and lemon vinaigrette. Whole octopus can be casseroled slowly in its own juices and ink, but be aware that the ink has a strong flavour which is not to everyone's taste. The Japanese are very fond of octopus and use the boiled tentacles for *sushi*.

OTHER EDIBLE SEA CREATURES

The sea is full of weird and wonderful creatures whose strange appearance belies their delicious taste. They may be soft and gelatinous like jellyfish, warty like sea cucumbers or menacingly spiny like sea urchins, but somewhere in the world, they will be regarded as a great delicacy. If ever you come across these unusual treats, they are well worth trying.

Jellyfish (*Scyphoza*)

These strange, transparent creatures, with their dangling tentacles, look like open parachutes, and can strike fear into the hearts of anyone who has been stung by them. They inhabit every ocean of the world, but are eaten almost exclusively in Asia, where they are dried and used to add texture and flavour to many seafood dishes.

Buying and using Dried jellyfish can be found in any Oriental food store, together with jellyfish preserved in brine. Both types must be soaked in water for several hours, changing the water often and squeezing the jellyfish each time to get rid of as much of the fishy smell as possible. In China, dried jellyfish slices are scalded in boiling water until they curl up, then drained and served in a dressing of soy sauce, sesame oil and rice vinegar. Dried jellyfish are also sliced and added to shellfish or chicken stir-fries, but they must be tossed in at the last moment as they will become rubbery if overcooked. In Japan, crisply fried strips of jellyfish are served with vinegar, and are sometimes combined with sea urchins.

Sea Cucumber (*Holothurioidea*)

It is hard to imagine why anyone would wish to eat these repulsive-looking, warty, cucumber-shaped marine animals, which rejoice in the alternative unattractive name of sea slugs, but they are considered a great delicacy in Japan and China, where they are reputed to be an aphrodisiac. The plethora of prickles along their backs are actually feet, which enable them to crawl along the sea bed. Sea cucumber is known in the Orient as *trepang*, *balatin* or *iriko*. In Japan, it is sliced and eaten raw as *sashimi*. Sea cucumber is available dried. It must be soaked in cold water for at least 24 hours to make it palatable. During soaking it will double in bulk and become very gelatinous. It is used in soup and in several complicated recipes, which take so long to prepare that one feels it must have charms that are not apparent to Western palates.

SEAWEED

This marine algae is not a sea creature but is much used in the Japanese diet. In fact, it is a very healthy option since it is rich in protein, very low in fat and packed full of vitamins, minerals and trace elements.

There are several species of seaweed and its popularity as a foodstuff is now spreading beyond the boundaries of Japan. It can be eaten fresh or it can be processed, dried or powdered to make a sort of seasoning. The best-known types are wakame, kombu *and* nori.

Seaweed can be poached and served as a vegetable on its own, added to salads and soups, used to flavour stocks, grilled (broiled) and crumbled over dishes or used to wrap sushi.

Sea Squirt (*Ascidiacea*)

There are over a thousand species of sea squirts: small invertebrates whose bodies are enclosed in thick leathery "tunics". They have two orifices or spouts through which they siphon water in and squirt it out, and they attach themselves to the sea bed or rocks and crevices. They are found in the Mediterranean, where they are a popular if esoteric food, particularly in Spain and the south of France, where the local name, *violet*, refers to the sea squirt's resemblance to a large purple fig. Enthusiasts eat them by splitting them in half, then scooping out the soft yellow part inside and eating it raw, despite the strong aroma of iodine. Sea squirts can accumulate toxins, so avoid them if they come from polluted waters.

Other names In French, sea squirt is known as *violet* or *figue de mer*; in Italian it is called *ovo di mare*.

Sea Urchin (*Echinoidea*)

One of the most unpleasant experiences a holidaymaker can have is to tread on the long, poisonous spines of a sea urchin. To lovers of seafood, however, eating these marine creatures are a great gastronomic pleasure. They are considered a delicacy in Japan and many Mediterranean countries. There are over eight-hundred species found all over the world, but only a few are edible. The most common European variety is the *Paracentrotus lividus*, which is a greenish- or purplish-black hemispherical creature measuring about 7.5cm/3in across, and whose shell is covered with long spines, rather like those of a hedgehog, which are intended to dissuade predators. The females are slightly larger than the males and are said to taste better. Only the orange or yellow ovaries or gonads (known as the coral) are eaten; these have a pungent taste reminiscent of iodine.

Other names In French, sea urchins are variously known as *oursin*, *châtaigne de mer* (sea chestnut) and *hérisson de mer* (sea hedgehog); in Italian, they are *riccio di mare*; in Spanish *erizo de mar*.

Buying Overfishing has made sea urchins rare and expensive. The best are the purple or green urchins with long spines; short-spined, whitish species have an extremely strong flavour and are best used in cooked dishes. Look for urchins with firm spines and a tightly closed mouth, which can be found on the underside. If you find a source of fresh sea urchins, they can be kept in the refrigerator for up to three days.

OPENING SEA URCHINS

Sea urchins are covered in prickly spines so always wear a pair of rubber gloves when handling. The best implement for opening sea urchins is a purpose-made coupe-orsin but sharp scissors will do.

1 Hold the sea urchin in the palm of your hand and carefully cut around the soft tissue on the underside, using a special knife or a pair of sharp, pointed scissors. Alternatively, slice off the top like a boiled egg to reveal the coral.

2 Lift off the top of the sea urchin and remove the mouth and innards, which are inedible. Keep the juices for flavouring shellfish sauces, egg dishes or soup.

3 Use a teaspoon to scoop out the bright orange coral.

Cooking Sea urchins can be eaten raw or used to flavour sauces, pasta, omelettes and scrambled eggs. They make wonderful soup, which can be served in small portions in the shell. The shells can also be used as containers for other seafood such as langoustines in a sea urchin sauce.

SOUPS

Fish and shellfish soups are always delicious and can be eaten either as a first course or as an entire meal. Light or chilled soups such as Hot & Sour Soup with Prawns and Chilled Cucumber & Prawn Soup are ideal for a summer appetizer. Chunky soups such as Louisiana Seafood Gumbo, Matelote and Bouillabaisse are perfect for winter and are so hearty that they can be eaten as a meal in themselves. Sophisticated soups such as Lobster Bisque and Scallop & Jerusalem Artichoke Soup are great for entertaining and are sure to impress guests.

CHILLED CUCUMBER & PRAWN SOUP

If you have never served a chilled soup before, this is the one to try. Delicious and light in both flavour and colour, it's the perfect way to celebrate summer.

SERVES 4

INGREDIENTS
25g/1oz/2 tbsp butter
2 shallots, finely chopped
2 garlic cloves, crushed
1 cucumber, peeled, seeded and diced
300ml/½ pint/1¼ cups milk
225g/8oz cooked, peeled prawns (shrimp)
15ml/1 tbsp each finely chopped fresh mint, dill, chives and chervil
300ml/½ pint/1¼ cups whipping cream
salt and ground white pepper

FOR THE GARNISH
30ml/2 tbsp crème fraîche or sour cream (optional)
4 large, cooked prawns (shrimp), peeled with tail intact
fresh dill and chives

1 Melt the butter in a pan and gently cook the shallots and garlic until soft. Add the cucumber and cook gently, stirring frequently, until tender.

2 Stir in the milk, bring almost to boiling point, then lower the heat and simmer for 5 minutes. Tip the soup into a blender or food processor and purée until very smooth. Season to taste.

3 Pour into a large bowl and leave to cool. Stir in the prawns, chopped herbs and cream. Cover, transfer to the refrigerator and chill for at least 2 hours.

4 To serve, ladle the soup into four individual bowls and top each portion with a dollop of crème fraîche or sour cream, if using, and place a prawn over the edge of each dish. Scatter a little extra chopped dill over each soup and tuck two or three chives under the prawns on the edge of the bowls to garnish. Serve at once.

Hot & Sour Soup
With Prawns

How hot this soup is depends upon the type of chilli used. If you want to make it really spicy try tiny Thai chillies.

Serves 6

Ingredients
225g/8oz raw prawns (shrimp), in shells
2 lemon grass stalks
1.5 litres/2½ pints/6¼ cups vegetable stock
4 kaffir lime leaves
2 slices of peeled fresh root ginger
60ml/4 tbsp Thai fish sauce (nam pla)
60ml/4 tbsp fresh lime juice
2 garlic cloves, crushed
6 spring onions (scallions), chopped
1 fresh red chilli, seeded and cut into thin strips
115g/4oz/generous 1½ cups oyster mushrooms, sliced
fresh coriander (cilantro) leaves and kaffir lime slices, to garnish

1 Peel the prawns and set them aside. Put the shells in a large pan. Lightly crush the lemon grass and add the stalks to the pan with the stock, lime leaves and ginger. Bring to the boil, lower the heat and simmer for 20 minutes.

2 Strain the stock into a clean pan, discarding the prawn shells and aromatics. Add the fish sauce, lime juice, garlic, spring onions, chilli and mushrooms. Bring to the boil, lower the heat and simmer for 5 minutes. Add the peeled prawns and cook for 2–3 minutes. Serve, garnished with coriander leaves and lime slices.

Cook's Tip
Prawns take very little time to cook and it is important that they are not overcooked, or they will become tough and rubbery. Boil them only until they change colour: 1–3 minutes depending upon their size.

CHINESE CRAB & CORN SOUP

Frozen white crab meat works as well as fresh in this delicately flavoured soup.
Be sure to use white crab meat, which comes from the claws and legs, rather than
brown crab meat from the shell.

SERVES 4

INGREDIENTS
600ml/1 pint/2½ cups fish or chicken stock
2.5cm/1in piece fresh root ginger, peeled and very finely sliced
400g/14oz can creamed corn
150g/5oz cooked white crab meat
15ml/1 tbsp arrowroot or cornflour (cornstarch)
15ml/1 tbsp rice wine or dry sherry
15–30ml/1–2 tbsp light soy sauce
1 egg white
salt and ground white pepper
shredded spring onions (scallions), to garnish

1 Put the stock and ginger in a large pan and bring to the boil. Stir in the creamed corn and bring back to the boil.

2 Remove the pan from the heat and add the crab meat. Put the arrowroot or cornflour in a cup and stir in the rice wine or sherry to make a smooth paste, then stir into the soup. Cook over a low heat for 3 minutes, stirring, until the soup has thickened and is slightly glutinous. Add soy sauce, salt and pepper to taste.

3 In a bowl, whisk the egg white to a stiff foam. Gradually fold it into the soup. Ladle the soup into heated bowls, garnish each portion with the shredded spring onions and serve.

COOK'S TIP
This delicious Chinese soup can be made with frozen or canned whole kernel corn, but creamed corn gives a better texture.

THAI FISH BROTH

Lemon grass stalks, chillies and galangal are among the aromatic Thai flavourings used in this fragrant soup. If you can't find fresh galangal, then use the same quantity of fresh root ginger instead.

SERVES 2–3

INGREDIENTS
1 litre/1¾ pints/4 cups fish or light chicken stock
4 lemon grass stalks
3 limes
2 small fresh hot red chillies, seeded and thinly sliced
2cm/¾in piece fresh galangal, peeled and thinly sliced
6 coriander (cilantro) stalks, with leaves
2 kaffir lime leaves, coarsely chopped (optional)
350g/12oz monkfish fillet, skinned and cut into 2.5cm/1in pieces
15ml/1 tbsp rice vinegar
45ml/3 tbsp Thai fish sauce (nam pla)
30ml/2 tbsp chopped coriander (cilantro) leaves, to garnish

1 Pour the stock into a pan and bring it to the boil. Meanwhile, slice the bulb end of each lemon grass stalk diagonally into pieces about 3mm/⅛ in thick. Peel off four wide strips of lime rind with a vegetable peeler, taking care to avoid the white pith underneath, which would make the soup bitter. Squeeze the limes and reserve the juice in a separate bowl.

2 Add the sliced lemon grass, lime rind, chillies, galangal and coriander stalks to the stock, with the kaffir lime leaves, if using. Simmer for 1–2 minutes.

3 Add the monkfish, rice vinegar and Thai fish sauce, with half the reserved lime juice. Simmer for about 3 minutes, until the fish is just cooked. Lift out and discard the coriander, taste the broth and add more lime juice if necessary; the soup should taste quite sour. Sprinkle with the coriander leaves and serve very hot.

Saffron & Fish Soup

Filling yet not too rich, this golden soup will make a delicious meal on early summer evenings, served with lots of hot fresh bread and a glass of dry white wine. When mussels are not available use prawns in their shells instead.

SERVES 4

INGREDIENTS
2 parsnips, quartered
2 carrots, quartered
1 onion, quartered
2 celery sticks, quartered
2 smoked bacon rashers (strips), rinds removed
juice of 1 lemon
pinch of saffron threads
450g/1lb fish heads
900ml/1½ pints/3¾ cups water
450g/1lb fresh mussels, scrubbed and beards removed
1 leek, shredded
2 shallots, finely chopped
30ml/2 tbsp chopped dill, plus extra sprigs to garnish
450g/1lb haddock, skinned and boned
3 egg yolks
30ml/2 tbsp double (heavy) cream
salt and ground black pepper

COOK'S TIP
Fish stock freezes very well and will keep for up to 6 months. Make double the amount needed for this recipe and store the rest in your freezer.

1 Make a stock by putting the parsnips, carrots, onion, celery, bacon, lemon juice, saffron threads and fish heads in a large pan with the water and bring to the boil. Boil gently for about 20 minutes, or until reduced by half.

2 Discard any mussels that are open and do not close when tapped sharply. Add the rest to the pan of stock. Cook for about 4 minutes, or until they have opened.

3 Strain the soup and return the liquid to the pan. Discard any unopened mussels, then remove the remaining ones from their shells and set aside.

4 Add the leeks and shallots to the soup, then bring the liquid to the boil and cook over a medium heat for 5 minutes. Add the chopped dill and haddock, and simmer for a further 5 minutes, or until the fish is tender.

5 Remove the haddock from the pan using a slotted spoon, then flake it into a bowl using a fork. Set aside with the mussels.

6 In another bowl, whisk together the egg yolks and cream. Whisk in a little of the hot soup, then whisk the mixture back into the hot but not boiling liquid. Gently heat the soup through for a few minutes, whisking continuously until it thickens slightly, but do not let it boil.

7 Add the flaked haddock and mussels to the soup and check the seasoning. Garnish with tiny sprigs of dill and serve piping hot.

LOBSTER BISQUE

Bisque is a luxurious, velvety soup, which can be made with any crustaceans. For this recipe, it is best to buy live lobster and cook it yourself.

SERVES 6

INGREDIENTS
500g/1¼lb freshly cooked lobster
75g/3oz/6 tbsp butter
1 onion, chopped
1 carrot, diced
1 celery stick, diced
45ml/3 tbsp brandy, plus extra for serving (optional)
250ml/8fl oz/1 cup dry white wine
1 litre/1¾ pints/4 cups fish stock
15ml/1 tbsp tomato purée (paste)
75g/3oz/scant ½ cup long grain rice
fresh bouquet garni
150ml/¼ pint/⅔ cup double (heavy) cream, plus extra to garnish (optional)
salt, ground white pepper and cayenne pepper

1 Cut the lobster into pieces. Melt half the butter in a large pan, add the vegetables and cook over a low heat until soft. Put in the lobster and stir until the shell on each piece turns red.

2 Pour over the brandy and set it alight. When the flames die down, add the wine and boil until reduced by half. Pour in the fish stock and simmer for about 2 minutes. Remove the lobster.

3 Stir in the tomato purée and rice, and add the bouquet garni. Meanwhile, remove the lobster meat from the shell and return the shells to the pan. Dice the lobster meat and set aside. When the rice is cooked, discard the larger bits of shell.

4 Tip the mixture into a food processor or blender and purée, then press through a fine sieve placed over the clean pan. Heat the mixture until almost boiling. Season with salt, pepper and cayenne, lower the heat and stir in the cream. Dice the remaining butter and whisk it into the bisque. Add the lobster meat and serve immediately. If you like, pour a small spoonful of brandy into each soup bowl and swirl in a little cream.

BOUILLABAISSE

Authentic bouillabaisse comes from the south of France and includes rascasse (scorpion fish) as an essential ingredient. It is, however, perfectly possible to make this wonderful main-course soup without it. Use as large a variety of fish as you can.

SERVES 4

INGREDIENTS
45ml/3 tbsp olive oil
2 onions, chopped
2 leeks, white parts only, chopped
4 garlic cloves, chopped
450g/1lb ripe tomatoes, peeled and chopped
3 litres/5 pints/12 cups boiling fish stock or water
15ml/1 tbsp tomato purée (paste)
large pinch of saffron threads
fresh bouquet garni, containing 2 thyme sprigs, 2 bay leaves
    and 2 fennel sprigs
3kg/6½lb mixed fish, cleaned and cut into large chunks
4 potatoes, peeled and thickly sliced
salt, pepper and cayenne pepper
30ml/2 tbsp chopped flat leaf parsley, to garnish
16 slices of French bread, toasted and rubbed with garlic, and a bowl of
    garlic mayonnaise, to serve

1 Heat the oil in a large pan. Add the onions, leeks, garlic and tomatoes. Cook until slightly softened. Stir in the stock or water, tomato purée and saffron. Add the bouquet garni and boil until the oil is amalgamated. Lower the heat; add the fish and potatoes.

2 Simmer the soup for 5–8 minutes, removing each type of fish as it becomes cooked. Continue to cook until the potatoes are very tender. Season well with salt, pepper and cayenne.

3 Put the fish and potatoes into soup plates, strain the soup and ladle over the fish and potatoes. Garnish with parsley and serve with toasted French bread and garlic mayonnaise.

MATELOTE

Traditionally this French fishermen's chunky soup is made from freshwater fish, including eel. Any firm fish can be used, but try to include at least some eel, and use a robust red or dry white wine for extra flavour.

SERVES 6

INGREDIENTS
1kg/2¼lb mixed fish, including 450g/1lb conger eel if possible
50g/2oz/¼ cup butter
1 onion, thickly sliced
2 celery sticks, thickly sliced
2 carrots, thickly sliced
1 bottle red or dry white wine
fresh bouquet garni, containing parsley, bay leaf and chervil
2 cloves
6 black peppercorns
beurre manié, for thickening (see Cook's Tip)
salt and cayenne pepper

FOR THE GARNISH
25g/1oz/2 tbsp butter
12 baby (pearl) onions, peeled
12 button (white) mushrooms
chopped fresh flat leaf parsley

COOK'S TIP
To make the beurre manié for thickening, mix 15g/½oz/1 tbsp softened butter with 15ml/1 tbsp plain (all-purpose) flour. Add to the boiling soup a pinch at a time, whisking constantly.

1 Cut all the fish into thick slices, removing any obvious bones. Melt the butter in a large pan, put in the fish and sliced vegetables and stir over a medium heat until lightly browned. Pour in the wine and enough cold water to cover. Add the bouquet garni and spices and season. Bring to the boil, lower the heat and simmer gently for 20–30 minutes, or until the fish is tender. Skim off froth occasionally.

2 Meanwhile, prepare the garnish. Heat the butter in a small frying pan, add the baby onions and sauté until golden and tender. Add the mushrooms and fry until golden. Season with salt and keep hot.

3 Strain the soup through a large sieve placed over a clean pan. Discard the bouquet garni and spices in the sieve, then divide the fish among deep soup plates (you can skin the fish if you wish, but this is not essential) and keep hot.

4 Reheat the soup until it reaches boiling point. Lower the heat and whisk in the beurre manié little by little until the soup thickens. Season the soup with salt, if necessary, and cayenne pepper, then pour it over the fish. Garnish each portion with the sautéed baby onions and mushrooms and sprinkle with chopped parsley.

Scallop & Jerusalem Artichoke Soup

The subtle sweetness of scallops combines well with the flavour of Jerusalem artichokes in this attractive golden soup. For an even more colourful version, substitute pumpkin for the artichokes and use extra stock instead of the milk.

SERVES 6

INGREDIENTS
1kg/2¼lb Jerusalem artichokes
juice of ½ lemon
115g/4oz/½ cup butter
1 onion, finely chopped
600ml/1 pint/2½ cups fish stock
300ml/½ pint/1¼ cups milk
generous pinch of saffron threads
6 large or 12 small scallops, with their corals
150ml/¼ pint/⅔ cup whipping cream
salt and ground white pepper
45ml/3 tbsp flaked (sliced) almonds and 15ml/1 tbsp finely chopped fresh chervil,
   to garnish

COOK'S TIP
If you prefer not to use scallop corals, substitute 12 small cooked, peeled prawns (shrimp). Chop roughly and cook briefly with the almonds.

---

1 Scrub and peel the Jerusalem artichokes, cut them into 2cm/¾in chunks and drop them into a bowl of cold water, which has been acidulated with the lemon juice. This will prevent the artichokes from discolouring.

2 Melt half the butter in a large, heavy pan, add the onion and cook over a low heat until softened. Drain the artichokes and add them to the pan. Cook gently for 5 minutes, stirring frequently. Pour in the stock and milk, add the saffron threads and bring to the boil. Lower the heat and simmer until the artichokes are tender but not mushy.

3 Meanwhile, carefully separate the scallop corals from the white flesh. Prick the corals and slice each scallop in half horizontally. Heat half the remaining butter in a frying pan, add the scallops and corals, if using, and cook very briefly (for about 1 minute) on each side. Dice the scallops and corals, keeping them separate, and set them aside until needed.

4 When the artichokes are cooked, tip the contents of the pan into a food processor or blender. Add half the white scallop meat and purée until very smooth. Return the soup to the clean pan, season with salt and white pepper and keep hot over a low heat while you prepare the garnish.

5 Heat the remaining butter in a frying pan, add the almonds and toss over a medium heat until golden brown. Add the diced scallop coral and cook for about 30 seconds. Stir the cream into the soup and add the remaining diced white scallop meat. Ladle the soup into individual bowls and garnish each serving with the almonds, scallop corals and a sprinkling of chopped chervil.

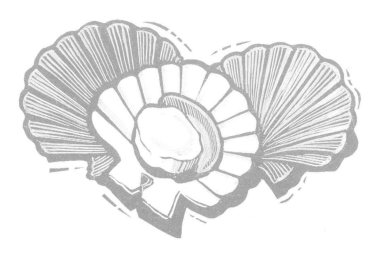

Fish & Okra Soup

The inspiration for this soup came from a traditional Ghanaian recipe. Leave the okra whole or chop them to achieve a more authentic consistency.

Serves 4

Ingredients
2 green bananas
50g/2oz/¼ cup butter
1 onion, finely chopped
2 tomatoes, skinned and finely chopped
115g/4oz okra, trimmed
225g/8oz smoked haddock or cod fillet, cut into bitesize pieces
900ml/1½ pints/3¾ cups fish stock
1 fresh chilli, seeded and chopped
salt and ground black pepper
chopped fresh flat leaf parsley, to garnish

1 Slit the banana skins, but do not peel them. Place the bananas in a large pan. Cover with water, bring to the boil and cook over a medium heat for about 25 minutes, or until tender. Transfer to a plate using a slotted spoon and leave to cool.

2 Melt the butter in a large pan, add the onion and sauté for about 5 minutes until softened. Stir in the chopped tomatoes and the okra and fry gently for a further 10 minutes.

3 Add the fish, fish stock, chilli and seasoning. Bring to the boil, then reduce the heat and simmer for about 20 minutes, or until the fish is cooked through and flakes easily with a fork.

4 Peel the cooked bananas and cut them into slices. Stir the banana slices into the soup and heat through for a few minutes. Ladle the soup into bowls, sprinkle with the chopped parsley and serve.

CLAM CHOWDER

If fresh clams are hard to find, use frozen or canned clams for this classic New England recipe. Large clams should be cut into chunky pieces. Reserve a few clams in their shells for garnish, if you like. Traditionally, the soup is served with savoury biscuits called saltine crackers. You should be able to find these in a delicatessen.

SERVES 4

INGREDIENTS
100g/3¾oz salt pork or thinly sliced unsmoked bacon, diced
1 large onion, chopped
2 potatoes, peeled and cut into 1cm/½in cubes
1 bay leaf
1 fresh thyme sprig
300ml/½ pint/1¼ cups milk
400g/14oz cooked clams, cooking liquid reserved
150ml/¼ pint/⅔ cup double (heavy) cream
salt, ground white pepper and cayenne pepper
finely chopped fresh flat leaf parsley, to garnish

1 Put the salt pork or unsmoked bacon in a pan, and heat gently, stirring frequently, until the fat runs and the meat is starting to brown. Add the chopped onion and fry over a low heat until softened but not browned.

2 Add the cubed potatoes, the bay leaf and thyme sprig, stir well to coat with fat, then pour in the milk and reserved clam liquid and bring to the boil. Lower the heat and simmer for about 10 minutes, or until the potatoes are tender but still firm. Lift out the bay leaf and thyme sprig and discard.

3 Remove the shells from most of the clams. Add all the clams to the pan and season to taste with salt, pepper and cayenne. Simmer gently for 5 minutes more, then stir in the cream. Heat until the soup is very hot, but do not allow it to boil. Ladle into soup bowls, garnish with the chopped parsley and serve.

LOUISIANA SEAFOOD GUMBO

Gumbo is a soup, but is served over rice as a main course. In Louisiana, oysters are cheap and prolific, and would be used here instead of mussels.

SERVES 6

INGREDIENTS
450g/1lb fresh mussels
450g/1lb large, raw prawns (shrimp), in the shell
1 cooked crab, about 1kg/2¼lb
small bunch of flat leaf parsley, leaves chopped and stalks reserved
150ml/¼ pint/⅔ cup vegetable oil
115g/4oz/1 cup plain (all-purpose) flour
1 green (bell) pepper, seeded and chopped
1 large onion, chopped
2 celery sticks, sliced
3 garlic cloves, finely chopped
75g/3oz smoked spiced sausage, skinned and sliced
275g/10oz/1½ cups long grain rice
6 spring onions (scallions), shredded
cayenne pepper and Tabasco sauce, to taste
salt

1 Wash the mussels in several changes of cold water, scrubbing them thoroughly and pulling away the "beards". Discard any mussels that are broken or do not close when you tap them firmly.

2 Bring 250ml/8fl oz/1 cup water to the boil in a deep pan. Add the mussels, cover the pan tightly and cook over a high heat, shaking frequently, for 3 minutes. As the mussels open, lift them out with a slotted spoon into a sieve set over a bowl. Discard any that fail to open.

3 Shell the mussels, discarding the shells. Return the liquid from the bowl to the pan and make the quantity up to 2 litres/3½ pints/8 cups with water.

4 Peel the prawns and set them aside, reserving a few for the garnish. Put the shells and heads into the pan. Remove all the meat from the crab, separating the brown and white meat. Add all the pieces of shell to the pan with 5ml/1 tsp salt.

5 Bring the shellfish stock to the boil, skimming it regularly. When there is no more froth on the surface, add the parsley stalks and simmer for 15 minutes. Cool the stock, then strain it into a measuring jug (cup) and make up to 2 litres/3½ pints/8 cups with water.

6 Heat the oil in a heavy pan and stir in the flour. Stir constantly over a medium heat with a wooden spoon or whisk until the roux reaches a golden-brown colour. Immediately add the pepper, onion, celery and garlic. Continue cooking for about 3 minutes, or until the onion has softened. Stir in the sausage. Reheat the stock.

7 Stir the brown crab meat into the roux, then ladle in the hot stock a little at a time, stirring constantly until it has all been smoothly incorporated. Bring to the boil, then reduce the heat, partially cover the pan and simmer the gumbo for 30 minutes.

8 Meanwhile, cook the rice in plenty of lightly salted boiling water for about 12 minutes, or until the grains are tender.

9 Add the prawns, mussels, white crab meat and spring onions to the gumbo. Return to the boil and season with salt if necessary, cayenne and a dash or two of Tabasco sauce. Simmer for a further minute, then add the chopped parsley leaves. Serve immediately, ladling the soup over the hot rice in soup plates.

COOK'S TIP
It is vital to stir constantly to darken the roux without burning as this impairs the flavour. Should black specks occur at any stage of cooking, discard the roux and start again. Have the onion, green pepper and celery ready to add to the roux the minute it reaches the correct golden-brown stage, as this stops it cooking further.

MALAYSIAN PRAWN LAKSA

The addition of coconut milk to this spicy prawn and noodle soup gives a wonderful, creamy result. It is quick and easy to prepare and makes a satisfying lunch or supper dish. Serve with prawn crackers for an authentic Malaysian feel.

SERVES 2–3

INGREDIENTS
115g/4oz rice vermicelli or stir-fry rice noodles
15ml/1 tbsp vegetable or groundnut (peanut) oil
600ml/1 pint/2½ cups fish stock
400ml/14fl oz/1⅔ cups thin coconut milk
30ml/2 tbsp Thai fish sauce (nam pla)
½ lime
16–24 cooked, peeled prawns (shrimp)
salt and cayenne pepper
60ml/4 tbsp fresh coriander (cilantro) sprigs and leaves, chopped, to garnish

FOR THE SPICE PASTE
2 lemon grass stalks, finely chopped
2 fresh red chillies, seeded and chopped
2.5cm/1in piece fresh root ginger, peeled and sliced
2.5ml/½ tsp dried shrimp paste
2 garlic cloves, chopped
2.5ml/½ tsp ground turmeric
30ml/2 tbsp tamarind paste

COOK'S TIP
This spicy soup tastes just as good when made with fresh crab meat or any flaked cooked fish. If you are short of time or cannot find all the spice paste ingredients, buy ready-made laksa paste, available from Asian stores.

1 Cook the rice vermicelli or noodles in a large pan of boiling salted water according to the instructions on the packet. Tip into a large sieve or colander, then rinse under cold water and drain. Keep warm.

2   To make the spice paste, place the lemon grass, chillies, root ginger, shrimp paste, garlic, turmeric and tamarind paste in a mortar and pound with a pestle until a smooth paste is formed. Alternatively, put the ingredients in a food processor or blender and whizz until smooth.

3   Heat the vegetable or groundnut oil in a large pan, add the spice paste and fry, stirring constantly, for a few moments to release all the flavours, but be careful not to let it burn.

4   Add the fish stock and coconut milk to the pan and bring to the boil. Stir in the Thai fish sauce, then simmer for 5 minutes. Season with salt and cayenne pepper to taste, adding a generous squeeze of lime. Add the peeled prawns and heat through for a few seconds.

5   Divide the noodles among two or three soup plates. Pour over the soup, making sure that each portion includes an equal number of prawns. Garnish with coriander and serve piping hot.

APPETIZERS

The delicate flavours and light textures of fish and shellfish make them the ideal appetizer. Cold marinated fish dishes such as Ceviche with Tomato & Anchovy Salsa and Potato Pancakes with Pickled Herrings & Onion are sure to whet the appetite. Light and refreshing salads such as Prawn Cocktail and Crab & Rocket Salad are perfect for summer. More substantial, deep-fried fish such as Devilled Whitebait and Breaded Sole Goujons, and baked dishes such as Gratin of Mussels with Pesto are great for those with hearty appetites.

Ceviche with Tomato & Avocado Salsa

You can use almost any firm-fleshed fish for this South American dish, provided that it is perfectly fresh. The fish is "cooked" by the action of the acidic lime juice. Adjust the amount of chilli according to your taste.

SERVES 6

INGREDIENTS
675g/1½lb halibut, sole, sea bass or salmon fillets, skinned
juice of 3 limes
1–2 fresh red chillies, seeded and very finely chopped
15ml/1 tbsp olive oil
salt
30ml/2 tbsp fresh coriander (cilantro) leaves, to garnish

FOR THE SALSA
4 large firm tomatoes, peeled, seeded and diced
1 ripe avocado, peeled and diced
15ml/1 tbsp lemon juice
30ml/2 tbsp olive oil

1 Cut the fish fillets into strips measuring about 5 × 1cm/2 × ½in. Lay these in a shallow dish and pour over the lime juice, turning the fish to coat all over in the juice. Cover with clear film (plastic wrap) and leave for 1 hour.

2 Meanwhile, make the salsa. Put the diced tomatoes, avocado, lemon juice and olive oil in a bowl and mix together well. Set aside.

3 Season the fish with salt and scatter over the chopped chillies. Drizzle with the olive oil. Toss the fish in the mixture, then replace the cover. Leave to marinate in the refrigerator for 15–30 minutes more.

4 To serve, divide the salsa among six plates. Spoon on the marinated fish strips, sprinkle with coriander leaves and serve.

MARINATED SMOKED HADDOCK FILLETS

This simple dish is also excellent made with kipper or smoked herring fillets. If you do try this version, use whisky instead of the rum or, if you prefer, omit the spirits and add a teaspoon of sugar to the marinade instead.

SERVES 6

INGREDIENTS
450g/1lb undyed smoked haddock fillets, skinned
1 onion, very thinly sliced into rings
5–10ml/1–2 tsp Dijon mustard
30ml/2 tbsp lemon juice
90ml/6 tbsp olive oil
45ml/3 tbsp dark rum
12 small new potatoes, scrubbed
30ml/2 tbsp chopped fresh dill, plus 6 dill sprigs to garnish
ground black pepper

1 Cut the fish fillets in half lengthways. Arrange the pieces in a single layer in a shallow non-metallic dish. Sprinkle the onion rings evenly over the top.

2 In a small bowl, whisk together the mustard, lemon juice and some pepper. Add the oil gradually, whisking. Pour two-thirds of the dressing over the fish. Cover the dish with clear film (plastic wrap) and leave the fish to marinate for 2 hours in a cool place. Sprinkle the rum over the fish and leave for 1 hour more.

3 Cook the potatoes in boiling salted water until tender. Drain, cut in half and tip into a bowl. Cool until warm, then toss in the remaining dressing. Stir in the chopped dill, cover the bowl and set aside.

4 Slice the haddock thinly, as for smoked salmon. Arrange the slices on small plates and spoon over some marinade and onion rings. Pile the potato halves on one side of each plate and garnish each portion with a sprig of dill. Serve chilled or at room temperature.

POTATO PANCAKES WITH PICKLED HERRING & ONION

These pancakes are full of delicious Scandinavian flavours. Serve them as a first course or as a light main course with salad. Small pancakes make excellent canapés to serve with ice-cold shots of vodka or other pre-dinner drinks.

SERVES 6

INGREDIENTS
275g/10oz peeled potatoes
2 eggs, beaten
150ml/¼ pint/⅔ cup milk
40g/1½oz/⅓ cup plain (all-purpose) flour
30ml/2 tbsp chopped fresh chives
vegetable oil or butter, for greasing
salt and ground black pepper
fresh dill sprigs and fresh chives or chive flowers, to garnish

FOR THE TOPPING
2 small red or yellow onions, thinly sliced into rings
60ml/4 tbsp sour cream or crème fraîche
5ml/1 tsp wholegrain mustard
15ml/1 tbsp chopped fresh dill
6 pickled herring fillets

1 Cut the potatoes into small chunks and cook them in a small pan of boiling salted water for about 15 minutes, or until they are tender, then drain and mash or sieve to form a smooth purée.

2 Meanwhile, prepare the topping. Place the red or yellow onions in a bowl and cover with boiling water. Allow to stand for 2–3 minutes, then drain thoroughly and dry on kitchen paper.

3 Mix the onions with the sour cream or crème fraîche, mustard and chopped dill. Season to taste. Then cut the pickled herring fillets into 12–18 pieces, using a sharp knife. Set them aside.

4 Put the potato purée in a bowl and beat in the eggs, milk and flour with a wooden spoon to make a batter. Season to taste with salt and pepper and stir in the chopped chives.

5 Heat a large, non-stick frying pan over a medium heat and grease it with a little oil or butter. Make the pancakes three or four at a time. Spoon about 30ml/ 2 tbsp of batter into the pan to make a pancake, measuring about 7.5cm/3in across. Cook for 3–4 minutes, or until the underside is set and golden brown. Turn the pancakes over and cook the other side for 3–4 minutes, or until golden brown. Transfer to a plate and keep warm while you make the remaining pancakes. The mixture will make 12 pancakes.

6 Place two pancakes on each of six warmed plates and distribute the pickled herring fillets and onions equally among them. Garnish with dill sprigs, fresh chives and/or chive flowers. Season with black pepper and serve immediately.

PRAWN COCKTAIL

There is no nicer appetizer than a good, fresh prawn cocktail – and nothing nastier than one in which soggy prawns swim in a thin, vinegary sauce embedded in limp lettuce. This recipe shows just how good a prawn cocktail can be.

SERVES 6

INGREDIENTS
60ml/4 tbsp double (heavy) cream
60ml/4 tbsp mayonnaise, preferably home-made
60ml/4 tbsp tomato ketchup
5–10ml/1–2 tsp Worcestershire sauce
juice of 1 lemon
½ cos (romaine) lettuce or other very crisp lettuce
450g/1lb cooked, peeled prawns (shrimp)
salt, ground black pepper and paprika
6 large, whole cooked prawns (shrimp) in the shell, to garnish (optional)
thinly sliced brown bread and butter, and lemon wedges, to serve

1 Place the cream in a small bowl and whip lightly. Add the mayonnaise and tomato ketchup and whisk to combine. Add Worcestershire sauce and lemon juice to taste. Finely shred the lettuce and fill six individual glasses one-third full.

2 Stir the prawns into the sauce, then check the seasoning and spoon the prawn mixture over the shredded lettuce. If you like, drape a cooked prawn over the edge of each glass and sprinkle each of the cocktails with pepper and/or paprika. Serve immediately, with brown bread, spread with butter, and lemon wedges.

COOK'S TIP
Partly peeled prawns make a pretty garnish. To prepare, remove the heads, then peel the body shell from the prawns, leaving the tail fan for decoration.

CRAB & ROCKET SALAD

The delicate flavour of crab goes wonderfully with fresh, peppery rocket leaves. A dressed crab is one that has had all the white and brown meat cooked and removed, and then put back into the emptied and cleaned shell. Use frozen crab meat, if fresh is not available, or substitute canned white crab meat.

SERVES 4

INGREDIENTS
white and brown meat from 4 small fresh crabs,
  about 450g/1lb
1 small red (bell) pepper, seeded and finely chopped
1 small red onion, finely chopped
30ml/2 tbsp drained, bottled capers
30ml/2 tbsp chopped fresh coriander (cilantro)
grated rind and juice of 2 lemons
Tabasco sauce
40g/1½oz rocket (arugula) leaves
30ml/2 tbsp sunflower oil
15ml/1 tbsp fresh lime juice
salt and ground black pepper
lemon rind strips, to garnish

1 Put the white and brown crab meat, red pepper, onion, capers and chopped coriander in a large bowl. Add the lemon rind and juice and toss gently to mix together. Season with a few drops of Tabasco sauce, according to taste, and a little salt and ground black pepper.

2 Wash the rocket leaves and pat dry on kitchen paper. Divide among four plates. Mix together the sunflower oil and lime juice in a small bowl. Pour the dressing over the rocket leaves, then pile the crab salad on top and serve immediately, garnished with lemon rind strips.

Red Mullet Dolmades

If you cannot find prepared vine leaves, use blanched cabbage or large spinach leaves instead. Plaice or lemon sole can be substituted for the red mullet or snapper.

Serves 4

Ingredients
225g/8oz red mullet or snapper fillets, scaled
45ml/3 tbsp dry white wine
115g/4oz/1 cup cooked long grain rice (40–50g/1½–2oz raw weight)
25g/1oz/⅓ cup pine nuts
45ml/3 tbsp chopped fresh flat leaf parsley
grated rind and juice of ½ lemon
8 vine leaves in brine, rinsed and dried
salt and ground black pepper

For the sauce
grated rind and juice of 2 oranges
2 shallots, very finely chopped
25g/1oz/2 tbsp chilled butter, diced

1 Preheat the oven to 200°C/400°F/Gas 6. Put the fillets in a shallow pan and season with salt and pepper. Pour over the wine, bring to the boil, then lower the heat and poach the fish gently for about 3 minutes. Strain, reserving the cooking liquid.

2 Remove the fish skin and flake the flesh into a bowl. Gently stir in the rice, pine nuts, parsley, and lemon rind and juice. Season to taste with salt and pepper.

3 Spoon 30–45ml/2–3 tbsp of the filling into the middle of each vine leaf. Roll up, tucking in the sides to make a secure package. Arrange the dolmades in a shallow ovenproof dish, with the joins underneath. Pour over the reserved cooking liquid and cook in the oven for about 5 minutes.

4 To make the sauce, mix the orange rind and juice and the shallots in a small pan and boil vigorously for a few minutes until the mixture is reduced and syrupy. Strain into a clean pan, discarding the shallots. Beat in the butter, one piece at a time. Reheat gently, then drizzle over the dolmades and serve at once.

SALMON & SCALLOP BROCHETTES

With their delicate colours and superb flavour, these skewers, drizzled with a light, tarragon sauce, make the perfect beginning to a sophisticated meal.

SERVES 4

INGREDIENTS
8 lemon grass stalks
225g/8oz salmon fillet, skinned
8 queen scallops, with their corals if possible
8 baby (pearl) onions, peeled and blanched
½ yellow (bell) pepper, cut into 8 squares
25g/1oz/2 tbsp butter
juice of ½ lemon
salt, ground white pepper and paprika

FOR THE SAUCE
30ml/2 tbsp dry vermouth
50g/2oz/¼ cup butter
5ml/1 tsp chopped fresh tarragon

1 Preheat the grill (broiler) to medium-high. Cut off the top 10cm/4in of each lemon grass stalk. Reserve the bulb ends for another dish. Cut the salmon fillet into twelve 2cm/¾in cubes. Thread the salmon cubes, scallops, corals if available, baby onions and pepper squares on to the lemon grass stalks and arrange the brochettes neatly in a grill (broiling) pan.

2 Melt the butter in a small pan, add the lemon juice and a pinch of paprika and then brush all over the brochettes. Grill (broil) for 2–3 minutes on each side, turning and basting the brochettes every minute, until the fish and scallops are just cooked, but are still very juicy. Transfer to a platter and keep hot while you make the tarragon butter sauce.

3 Pour the vermouth and all the leftover cooking juices from the brochettes into a small pan and boil quite fiercely to reduce by half. Add the butter and melt, stirring constantly. Stir in the chopped tarragon and add salt and pepper to taste. Pour the tarragon butter sauce over the brochettes and serve.

BREADED SOLE GOUJONS

Goujons are tiny fish that are fried and eaten whole. In this dish, sole fillets are cut into strips that, when cooked, resemble goujons. You could say that the French manage to bring a sense of style even to fish fingers.

SERVES 4

INGREDIENTS
275g/10oz lemon sole fillets, skinned
2 eggs
120g/4oz/1½ cups fine fresh breadcrumbs
85g/3oz/6 tbsp plain (all-purpose) flour
vegetable oil, for frying
salt and ground black pepper
tartar sauce and lemon wedges, to serve

1 Cut the fish fillets into long diagonal strips about 2cm/¾in wide. Break the eggs into a shallow dish, add a little salt and beat well with a fork. Place the breadcrumbs in another shallow dish. Put the flour in a large plastic bag and season with salt and ground black pepper.

2 Dip the fish strips in the egg, turning to coat them well. Place the strips in a single layer on a large plate and then, taking a few at a time, shake them in the bag of flour. Dip the fish strips in the egg again and then in the breadcrumbs, turning to coat them well. Place on a tray in a single layer, not touching. Let the coating set for at least 10 minutes.

3 Heat 1cm/⅜in oil in a large frying pan over a medium-high heat. When the oil is hot (a cube of bread will sizzle when dropped into the oil) add the fish strips in batches and fry for about 2–2½ minutes, turning once, taking care not to overcrowd the pan. Drain on kitchen paper and keep warm. Serve the fish with tartar sauce and lemon wedges.

DEVILLED WHITEBAIT

The tiny, silvery fry of the herring, whitebait are eaten whole. These deliciously crisp little fish are wonderful served with lemon wedges and thinly sliced brown bread and butter, and eaten with your fingers.

SERVES 4

INGREDIENTS
vegetable oil, for deep-frying
150ml/¼ pint/⅔ cup milk
115g/4oz/1 cup plain (all-purpose) flour
450g/1lb whitebait
salt, ground black pepper and cayenne pepper
thinly sliced brown bread and butter, and lemon wedges, to serve

1 Heat the oil in a large pan or deep-fryer. Put the milk in a shallow bowl. Spoon the flour into a paper bag and season with salt, pepper and a little cayenne.

2 Dip a handful of the whitebait into the milk, drain well, then pop them into the paper bag. Shake gently to coat in flour. Repeat until all the fish have been coated. Do not add too many at once, or they will stick together.

3 Heat the oil for deep-frying to 190°C/375°F or until a cube of stale bread, dropped into the oil, browns in 20 seconds. Add a batch of whitebait and fry for 2–3 minutes, or until golden. Drain and keep hot while you fry the rest. Sprinkle with cayenne and serve hot with brown bread and butter, and lemon wedges.

COOK'S TIP
Whitebait are usually sold frozen. Thaw them before use and dry them thoroughly on kitchen paper, making sure to keep them separate.

Prawns & Baby Vegetables with Hot Garlic Dip

This hot garlic dip from Piedmont in northern Italy is very rich. It is traditionally eaten to celebrate the end of the grape harvest.

Serves 4

Ingredients
a selection of vegetables, such as new potatoes, baby artichokes, cauliflower florets,
   fennel, celery sticks, baby carrots
crusty bread
8 large cooked prawns (shrimp), peeled

For the dip
150ml/¼ pint/⅔ cup extra virgin olive oil
5cm/2in sprig of fresh rosemary
6 garlic cloves, thinly sliced or finely chopped
50g/2oz can anchovy fillets, drained and chopped
90g/3½oz/7 tbsp unsalted butter, diced
75ml/5 tbsp double (heavy) cream (optional)
ground black pepper

1 Prepare and, if necessary, cook the vegetables. Cut the bread and any large vegetables into small portions. For the dip, place the oil in a small pan over a very low heat, then add the rosemary and garlic. Keep the heat low for 5 minutes to allow the garlic to flavour the oil, but do not allow it to brown. Remove the rosemary.

2 Add the anchovies and cook very gently for another 3–5 minutes, mashing the anchovies into the oil with a wooden spoon or spatula. When the anchovies have broken down completely, add the butter and cream and whisk gently until the butter has melted. Season to taste with a little pepper.

3 Pour the hot butter mixture into a fondue pan or small flameproof earthenware dish and stand this over a spirit stove or nightlight to keep the dip warm. Serve immediately with the bread, vegetables and prawns for dipping.

Soft-shell Crabs with Chilli & Salt

If fresh soft-shell crabs are unavailable, you can buy frozen ones in Asian supermarkets. Allow two small crabs per serving, or one if they are large.

SERVES 4

INGREDIENTS
8 small soft-shell crabs, thawed if frozen
50g/2oz/½ cup plain (all-purpose) flour
60ml/4 tbsp groundnut (peanut) or vegetable oil
2 large fresh red chillies, or 1 green and 1 red, seeded and thinly sliced
4 spring onions (scallions) or a small bunch of garlic chives, chopped
coarse sea salt and ground black pepper

TO SERVE
shredded lettuce, mooli (daikon) and carrot
light soy sauce

1 Pat the crabs dry with kitchen paper. Season the flour with pepper and coat the crabs lightly with the mixture.

2 Heat the oil in a shallow pan until very hot, then put in the crabs. Fry for about 3 minutes on each side, until the crabs are golden brown but still juicy in the middle. Drain the cooked crabs on kitchen paper and keep hot.

3 Add the sliced chillies and spring onions or garlic chives to the pan and cook gently for about 2 minutes. Add salt, then spread the mixture on to the crabs.

4 Mix together the shredded lettuce, mooli and carrot. Arrange on plates, top each portion with two crabs and serve with light soy sauce for dipping.

COOK'S TIP
The shredded vegetables make a colourful bed for the crabs. If you can't find mooli, use celeriac instead.

CRAB EGG ROLLS

These wonderful crab rolls are very similar to authentic Chinese spring rolls. They are made with wafer-thin egg pancakes, which provide the very crisp case for the filling.

MAKES ABOUT 12

INGREDIENTS
3 eggs
450ml/³/₄ pint/scant 2 cups water
175g/6oz/1½ cups plain (all-purpose) flour
2.5ml/½ tsp salt
oil, for deep-frying (optional)
45ml/3 tbsp light soy sauce mixed with 5ml/1 tsp sesame oil, for dipping
lime wedges, to serve

FOR THE FILLING
225g/8oz/1⅓ cups white crab meat or small cooked, peeled
   prawns (shrimp)
3 large spring onions (scallions), shredded
2.5cm/1in piece fresh root ginger, grated
2 large garlic cloves, chopped
115g/4oz bamboo shoots, chopped, or beansprouts
15ml/1 tbsp soy sauce
10–15ml/2–3 tbsp cornflour (cornstarch) blended with 15ml/1 tbsp water
1 egg, separated
salt and ground black pepper

> COOK'S TIP
> *If you want to make 18–20 smaller, bitesize rolls, prepare smaller egg wrappers using an omelette pan 12.5–15cm/5–6in in diameter.*

1 Make the egg pancakes. Lightly beat the eggs and gradually stir in the water. Sift the flour and salt into another bowl and whisk in the egg and water mixture. Blend to make a smooth batter. Leave to rest for 20 minutes. When ready to use, whisk the mixture and stir in 15ml/1 tbsp cold water.

2 Lightly grease a 25cm/10in non-stick frying pan and heat gently. To make smooth, pale wrappers, the frying pan must be hot enough to set the batter, but not hot enough for the batter to brown, bubble or develop holes.

3 Pour about 45ml/3 tbsp batter into the heated pan and swirl round to spread evenly and very thinly. Cook for 2 minutes, or until the pancake loosens from the pan. There is no need to cook the pancake on the other side.

4 Stack the pancakes as they are cooked, cooked-side upwards, between sheets of baking parchment. Set aside until ready to use.

5 Combine the crab or prawns, spring onions, ginger, garlic, bamboo shoots or beansprouts, soy sauce, cornflour, egg yolk and seasoning.

6 Lightly beat the egg white. Place a spoonful of filling in the middle of each pancake, brush the edges with egg white and fold into neat parcels, tucking in the sides well.

7 Using a stacking bamboo steamer, arrange four parcels in each layer, cover with a lid and steam for 30 minutes. Alternatively, heat the oil in a deep-frying pan and, when a small piece of bread turns light golden in 1 minute, carefully add four of the parcels, fold-side downwards. Cook for 1–2 minutes, or until golden and crisp.

8 Remove with a draining spoon and place on kitchen paper. Keep warm in the oven while you cook the remaining egg rolls. Serve with the thoroughly combined dipping sauce and wedges of lime.

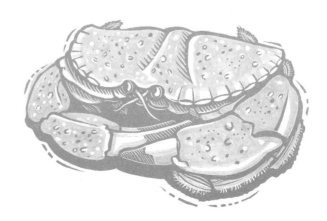

GRATIN OF MUSSELS WITH PESTO

This is the perfect appetizer for serving when you do not have a lot of time, as both the pesto and the mussels can be prepared in advance, and the dish assembled and cooked at the last minute.

SERVES 4

INGREDIENTS
36 large fresh mussels, scrubbed and beards removed
105ml/7 tbsp dry white wine
60ml/4 tbsp finely chopped fresh flat leaf parsley
1 garlic clove, finely chopped
30ml/2 tbsp fresh white breadcrumbs
60ml/4 tbsp olive oil
chopped fresh basil, to garnish
hot crusty bread, to serve

FOR THE PESTO
2 fat garlic cloves, chopped
2.5ml/½ tsp coarse sea salt
100g/3¾oz/3 cups basil leaves
25g/1oz/⅓ cup pine nuts, chopped
50g/2oz/⅔ cup freshly grated Parmesan cheese
120ml/4fl oz/½ cup extra virgin olive oil

COOK'S TIP
Home-made pesto is best but when basil is out of season – or you are in a hurry – a jar of ready-made pesto may be used instead. Once opened, it will keep in the refrigerator for a few weeks.

1 Discard any open mussels that do not close when sharply tapped. Put the remaining mussels in a pan with the wine, clamp on the lid and shake over a high heat for 3–4 minutes, or until the mussels have opened. Any that remain closed should be discarded.

2 As soon as the mussels are cool enough to handle, lift them out of the cooking liquid. Pull the top shells off the mussels and discard the cooking liquid and the empty half-shells. Arrange the mussels in their half-shells in a single layer in four individual gratin dishes. Cover and set aside while you make the pesto.

3 To make the pesto, put the chopped garlic and salt in a mortar and pound to a purée with a pestle. Add the basil leaves and chopped pine nuts and crush to a thick paste. Work in the Parmesan cheese, and finally gradually drip in enough of the extra virgin olive oil to make a smooth and creamy paste. Alternatively, use a food processor: process the garlic, salt, basil and pine nuts to make a smooth paste. Add the Parmesan and pulse to mix, then, with the motor running, drizzle in the oil.

4 Spoon the pesto over the mussels in the gratin dishes. In a small bowl, mix together the parsley, garlic and breadcrumbs, then sprinkle evenly over the mussels. Drizzle with the olive oil.

5 Preheat the grill (broiler) to high. Stand the gratin dishes on a baking sheet and grill (broil) for 3 minutes. Scatter some chopped basil over the top and serve with hot crusty bread.

MOULES PROVENÇALES

Eating these garlic-and-herb-flavoured mussels is a messy affair, which is part of their charm. Hand round plenty of crusty French bread for mopping up the juices and don't forget to provide big napkins, fingerbowls and a deep plate for discarded shells.

SERVES 4

INGREDIENTS
30ml/2 tbsp olive oil
200g/7oz rindless unsmoked streaky (fatty) bacon, diced
1 onion, finely chopped
3 garlic cloves, finely chopped
1 bay leaf
15ml/1 tbsp chopped fresh mixed provençal herbs, such as thyme, marjoram, basil, oregano and savory
15–30ml/1–2 tbsp sun-dried tomatoes in oil, drained and chopped
4 large, very ripe tomatoes, peeled, seeded and chopped
50g/2oz/½ cup pitted black olives, chopped
105ml/7 tbsp dry white wine
2.25kg/5–5¼lb fresh mussels, scrubbed and beards removed
salt and ground black pepper
60ml/4 tbsp coarsely chopped fresh flat leaf parsley, to garnish

1 Heat the oil in a large pan, add the bacon and fry until golden and crisp. Remove with a slotted spoon and set aside. Add the onion and garlic to the pan and cook gently until softened. Add the herbs with both types of tomatoes, and fry gently for 5 minutes, stirring frequently. Stir in the olives and add seasoning to taste.

2 Put the wine and mussels in another pan. Cover and shake over a high heat for about 5 minutes, or until the mussels open. Discard any that remain closed.

3 Strain the cooking liquid into the pan containing the tomato sauce and boil until reduced by about one-third. Add the mussels and stir to coat them thoroughly with the sauce. Take out the bay leaf.

4 Divide the mussels and sauce among four heated dishes. Scatter over the fried bacon and chopped parsley and serve piping hot.

Scallops with Samphire & Lime

Samphire is a seashore plant with a wonderful taste and aroma of the sea. It is the perfect complement to scallops and helps to create a very attractive first course.

SERVES 4

INGREDIENTS
225g/8oz fresh samphire
12 large or 24 queen scallops
300ml/½ pint/1¼ cups dry white wine
juice of 2 limes
15ml/1 tbsp groundnut (peanut) or vegetable oil
½ cucumber, peeled, seeded and diced
ground black pepper
chopped fresh flat leaf parsley, to garnish

1 Wash the fresh samphire in several changes of cold water. Drain, then trim off any woody ends. Bring a pan of water to the boil, then drop in the samphire and cook for 3–5 minutes, or until tender but still crisp. Drain, refresh under cold water and drain again.

2 If the scallops are large, cut them in half horizontally. Detach the corals. In a shallow pan, bring the wine to the boil and cook until it is reduced by about one-third. Lower the heat and add the lime juice to the pan.

3 Add the scallops and corals and poach gently for 3–4 minutes, or until the scallops are just cooked, but still opaque. Using a slotted spoon, lift out the scallops and corals and set aside.

4 Leave the cooking liquid to cool until lukewarm, then whisk in the groundnut or vegetable oil. Add the samphire, cucumber, scallops and corals and toss lightly to mix. Grind over some black pepper, cover and leave at room temperature for about 1 hour – this will allow the flavours to develop. Divide the mixture among four individual dishes and then garnish each with a little chopped fresh parsley. Serve at room temperature.

OYSTERS ROCKEFELLER

This is the perfect dish for those who prefer their oysters lightly cooked rather than raw. As a cheaper alternative, for those who are not "as rich as Rockefeller", give mussels or clams the same treatment; they will also taste delicious.

SERVES 6

INGREDIENTS
450g/1lb/3 cups coarse sea salt, plus extra to serve
24 oysters, opened
115g/4oz/½ cup butter
2 shallots, finely chopped
500g/1¼lb spinach leaves, finely chopped
60ml/4 tbsp chopped fresh flat leaf parsley
60ml/4 tbsp chopped celery leaves
90ml/6 tbsp fresh white breadcrumbs
Tabasco sauce or cayenne pepper
10–20ml/2–4 tsp Pernod or Ricard
salt and ground black pepper
lemon wedges, to serve

1 Preheat the oven to 220°C/425°F/Gas 7. Make a bed of coarse salt on two large baking sheets. Set the oysters in the half-shell in the bed of salt to keep them steady. Set aside.

2 Melt the butter in a frying pan. Add the finely chopped shallots and cook them over a low heat for 2–3 minutes, or until they are softened. Stir in the chopped spinach and allow it to wilt.

3 Add the parsley, celery leaves and breadcrumbs to the pan and fry gently for 5 minutes. Season with salt, pepper and Tabasco or cayenne.

4 Divide the stuffing among the oysters. Drizzle a few drops of Pernod or Ricard over each oyster, then bake for about 5 minutes, or until bubbling and golden brown. Serve on a heated platter on a shallow salt bed with lemon wedges.

FLASH-FRIED SQUID
WITH PAPRIKA & GARLIC

These quick-fried squid are good served with a dry sherry or manzanilla as an appetizer or as part of mixed tapas. Alternatively, serve them on a bed of salad leaves and offer warm bread as an accompaniment for a more substantial first course.

SERVES 6–8 AS AN APPETIZER, 4 AS A FIRST COURSE

INGREDIENTS
500g/1¼lb very small squid, cleaned
90ml/6 tbsp olive oil, plus extra
1 red chilli, seeded and finely chopped
10ml/2 tsp Spanish mild smoked paprika (pimentón)
30ml/2 tbsp plain (all-purpose) flour
2 garlic cloves, finely chopped
15ml/1 tbsp sherry vinegar
5ml/1 tsp grated lemon rind
30–45ml/2–3 tbsp finely chopped fresh flat leaf parsley
salt and ground black pepper

1 Choose small squid that are no longer than 10cm/4in. Cut the body sacs into rings and cut the tentacles into bitesize pieces. Place the squid in a bowl and add 30ml/2 tbsp of the oil, half the chilli and the paprika. Season with a little salt and some pepper, cover and marinate for 2–4 hours in the refrigerator.

2 Toss the squid in the flour and divide it into two batches. Heat the remaining oil in a preheated wok or deep frying pan over a high heat until very hot. Add the first batch of squid and stir-fry for 1–2 minutes, or until the squid becomes opaque and the tentacles have curled.

3 Sprinkle in half the garlic. Stir, then quickly tip out on to a serving plate. Keep warm. Repeat with the second batch, adding more oil if needed. Sprinkle over the sherry vinegar, lemon rind, parsley and the remaining chilli. Season and serve hot, or leave to cool to serve with salad leaves.

Mousses, Terrines & Pates

Fish and shellfish are the ideal ingredients for mousses, terrines and pâtés. Fresh and smoked fish can add a distinctive flavour, and the different colours and textures of the flesh can be used to create pretty terrines and roulades. Smoked Fish & Asparagus Mousse and Smoked Mackerel Pâté have a wonderfully delicate flavour and are delicious for a first course or light snack. Terrines such as Haddock & Smoked Salmon Terrine make stunning centrepieces for a buffet table, and taste delicious. Many of the recipes in this chapter are ideal for entertaining as they can be prepared in advance and chilled until ready to serve.

SEA TROUT MOUSSE

This deliciously creamy mousse makes a little sea trout go a long way. The flesh of
the sea trout is pink and similar in flavour to salmon, which can be used instead.
Both give the mousse a wonderfully subtle hue.

SERVES 6

INGREDIENTS
250g/9oz sea trout fillet
120ml/4fl oz/½ cup fish stock
15ml/1 tbsp powdered gelatine
juice of ½ lemon
30ml/2 tbsp dry sherry or dry vermouth
30ml/2 tbsp freshly grated Parmesan cheese
300ml/½ pint/1¼ cups whipping cream
2 egg whites
15ml/1 tbsp sunflower oil
salt and ground white pepper
5cm/2in piece of cucumber, with peel, thinly sliced and halved,
    and fresh dill or chervil, to garnish

1 Put the sea trout in a shallow pan. Pour in the fish stock and heat to simmering
point. Poach the fish for about 3–4 minutes, or until it is lightly cooked. Strain
the stock into a jug (pitcher) and leave the trout to cool slightly.

2 Sprinkle the gelatine over the lemon juice and 15ml/1 tbsp water in a small
bowl and leave until spongy. Add the gelatine to the hot stock in the jug and
stir until it has dissolved completely. Set aside until required. When the trout is cool
enough to handle, remove the skin and flake the flesh.

3 Pour the stock into a food processor or blender. Process briefly, then gradually
add the flaked trout, sherry or vermouth and Parmesan through the feeder
tube, continuing to process the mixture until it is smooth. Scrape into a large bowl
and leave to cool completely.

4 Lightly whip the cream in a bowl, then fold it into the cold trout mixture.
Season to taste, then cover with clear film (plastic wrap) and chill until the
mousse is just beginning to set. It should have the consistency of mayonnaise.

5 In a grease-free bowl, whisk the egg whites with a pinch of salt until softly peaking. Using a large metal spoon, stir one-third of the beaten whites into the trout mixture to slacken it, then gently fold in the rest.

6 Lightly grease six ramekins with the sunflower oil. Divide the mousse among the ramekins and level the surface. Place in the refrigerator for 2–3 hours, or until set. Just before serving, arrange a few slices of cucumber and a small herb sprig on each mousse and add a little chopped dill or chervil.

COOK'S TIP
Serve the mousse with Melba toast, if you like. Toast thin slices of bread on both sides under the grill (broiler), then cut off the crusts and carefully slice each piece of toast in half horizontally, then cut each slice into triangles. Return to the grill pan, untoasted sides up, and cook under a medium-low heat until the toast is curled and pale golden. The thin slices will swiftly brown and curl, so watch them closely.

Smoked Fish & Asparagus Mousse

This elegant mousse looks very special with its studding of asparagus and smoked salmon. Serve a mustard and dill dressing separately if you like.

SERVES 8

INGREDIENTS

15ml/1 tbsp powdered gelatine
juice of 1 lemon
105ml/7 tbsp fish stock
50g/2oz/¼ cup butter, plus extra for greasing
2 shallots, finely chopped
225g/8oz smoked trout fillets
105ml/7 tbsp sour cream
225g/8oz/1 cup low-fat cream cheese or cottage cheese
1 egg white
12 spinach leaves, blanched
12 fresh asparagus spears, lightly cooked
115g/4oz smoked salmon, cut into long strips
salt
shredded raw beetroot (beet) and salad leaves, to garnish

1 Sprinkle the gelatine over the lemon juice in a small bowl and leave until spongy. Heat the fish stock, add the gelatine and stir to dissolve. Melt the butter in a small pan, add the shallots and cook gently until softened. Flake the fish fillets and blend them until smooth with the shallots, sour cream, stock mixture and cream or cottage cheese. Spoon it all into a bowl.

2 Whisk the egg white with a pinch of salt to soft peaks. Fold into the fish. Cover and chill for 30 minutes, or until starting to set. Grease a 1 litre/1¾ pint/4 cup loaf tin (pan) with butter, then line it with the spinach leaves. Spread half the mousse over the base, arrange the asparagus on top, then cover with the remaining mousse.

3 Arrange the smoked salmon strips lengthways on the mousse and fold over the spinach leaves. Cover with clear film (plastic wrap) and chill for 4 hours, or until set. Turn out on to a serving dish and garnish with the beetroot and salad leaves.

Prawn, Egg & Avocado Mousses

Light and creamy, with lots of texture and a delicious combination of flavours, these little mousses are best served on the day you make them, but chill really well first.

SERVES 6

INGREDIENTS
olive oil, for greasing
15ml/1 tbsp powdered gelatine
juice and rind of 1 lemon
60ml/4 tbsp good mayonnaise
60ml/4 tbsp chopped fresh dill
5ml/1 tsp anchovy essence (paste)
5ml/1 tsp Worcestershire sauce
4 eggs, hard-boiled (hard-cooked), peeled and chopped
175g/6oz/1 cup cooked, peeled prawns (shrimp), roughly chopped if large
1 large ripe but just firm avocado, peeled, stoned (pitted) and diced
250ml/8fl oz/1 cup double (heavy) or whipping cream, lightly whipped
2 egg whites
salt and ground black pepper
sprigs of dill, to garnish
hot bread or toast, to serve

1 Lightly grease six small ramekins, then wrap a piece of baking parchment tightly around each of the dishes. Ensure it comes well above the top of the dish. Secure firmly with tape so that the paper will support the mousse as it sets. If you prefer, prepare one small soufflé dish rather than individual ramekins.

2 Sprinkle the gelatine over the lemon juice and 15ml/1 tbsp hot water in a small bowl and leave until spongy. Place over a pan of hot water and stir until the mixture becomes clear. Cool slightly, then blend in the lemon rind, mayonnaise, dill and sauces.

3 Mix the eggs, prawns and avocado in a medium bowl. Stir in the gelatine mixture, then fold in the cream. Whisk the egg whites until holding soft peaks and fold into the mixture with seasoning to taste. Spoon into the ramekins and chill for about 4 hours. Garnish with dill and serve with hot bread or toast.

QUENELLES OF SOLE

Traditionally, these light fish dumplings are made with pike, but they are even better made with sole or other white fish. If you are feeling extravagant, serve them with a creamy shellfish sauce studded with crayfish tails or prawns.

SERVES 6

INGREDIENTS
450g/1lb sole fillets, skinned and cut into large pieces
4 egg whites
600ml/1 pint/2½ cups double (heavy) cream
salt, ground white pepper and grated nutmeg

FOR THE SAUCE
1 small shallot, finely chopped
60ml/4 tbsp dry vermouth, such as Noilly Prat
120ml/4fl oz/½ cup fish stock
150ml/¼ pint/⅔ cup double (heavy) cream
50g/2oz/¼ cup butter, chilled and diced
chopped fresh flat leaf parsley, to garnish

COOK'S TIP
When poaching quenelles, keep the heat very low to ensure the water remains at a very gentle simmer. Quenelles are very delicate and tend to disintegrate in rapidly boiling water.

1 Check the sole for stray bones, then put the pieces in a food processor or blender. Add a generous pinch of salt and a grinding of pepper. Switch on and, with the motor running, add the egg whites one at a time through the feeder tube to make a smooth purée.

2 Tip the fish purée into a metal sieve placed over a large bowl. Press the purée through the sieve with the back of a spoon. Stand the bowl of purée in a larger bowl and surround it with plenty of crushed ice or ice cubes. Set aside.

3 Whip the cream until thick and floppy, but not stiff. Fold it into the fish mousse, making sure each spoonful has been absorbed before adding the next. Season with salt and pepper, then stir in nutmeg to taste. Cover the bowl of mousse and transfer it, still in its bowl of ice, to the refrigerator. Chill for several hours.

4 To make the sauce, combine the shallot, vermouth and fish stock in a small pan. Bring to the boil and cook until reduced by half. Add the cream and boil again until the sauce has the consistency of single cream. Strain, then return the sauce to the pan and whisk in the butter, one piece at a time, until the sauce is very creamy. Season and keep hot, but do not let it boil.

5 Bring a wide, shallow pan of lightly salted water to the boil, then reduce the heat so that the water surface barely trembles. Using two tablespoons dipped in hot water, shape the fish mousse into ovals. As each quenelle is shaped, slip it into the gently simmering water.

6 Poach the quenelles in batches for 8–10 minutes, or until they feel just firm to the touch, but are still slightly creamy inside. As each is cooked, lift it out with a slotted spoon, drain on kitchen paper and keep hot. When all the quenelles are cooked, arrange them on heated plates. Pour the sauce around and serve garnished with chopped parsley.

HADDOCK & SMOKED SALMON TERRINE

This substantial terrine makes a superb dish for a summer lunch party, accompanied by dill mayonnaise and peppery rocket leaves. The white and pink flesh of the two fish ensure that this terrine will make a decorative centrepiece for any table.

SERVES 10–12 AS A FIRST COURSE, 6–8 AS A MAIN COURSE

INGREDIENTS
15ml/1 tbsp sunflower oil, for greasing
350g/12oz thinly sliced smoked salmon
900g/2lb haddock fillets, skinned
2 eggs, lightly beaten
105ml/7 tbsp crème fraîche
30ml/2 tbsp drained, bottled capers
30ml/2 tbsp drained, bottled green or pink peppercorns
salt and ground white pepper
crème fraîche, fresh dill and rocket (arugula), to garnish

VARIATION
If you prefer, you can use any thick white fish fillets for this terrine: try halibut or Arctic bass, or ask your fishmonger to recommend a firm, white fish.

1 Preheat the oven to 200°C/400°F/Gas 6. Grease a 1 litre/1¾ pint/4 cup loaf tin (pan) or terrine with the oil. Use some of the salmon to line the tin or terrine; let some of the ends overhang the mould. Reserve the remaining smoked salmon.

2 Cut two long slices of haddock the length of the tin or terrine and set aside. Cut the rest of the haddock into small pieces. Season it all with salt and pepper.

3 Combine the eggs, crème fraîche, capers and green or pink peppercorns in a bowl. Season with salt and white pepper and then stir in the small pieces of haddock. Spoon the mixture into the mould until it is one-third full. Smooth the surface with a metal spatula.

4 Wrap the long haddock fillets in the reserved smoked salmon. Lay them on top of the layer of the fish mixture in the tin or terrine. Fill the tin or terrine with the rest of the fish mixture, smooth the surface and fold the overhanging pieces of smoked salmon over the top. Cover tightly with a double thickness of foil. Tap the terrine to settle the contents.

5 Stand the terrine in a roasting pan and pour in boiling water to come halfway up the sides. Place the pan and terrine in the preheated oven and cook for 45 minutes–1 hour, or until the filling is just set.

6 Take the terrine out of the roasting pan, but do not remove the foil cover. Place two or three large heavy cans of food on the foil to weight it and leave until cold. Chill in the refrigerator for 24 hours.

7 About an hour before serving, remove the terrine from the refrigerator, lift off the weights and remove the foil. Carefully invert the terrine on to a serving plate and lift off the tin or terrine.

8 Cut the terrine into thick slices using a sharp knife and serve, garnished with crème fraîche, fronds of dill, and rocket leaves.

STRIPED FISH TERRINE

Serve this attractive terrine cold or just warm. A hollandaise sauce complements it very nicely. It is ideal as an appetizer or light lunch dish, served in slices.

SERVES 8

INGREDIENTS
15ml/1 tbsp sunflower oil
450g/1lb salmon fillet, skinned
450g/1lb sole fillets, skinned
3 egg whites
105ml/7 tbsp double (heavy) cream
15ml/1 tbsp fresh chives, finely chopped
juice of 1 lemon
115g/4oz/scant 1 cup fresh or frozen peas, cooked
5ml/1 tsp chopped fresh mint leaves
salt, ground white pepper and grated nutmeg
thinly sliced cucumber, salad cress and chives, to garnish

1 Grease a 1 litre/1¾ pint/4 cup loaf tin (pan) or terrine with the oil. Slice the salmon thinly (see Cook's Tip); cut it and the sole into long strips, 2.5cm/1in wide. Preheat the oven to 200°C/400°F/Gas 6.

2 Line the terrine neatly with alternate slices of salmon and sole leaving the ends overhanging the edge. You should be left with about a third of the salmon and half the sole. Put these aside for later.

3 In a bowl, beat the egg whites with a pinch of salt until they form soft peaks. Purée the remaining sole in a food processor. Spoon into a mixing bowl, season, then fold in two-thirds of the egg whites, followed by two-thirds of the cream.

4 Put half the mixture into a second bowl and stir in the chives. Add nutmeg to the first bowl and gently mix it in. Purée the remaining salmon, spoon it into a bowl and add the lemon juice. Fold in the remaining whites, then the cream.

5 Purée the peas with the mint. Season the mixture and spread it over the base of the tin or terrine, smoothing the surface with a spatula. Spoon the sole with chive mixture on top and spread evenly.

6 Add the salmon mixture, then finish with the plain sole mixture. Cover with the overhanging fish fillets and make a lid of oiled foil. Stand the terrine in a roasting pan and pour in enough boiling water to come halfway up the sides.

7 Bake for 15–20 minutes, or until the top fillets are just cooked and the mousse feels springy. Remove the foil, lay a wire rack over the top of the terrine and invert both rack and terrine on to a lipped baking sheet to catch the cooking juices that drain out. Keep these to make fish stock or soup.

8 Leaving the loaf tin in place, let the terrine stand for about 15 minutes, then turn the terrine over again. Invert it on to a serving dish and lift off the loaf tin carefully. Serve warm, or place in the refrigerator to chill first and serve cold. Garnish with thinly sliced cucumber, salad cress and chives before serving.

COOK'S TIPS
- *Pop the salmon into the freezer about an hour before slicing it. If it is almost frozen, it will be much easier to slice. This method is often used by Japanese sashimi chefs to get really thin slices.*
- *You can line the tin or terrine with oven-safe clear film (plastic wrap) after greasing and before adding the salmon and sole strips. This makes it easier to turn out the terrine but is not strictly necessary.*

SMOKED SALMON & HERB ROULADE

A little smoked salmon goes a long way in the filling for this delicately flavoured roulade. Make the roulade in advance to give it time to cool, but do not put it in the refrigerator or the roulade will lose its light texture.

SERVES 6–8

INGREDIENTS
25g/1oz/2 tbsp butter
25g/1oz/¼ cup plain (all-purpose) flour
175ml/6fl oz/¾ cup milk, warm
3 large eggs, separated
50g/2oz/⅔ cup freshly grated Parmesan cheese
30ml/2 tbsp chopped fresh dill
30ml/2 tbsp chopped fresh flat leaf parsley
150ml/¼ pint/⅔ cup crème fraîche
115g/4oz smoked salmon, coarsely chopped
salt and ground black pepper
lamb's lettuce, to garnish

1 Melt the butter in a heavy pan, blend in the flour and cook over a low heat to a thick paste. Gradually stir in the milk, whisking as it thickens, and cook for 1–2 minutes to make a thick sauce. Stir in the egg yolks, two-thirds of the Parmesan cheese, half the dill, the parsley and salt and pepper to taste.

2 Prepare a 33 × 28cm/13 × 11in Swiss (jelly) roll tin (pan) and preheat the oven to 180°C/350°F/Gas 4. Whisk the egg whites and fold into the yolk mixture, then pour into the tin and bake for 12–15 minutes. Leave, covered with baking parchment, for 10–15 minutes, then tip out on to a sheet of baking parchment sprinkled with a little of the remaining grated Parmesan. Allow to cool.

3 Mix together the crème fraîche, chopped smoked salmon, chopped dill and seasoning. Spread over the roulade and roll up, then leave to firm up in a cold place. Sprinkle with the rest of the Parmesan. Cut into thick slices and serve garnished with lamb's lettuce.

Smoked Mackerel Pâté

Some of the most delicious dishes are also the simplest to make. Serve this tasty pâté with warmed Melba toast as an appetizer, or for a light lunch with ciabatta toast. Decorate the surface of the pâté with indentations made using a blunt-edged knife.

Serves 6

Ingredients
4 smoked mackerel fillets, skinned
225g/8oz/1 cup cream cheese
1–2 garlic cloves, finely chopped
juice of 1 lemon
30ml/2 tbsp chopped fresh chervil, flat leaf parsley or chives
15ml/1 tbsp Worcestershire sauce
salt and cayenne pepper
fresh chives, to garnish
warmed Melba toast or toasted ciabatta, to serve

1 Break up the mackerel and put it in a food processor. Add the cream cheese, garlic, lemon juice and herbs.

2 Process the mixture until it is fairly smooth but still has a slightly chunky texture, then add the Worcestershire sauce, and salt and cayenne pepper to taste. Process to mix, then spoon the pâté into a dish, cover with clear film (plastic wrap) and chill. Garnish with chives and serve with Melba toast or toasted ciabatta.

BRANDADE OF SALT COD

There are almost as many versions of this creamy salt cod purée as there are regions of France. Some contain mashed potatoes, others truffles. This comparatively light recipe includes garlic, but you can omit it and serve the brandade on toasted slices of French bread rubbed with garlic if you prefer.

SERVES 6

INGREDIENTS
200g/7oz salt cod
250ml/8fl oz/1 cup extra virgin olive oil
4 garlic cloves, crushed
250ml/8fl oz/1 cup double (heavy) or whipping cream
freshly ground white pepper
shredded spring onions (scallions), to garnish
herbed crispbread, to serve

1 Soak the fish in cold water for 24 hours, changing the water often. Drain. Cut into pieces, place in a shallow pan and pour in cold water to cover. Heat the water until simmering, then poach the fish for 8 minutes, or until it is just cooked. Drain the fish, then remove the skin and bones.

2 Combine the olive oil and garlic in a small pan and heat to just below boiling point. In another pan, heat the cream until it starts to simmer.

3 Put the cooked cod into a food processor or blender, process briefly, then gradually add alternate amounts of the garlic-flavoured olive oil and hot cream, while continuing to process the mixture. The aim is to create a smooth purée with the consistency of mashed potatoes.

4 Add ground white pepper to taste, then scoop the brandade into a serving bowl and smooth the surface with a metal spatula. Garnish with shredded spring onions and serve warm with herbed crispbread.

TARAMASALATA

This rich-tasting, slightly tangy spread is made from hard fish roes, generally from grey mullet or cod, to which salt has been added as a preservative. Covered, the dish will keep for about 5 days in the refrigerator.

SERVES 4–6

INGREDIENTS
115g/4oz/8 tbsp smoked tarama (mullet roe) or cod's roe
15ml/1 tbsp lemon juice
175ml/6fl oz/³/4 cup olive oil, plus a little extra for drizzling
20g/³/4oz finely grated onion
15–25ml/1–1¹/2 tbsp boiling water
paprika, for sprinkling
black olives and celery leaves, to garnish
toast, to serve

1 Soak the tarama or cod's roe in cold water for 2 hours. Drain, then peel off any outer skin and membrane from the roe and discard it. Process the roe in a food processor or blender at a low speed.

2 Add the lemon juice to the puréed roe, then, with the motor still running, slowly add the olive oil through the feeder tube until the mixture thickens.

3 Beat in the grated onion and water into the fish mixture. Spoon into a serving bowl and chill well. Sprinkle with a little paprika. Garnish with the olives and celery leaves. Drizzle with a little oil and serve with toasted bread.

COOK'S TIP
Smoked cod's roe is paler than the burnt-orange colour of mullet roe. It is much cheaper than mullet roe and gives very good results.

SALADS

Tasty salads are a great way to enjoy really fresh fish and shellfish. The combination of imaginative ingredients, fresh flavours and mouth-watering textures is always unbeatable. Simple dishes such as Fresh Tuna Salad Niçoise and Black Olive, Tomato & Sardine Salad make perfect lunch or supper dishes. They are made with simple ingredients and take little time to prepare yet taste sensational. More sophisticated salads such as Warm Scallop & Green Bean Salad with Hazelnut Dressing and Red Mullet Salad with Raspberry Dressing are great for dinner parties, and are sure to impress.

Red Mullet Salad with Raspberry Dressing

The combination of red mullet and raspberry vinegar is delicious in this salad. Keep to the "red" theme by including salad leaves such as red oakleaf lettuce and red-stemmed baby chard. If red mullet is not available, use small red snapper fillets.

Serves 4

Ingredients

8 red mullet or snapper fillets, scaled
15ml/1 tbsp olive oil
15ml/1 tbsp raspberry vinegar
175g/6oz mixed dark green and red salad leaves, such as lamb's lettuce,
  radicchio, oakleaf lettuce and rocket (arugula)
salt and ground black pepper

For the dressing

115g/4oz/1 cup raspberries, puréed and sieved
30ml/2 tbsp raspberry vinegar
60ml/4 tbsp extra virgin olive oil
1.5–2.5ml/¼–½ tsp caster (superfine) sugar

1 Lay the red mullet or snapper fillets in a shallow dish. Whisk together the olive oil and raspberry vinegar, add a pinch of salt and drizzle the mixture over the fish. Cover and leave to marinate for 1 hour.

2 Whisk together the dressing ingredients and season to taste. Wash and dry the salad leaves, put them in a bowl, pour over most of the dressing and toss lightly.

3 Heat a ridged griddle pan or frying pan until very hot, put in the red mullet or snapper fillets and fry for 2–3 minutes on each side, until just cooked. Cut the fillets diagonally in half to make rough diamond shapes.

4 Arrange a tall heap of salad in the middle of each serving plate. Prop up 4 red mullet fillet halves on the salad on each plate. Spoon around the reserved dressing and serve at once.

Black Olive, Tomato & Sardine Salad

These wonderful Mediterranean ingredients bring a real burst of rich flavour and colour to a delightful light summer salad. It is the perfect dish for al fresco *dining, served with plenty of Mediterranean bread, such as ciabatta or focaccia.*

Serves 6

INGREDIENTS
8 large firm ripe tomatoes
1 large red onion
60ml/4 tbsp wine vinegar
90ml/6 tbsp extra virgin olive oil
18–24 small sardines, cooked
75g/3oz/³⁄₄ cup pitted black olives, drained well
salt and ground black pepper
45ml/3 tbsp chopped fresh flat leaf parsley, to garnish

1 Slice the tomatoes into 5mm/¼in slices. Slice the onion thinly into rings. Arrange the tomatoes on a serving plate, overlapping the slices, and top with the red onion rings.

2 Mix together the wine vinegar, olive oil and seasoning to taste and spoon over the tomatoes. Arrange the sardines and black olives on top of the tomatoes and sprinkle with the chopped parsley just before serving.

WARM SWORDFISH & ROCKET SALAD

Swordfish is robust enough to take the sharp flavours of rocket and Pecorino cheese. If you can't find Pecorino, use a good Parmesan instead.

SERVES 4

INGREDIENTS
4 swordfish steaks, about 175g/6oz each
75ml/5 tbsp extra virgin olive oil, plus extra for serving
juice of 1 lemon
30ml/2 tbsp finely chopped fresh flat leaf parsley
115g/4oz rocket (arugula)
115g/4oz Pecorino cheese
salt and ground black pepper

1 Lay the swordfish steaks in a shallow dish. Mix 60ml/4 tbsp of the olive oil with the lemon juice. Pour over the fish. Season, sprinkle the parsley on top and turn the fish to coat, cover with clear film (plastic wrap) and leave to marinate in a cool place for 10 minutes.

2 Heat a ridged griddle pan or the grill (broiler) until very hot. Take the fish out of the marinade and pat it dry with kitchen paper. Grill for 2–3 minutes on each side until the swordfish is just cooked through, but still juicy.

3 Meanwhile, put the rocket leaves in a bowl and season with a little salt and plenty of pepper. Add the remaining 15ml/1 tbsp olive oil and toss well. Shave the Pecorino over the top.

4 Place the swordfish steaks on four individual plates and arrange a little pile of salad on each steak. Serve extra olive oil separately to drizzle over the swordfish.

VARIATION
If you have trouble finding swordfish, tuna, marlin or shark steaks would be equally good in this recipe.

WARM MONKFISH SALAD

Monkfish has a flavour that cannot be matched. It benefits from being cooked simply. Teaming it with wilted baby spinach and toasted pine nuts is inspirational.

SERVES 4

INGREDIENTS
2 monkfish fillets, about 350g/12oz each
25g/1oz/⅓ cup pine nuts
15ml/1 tbsp olive oil
15g/½oz/1 tbsp butter
225g/8oz baby spinach leaves
salt and ground black pepper

FOR THE DRESSING
5ml/1 tsp Dijon mustard
5ml/1 tsp sherry vinegar
60ml/4 tbsp olive oil
1 garlic clove, crushed

1 Remove the membrane covering the fish. Holding the knife at a slight angle, cut each monkfish fillet into 12 diagonal slices. Season lightly and set aside.

2 Heat an empty frying pan, put in the pine nuts and shake them about for a few minutes, until golden brown. Do not allow them to burn. Transfer to a plate and set aside.

3 Make the dressing by whisking all the ingredients together until smooth and creamy. Pour the dressing into a small pan, season to taste with salt and pepper and heat gently.

4 Heat the oil and butter in a ridged griddle pan or frying pan until sizzling. Add the fish and sauté for 20–30 seconds on each side, or until just cooked.

5 Put the spinach leaves in a large bowl and pour the warm dressing over the top. Sprinkle on the toasted pine nuts, reserving a few, and toss together well. Divide the dressed spinach leaves among four serving plates and arrange the monkfish slices on top. Scatter the reserved pine nuts on top and serve.

Poached Skate with Bitter Salad Leaves

Skate has a deliciously sweet flavour that contrasts well with the bitterness of salad leaves such as escarole, rocket, frisée and radicchio. Serve with toasted French bread for a delicious and light salad.

Serves 4

Ingredients
800g/1¾lb skate wings
15ml/1 tbsp white wine vinegar
4 black peppercorns
1 fresh thyme sprig
175g/6oz bag of ready-prepared bitter salad leaves, such as frisée, rocket (arugula), radicchio, escarole and lamb's lettuce
1 orange
2 tomatoes, peeled, seeded and diced

For the dressing
15ml/1 tbsp white wine vinegar
45ml/3 tbsp olive oil
2 shallots, finely chopped
salt and ground black pepper

1 Put the skate wings into a large shallow pan, cover with cold water and add the vinegar, peppercorns and thyme. Bring to the boil, then poach the fish gently for 8–10 minutes, or until the flesh comes away easily from the bones.

2 Meanwhile, make the salad dressing. Whisk together the vinegar, olive oil and shallots in a bowl and season to taste. Tip the salad leaves into a bowl, pour over the dressing and toss well.

3 Using a zester, remove the outer rind from the orange, then peel the orange, removing all the white pith. Slice the orange into thin rounds.

4 When the skate is cooked, flake the flesh and mix it into the salad. Add the orange rind shreds, the orange slices and tomatoes, toss gently and serve.

SMOKED EEL SALAD WITH CITRUS DRESSING

Smoked eel has become increasingly popular recently and is seen on some of the most sophisticated tables. It tastes marvellous in a salad with chicory and radicchio.

SERVES 4

INGREDIENTS
450g/1lb smoked eel fillets, skinned
2 large heads of chicory (Belgian endive), separated into leaves
4 radicchio leaves
fresh flat leaf parsley leaves, to garnish

FOR THE DRESSING
1 lemon
1 orange
5ml/1 tsp sugar
5ml/1 tsp Dijon mustard
90ml/6 tbsp sunflower oil
15ml/1 tbsp chopped fresh flat leaf parsley
salt and ground black pepper

1 Cut the eel fillets diagonally into eight pieces. Make the dressing. Using a zester, carefully remove the outer rind in strips from the lemon and the orange. Squeeze the juice of both fruit. Set the lemon juice aside and pour the orange juice into a small pan. Stir in the rinds and sugar. Bring to the boil and reduce by half. Leave to cool.

2 Whisk the Dijon mustard, reserved lemon juice and the sunflower oil together in a bowl. Add the orange juice mixture, then stir in the chopped fresh parsley. Season to taste with salt and ground black pepper and whisk again.

3 Arrange the chicory leaves in a circle on individual plates, with the pointed ends radiating outwards like the spokes of a wheel. Take the radicchio leaves and arrange them on the plates, between the chicory leaves. Drizzle a little dressing over the salad leaves and divide the pieces of eel among the plates, placing them on the salad. Garnish with parsley and serve. Offer the remaining dressing separately.

Provençal Aioli with Salt Cod & Spring Vegetables

This substantial salad constitutes a meal on its own and is one of the nicest dishes for summer entertaining. Vary the vegetables according to what is in season; if you prefer raw vegetables, include radishes, yellow pepper and celery sticks for colour contrast.

SERVES 6

INGREDIENTS
1kg/2¼ lb salt cod, soaked in water for 24 hours
bouquet garni
18 small new potatoes, scrubbed
1 large fresh mint sprig, torn
225g/8oz green beans, trimmed
225g/8oz broccoli florets
6 hard-boiled (hard-cooked) eggs
12 baby carrots, with leaves if possible, scrubbed
1 large red (bell) pepper, seeded and cut into strips
2 fennel bulbs, cut into strips
18 red or yellow cherry tomatoes
6 large cooked prawns (shrimp) or langoustines, in the shell, to garnish (optional)

FOR THE AIOLI
600ml/1 pint/2½ cups home-made mayonnaise
2 fat garlic cloves (or more if you are feeling brave), crushed
cayenne pepper

COOK'S TIP
Before soaking and cooking, salt cod looks rather unappealing – like a flat grey board. Don't be put off though, as it tastes absolutely delicous.

1 Drain the cod and put it into a shallow pan. Pour in enough water barely to cover the fish and add the bouquet garni. Bring to the boil, then cover and poach very gently for about 10 minutes, or until the fish flakes easily when tested with the tip of a sharp knife. Drain and set aside until required.

2 Place the new potatoes in a large pan of lightly salted water with the torn mint and bring to the boil. Cook for about 15 minutes, or until just tender when speared with a sharp knife. Drain and set aside.

3 Cook the beans and broccoli in separate pans of lightly salted boiling water for about 3–5 minutes. They should still be very crisp. Refresh under cold water and drain again, then set aside.

4 Remove the skin from the cod and break the flesh into large flakes. Shell the hard-boiled eggs and halve them lengthways.

5 Pile the cod in the middle of a large serving platter and arrange the eggs and all the vegetables around the edges or randomly. Garnish with the prawns or langoustines, if you are using them.

6 To make the aioli, put the home-made mayonnaise in a bowl and stir in the crushed garlic and cayenne pepper to taste. Serve in individual bowls or one large bowl to hand round.

Fresh Tuna Salad Niçoise

This classic, colourful salad from the south of France is transformed into something really special by the addition of fresh, rather than canned, tuna. Served with chunks of warm bread it will make a substantial meal in itself.

SERVES 4

INGREDIENTS
4 tuna steaks, about 150g/5oz each
30ml/2 tbsp olive oil
225g/8oz fine green beans, trimmed
1 small cos (romaine) lettuce or 2 Little Gem (Bibb) lettuces
4 new potatoes, boiled
4 ripe tomatoes, or 12 cherry tomatoes
2 red (bell) peppers, seeded and cut into thin strips
4 hard-boiled (hard-cooked) eggs, sliced
8 drained anchovy fillets in oil, halved lengthways
16 large black olives
salt and ground black pepper
12 fresh basil leaves, to garnish

FOR THE DRESSING
15ml/1 tbsp red wine vinegar
90ml/6 tbsp olive oil
1 fat garlic clove, crushed

COOK'S TIP
To intensify the flavour of the red peppers and improve their texture, grill them until the skins are charred, then put them in a bowl and cover with several layers of kitchen paper. Leave for about 15 minutes, then rub off the skins.

1 Brush the tuna steaks on both sides with a little olive oil and season with salt and pepper. Heat a ridged griddle pan or the grill (broiler) until very hot, then cook the tuna steaks for 1–2 minutes on each side; the flesh should still be pink and juicy in the middle. Set aside.

2 Cook the beans in a pan of lightly salted boiling water for 4–5 minutes, or until only just tender. Drain, refresh under cold water and drain again.

3 Separate the lettuce leaves and wash thoroughly in cold water. Pat dry with a clean dishtowel and place in a large salad bowl.

4 Slice the boiled potatoes and tomatoes, if large (leave cherry tomatoes whole), and add them to the bowl of lettuce leaves. Add the green beans and red pepper strips and toss gently to mix.

5 Shell the hard-boiled eggs and cut them into quarters lengthways. Divide the salad among four serving plates and top each with four egg quarters and four pieces of anchovy fillet. Scatter four olives on to each plate.

6 To make the dressing, put the vinegar, olive oil and garlic in a jug (pitcher) or bowl, whisk them together and season to taste. Drizzle over the salads, place a tuna steak on each plate, scatter over the basil and serve.

Hake & Potato Salad with Yogurt Dressing

Meaty and white-fleshed, hake is excellent served cold in a salad. Here the flavour is enhanced with a piquant dressing. The white of the fish and potatoes, the red of the pepper and lettuce and the green of the peas and cucumber make this a very attractive dish. It makes a perfect lunch or supper.

SERVES 4

INGREDIENTS
450g/1lb hake fillets
150ml/¼ pint/⅔ cup court-bouillon or fish stock
1 onion, thinly sliced
1 bay leaf
450g/1lb cooked baby new potatoes, halved unless tiny
1 red (bell) pepper, seeded and diced
115g/4oz/1 cup petits pois (baby peas), cooked
2 spring onions (scallions), thinly sliced
½ cucumber, unpeeled and diced
4 large red lettuce leaves, such as lollo rosso or oakleaf lettuce
salt and ground black pepper

FOR THE DRESSING
150ml/¼ pint/⅔ cup Greek (US strained plain) yogurt
30ml/2 tbsp olive oil
juice of ½ lemon
15–30ml/1–2 tbsp capers, chopped

FOR THE GARNISH
2 hard-boiled (hard-cooked) eggs, finely chopped
15ml/1 tbsp finely chopped fresh flat leaf parsley
15ml/1 tbsp finely chopped fresh chives

1 Put the hake in a shallow pan with the court-bouillon or stock, onion slices and bay leaf. Bring to the boil over a medium heat. Lower the heat and poach the fish gently for about 10 minutes, or until it flakes easily when tested with the tip of a sharp knife. Leave it to cool, then remove the skin and bones, and separate the flesh into large flakes.

2 Put the baby new potatoes in a large bowl with the diced red pepper, petits pois, spring onions and cucumber. Gently stir in the flaked hake and season with salt and ground black pepper to taste.

3 Make the dressing. Place the yogurt, olive oil, lemon juice and chopped capers in a bowl or jug (pitcher) and mix together until well blended. Season to taste with salt and ground black pepper, then spoon or pour the dressing over the salad. Toss gently but thoroughly.

4 Place a lettuce leaf on each plate and spoon the salad over it. Make the garnish; mix the finely chopped hard-boiled eggs with the parsley and chives. Scatter the mixture over each salad and serve immediately.

VARIATIONS
- *This salad is equally good made with halibut, monkfish or cod.*
- *For a slightly richer dressing with a milder flavour, try mayonnaise mixed with the chopped capers.*

Potato & Mussel Salad with Shallot Dressing

Shallot and chives in a creamy dressing add bite to this salad of potato and sweet mussels. Serve with a bowl of full-flavoured watercress and plenty of wholemeal bread for a delicious summer lunch.

SERVES 4

INGREDIENTS
675g/1½lb salad potatoes
1kg/2¼lb mussels, scrubbed and beards removed
200ml/7fl oz/scant 1 cup dry white wine
15g/½oz fresh flat leaf parsley, chopped
salt and ground black pepper
chopped fresh chives or chive flowers, to garnish

FOR THE DRESSING
105ml/7 tbsp mild olive oil
15–30ml/1–2 tbsp white wine vinegar
5ml/1 tsp Dijon mustard
1 large shallot, very finely chopped
15ml/1 tbsp chopped fresh chives
45ml/3 tbsp double (heavy) cream
pinch of caster (superfine) sugar (optional)

> COOK'S TIP
> *Potato salads, such as this one, should not be chilled if at all possible as the cold alters the texture of the potatoes and of the creamy dressing. For the best flavour and texture, serve this salad just cool or at room temperature.*

1 Cook the potatoes in boiling, salted water for 15–20 minutes, or until tender. Drain, leave to cool, then peel. Slice the potatoes into a bowl and toss with 30ml/2 tbsp of the oil for the dressing.

2 Discard any open mussels that do not close when sharply tapped. Bring the white wine to the boil in a large, heavy pan. Add the mussels, cover and cook over a high heat, shaking the pan occasionally, for 3–4 minutes, or until the mussels have opened.

3 Discard any mussels that have not opened. Drain and shell the cooked mussels, reserving the cooking liquid. Set aside.

4 Boil the reserved cooking liquid until reduced to about 45ml/3 tbsp. Strain this through a fine sieve and pour over the potatoes. Toss to mix.

5 To make the dressing, whisk together the remaining oil with 15ml/1 tbsp of the vinegar, the mustard, chopped shallot and chives. Add the cream and whisk again to form a thick dressing. Adjust the seasoning, adding salt and pepper and more vinegar and/or a pinch of sugar to taste.

6 Toss the mussels with the potatoes, then pour over the dressing and chopped parsley and toss lightly. Serve sprinkled with extra chopped chives or chive flowers separated into tiny florets.

THAI PRAWN SALAD WITH GARLIC DRESSING

In this intensely flavoured salad, sweet prawns and mango are partnered with a sweet-sour garlic dressing heightened with the hot taste of chilli. Fresh coriander and mint add an extra, refreshing zest and go perfectly with the other flavours.

SERVES 4–6

INGREDIENTS
675g/1½lb medium-size raw prawns (shrimp), shelled
  and deveined with tails on
finely shredded rind of 1 lime
½ fresh red chilli, seeded and finely chopped
30ml/2 tbsp olive oil, plus extra for brushing
1 ripe but firm mango
2 carrots, cut into long thin shreds
10cm/4in piece cucumber, sliced
1 small red onion, halved and thinly sliced
a few sprigs of fresh coriander (cilantro)
a few sprigs of fresh mint
45ml/3 tbsp roasted peanuts, roughly chopped
4 large shallots, thinly sliced and fried until crisp
  in 30ml/2 tbsp groundnut (peanut) oil
salt and ground black pepper

FOR THE DRESSING
1 large garlic clove, chopped
10–15ml/2–3 tsp caster (superfine) sugar
juice of 2 limes
15–30ml/1–2 tbsp Thai fish sauce (nam pla)
1 red chilli, seeded
5–10ml/1–2 tsp light rice vinegar

1 Place the prawns in a glass or china dish and add the lime rind and chilli. Season with salt and pepper and spoon the oil over them. Toss to mix and leave to marinate for 30–40 minutes.

2 To make the dressing, pound the garlic in a mortar with 10ml/2 tsp sugar until smooth, then add the juice of 1½ limes and 15ml/1 tbsp of the Thai fish sauce.

3 Transfer the dressing to a jug (pitcher). Finely chop half the chilli and add it to the dressing. Taste the dressing and add more sugar, lime juice, fish sauce and the rice vinegar to taste.

4 Peel and stone (pit) the mango, then cut it into very fine strips. Toss together the mango, carrots, cucumber and onion with half of the dressing. Arrange the salad on individual plates or in bowls.

5 Heat a ridged, griddle pan or heavy frying pan until very hot. Brush with a little oil, then sear the prawns for 2–3 minutes on each side, or until they turn pink and are patched with brown on the outside. Arrange the prawns on the salads.

6 Sprinkle the remaining dressing over the salads and scatter the sprigs of coriander and mint over the top. Finely shred the remaining chilli and sprinkle it over the salads with the peanuts and crisp-fried shallots. Serve immediately.

COOK'S TIPS
• For an authentic flavour, try to use Pacific prawns. When searing them, make sure that they have all turned pink, because undercooked prawns may be dangerous and are unpleasant to eat. However, do not overcook, as this spoils the texture.
• The crisp, frizzled shallots sprinkled over this dish are a traditional addition to Thai salads.

Asparagus, Tarragon & Langoustine Salad

For a really extravagant treat, you could make this attractive salad with medallions of lobster. For a cheaper version, use large prawns, allowing six per serving.

SERVES 4

INGREDIENTS
16 langoustines
16 fresh asparagus spears, trimmed
2 carrots
30ml/2 tbsp olive oil
1 garlic clove, peeled
4 fresh tarragon sprigs and 15ml/1 tbsp chopped fresh tarragon, to garnish

FOR THE DRESSING
30ml/2 tbsp tarragon vinegar
120ml/4fl oz/½ cup olive oil
salt and ground black pepper

1 Shell the langoustines and set aside. Steam the asparagus until just tender, but still a little crisp. Refresh under cold water, drain and place in a shallow dish.

2 Peel the carrots and cut into fine julienne shreds. Cook in a pan of lightly salted boiling water for about 3 minutes, or until tender but still crunchy. Drain, refresh under cold water and drain again. Place in the dish with the asparagus.

3 To make the dressing, whisk the tarragon vinegar with the oil in a small bowl. Season to taste. Pour over the asparagus and carrots and leave to marinate. Meanwhile, heat the oil with the garlic in a frying pan until very hot. Add the langoustines and sauté quickly until just heated through. Discard the garlic.

4 Cut the asparagus spears in half and arrange on plates with the carrots. Drizzle over the dressing left in the dish and top each portion with four langoustine tails. To serve, top with the tarragon sprigs and scatter the chopped tarragon on top.

WARM SCALLOP & GREEN BEAN SALAD WITH HAZELNUT DRESSING

Lightly cooked scallops and green beans are combined with crisp lettuce leaves in a sweet, hazelnut dressing to make a wonderful summer salad.

SERVES 4

INGREDIENTS
115g/4oz fine green beans, trimmed
2 good handfuls of frisée or Batavia lettuce leaves, finely shredded
15g/½oz/1 tbsp butter
15ml/1 tbsp hazelnut oil
20 shelled queen scallops, with corals if possible
2 spring onions (scallions), very thinly sliced
salt and ground black pepper
4 fresh chervil sprigs, to garnish

FOR THE DRESSING
10ml/2 tsp sherry vinegar
30ml/2 tbsp hazelnut oil
15ml/1 tbsp finely chopped fresh mint leaves

1 Cook the beans in a pan of lightly salted boiling water for about 5 minutes, or until only just tender. Drain, refresh under cold water, drain again and set aside.

2 Put the finely shredded salad leaves into a bowl. Mix the dressing ingredients together, season, pour over the salad and toss. Divide the salad among four serving plates.

3 Heat the butter and hazelnut oil in a frying pan until sizzling, then add the scallops and their corals. Sauté for about 1 minute, tossing the scallops in the fat until they have just turned opaque.

4 Add the beans and spring onions to the scallops and stir to combine. Spoon the vegetables over the salad and pile the scallops and corals into a tower. Garnish with sprigs of chervil and serve immediately.

INSALATA DI MARE

You will find countless variations of this classic seafood salad all along Italy's coastline. This includes spicy dried chillies and is good warm or cold.

SERVES 6 AS A FIRST COURSE, 4 AS A MAIN COURSE

INGREDIENTS
450g/1lb fresh mussels, scrubbed and beards removed
450g/1lb small clams, scrubbed
105ml/7 tbsp dry white wine
225g/8oz squid, cleaned
4 large scallops, with their corals
30ml/2 tbsp olive oil
2 garlic cloves, finely chopped
1 small dried red chilli, crumbled
225g/8oz cooked prawns (shrimp), in the shell
6–8 large chicory (Belgian endive) leaves
6–8 radicchio leaves
15ml/1 tbsp chopped fresh flat leaf parsley, to garnish

FOR THE DRESSING
5ml/1 tsp Dijon mustard
30ml/2 tbsp white wine or cider vinegar
5ml/1 tsp lemon juice
120ml/4fl oz/½ cup extra virgin olive oil
salt and ground black pepper

VARIATION
You can vary the seafood in this Italian salad according to what is available, but try to include at least two kinds of shellfish and some squid.

---

1 Put the mussels and clams in a large pan with the white wine. Cover and cook over a high heat, shaking the pan occasionally, for about 4 minutes, or until they have opened. Discard any that remain closed. Use a slotted spoon to transfer the shellfish to a bowl, then strain and reserve the cooking liquid and set it aside.

2 Cut large squid into thin rings and then chop the tentacles. Leave small squid whole. Halve the scallops horizontally.

3 Heat the oil in a frying pan, add the garlic, chilli, squid, scallops and corals, and sauté for 2 minutes, or until just cooked and tender. Lift the squid and scallops out of the pan using a slotted spoon. Reserve the oil.

4 When the shellfish are cool enough to handle, shell them, keeping a dozen of each in the shell. Peel all but 6–8 of the prawns. Pour the shellfish cooking liquid into a small pan set over a high heat, and cook until reduced by half. Mix all the shelled and unshelled mussels and clams with the squid and scallops, then add the prawns.

5 To make the dressing, whisk the mustard with the vinegar and lemon juice in a small bowl and season with salt and pepper to taste. Add the olive oil, whisk vigorously, then whisk in the reserved cooking liquid and the oil from the frying pan. Pour the dressing over the seafood mixture and toss lightly to coat well.

6 Arrange the chicory and radicchio leaves around the edge of a large serving dish and pile the mixed seafood salad into the centre. Sprinkle with the chopped flat leaf parsley and serve immediately.

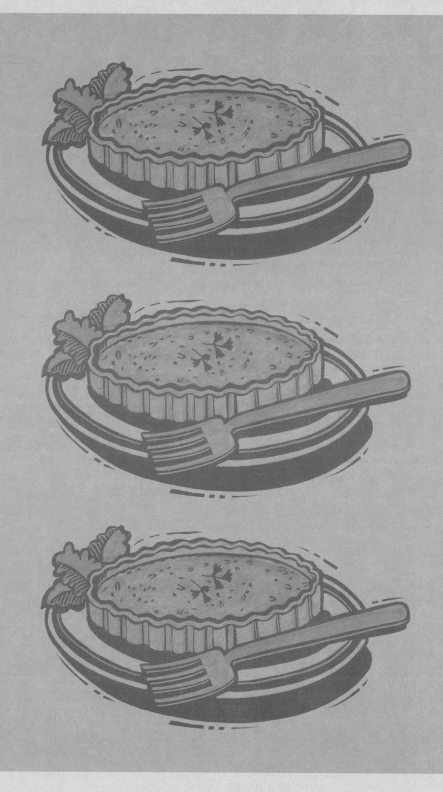

PASTRIES & TARTS

Crisp on the outside, creamy in the middle, pastries and tarts that are filled with fish and shellfish make the perfect meal, whether it is a first course, light lunch or evening meal main course. Small tartlets, such as Crab, Ricotta & Parmesan Cheese Tartlets and Mussel, Leek, Pepper & Saffron Tarts, make wonderful appetizers or snacks to be served with drinks. Elegant pastries such as Egg & Salmon Puff Parcels and Thai-style Seafood Turnovers make a great lunch or supper served with plenty of crisp green salad, while large tarts, such as Tuna & Egg Galette and Smoked Salmon Quiche with Potato Pastry, are great for picnics and buffets.

Trout with Filo Pastry & Almond Crust

Wrapped in pastry and filled with an almond stuffing, this trout is transformed into a special dish that makes a filling main course for any party. You can delight your guests with this impressive recipe which is very simple to make.

SERVES 4

INGREDIENTS
4 trout, about 175g/6oz each, gutted
75g/3oz/6 tbsp butter
1 small onion, finely chopped
115g/4oz/1 cup ground almonds
30ml/2 tbsp chopped fresh flat leaf parsley
finely grated rind of 1 lemon
12 sheets filo pastry, thawed if frozen
salt and ground black pepper

1 Preheat the oven to 200°C/400°F/Gas 6. Season the trout well and put them to one side. Melt 25g/1oz/2 tbsp of the butter in a large, heavy pan and cook the onion until soft but not coloured. Add 75g/3oz/¾ cup of the ground almonds with the parsley and lemon rind. Use this mixture to stuff the inside cavities of the fish.

2 Melt the remaining butter. Cut the filo pastry into strips and brush with the butter. Wrap the strips around the fish to enclose each trout completely. Place the fish on a baking tray.

3 Sprinkle the remaining ground almonds over the pastry and bake for about 20 minutes, or until the fish is cooked through and the pastry is golden brown. Serve the trout immediately.

COOK'S TIP
Paper-thin filo pastry should be handled with care. Keep it wrapped in clear film (plastic wrap) until you need it or it will dry out and become brittle.

Egg & Salmon Puff Parcels

These parcels hide a mouth-watering collection of flavours, and make a delicious starter or lunch dish. Serve with curry-flavoured mayonnaise or hollandaise sauce.

SERVES 6

INGREDIENTS
75g/3oz/scant ½ cup long grain rice
300ml/½ pint/1¼ cups fish stock
350g/12oz tail piece of salmon
juice of ½ lemon
15ml/1 tbsp chopped fresh dill
15ml/1 tbsp chopped fresh flat leaf parsley
10ml/2 tsp mild curry powder
6 small eggs, soft-boiled (soft-cooked) and cooled
425g/15oz flaky or puff pastry, thawed if frozen
1 small (US medium) egg, beaten
salt and ground black pepper

1 Cook the rice in the fish stock according to the packet instructions, then drain and set aside to cool. Preheat the oven to 220°C/425°F/Gas 7.

2 Place the salmon in a large pan and cover with cold water. Gently heat until not quite simmering and cook for 8–10 minutes. Lift the fish out of the pan with a metal spatula, and remove the bones and skin. Flake the fish into the rice, add the lemon juice, herbs, curry powder and seasoning, and mix well. Peel the eggs.

3 Roll out the pastry thinly and cut into six 14–15cm/5½–6in squares. Brush the edges with the beaten egg. Place a spoonful of the rice mixture in the middle of each square, push an egg into the centre and top with a little more of the rice mixture. Pull over the pastry corners to the middle to form a square parcel, pressing the joins together firmly to seal.

4 Brush the tops of the parcels with more beaten egg, place on a baking sheet and bake for 20 minutes, then reduce the oven temperature to 190°C/375°F/Gas 5 and cook for a further 10 minutes, or until golden and crisp underneath. Cool slightly before serving.

THAI-STYLE SEAFOOD TURNOVERS

Rice, white fish and prawns are combined with fragrant Thai flavourings to make a filling for these tiny pastry puffs. They make perfect finger food for a party.

MAKES 18

INGREDIENTS
plain (all-purpose) flour, for dusting
500g/1¼lb puff pastry, thawed if frozen
1 egg, beaten with 30ml/2 tbsp water
fresh coriander (cilantro) leaves and lime twists, to garnish

FOR THE FILLING
275g/10oz skinned white fish fillets, such as cod or haddock
plain (all-purpose) flour seasoned with salt and ground black pepper
8–10 large raw prawns (shrimp)
15ml/1 tbsp sunflower oil
about 75g/3oz/6 tbsp butter
6 spring onions (scallions), finely sliced
1 garlic clove, crushed
225g/8oz/2 cups cooked Thai fragrant rice (about 90g/3½oz raw weight)
4cm/1½in piece of fresh root ginger, grated
10ml/2 tsp finely chopped fresh coriander (cilantro)
5ml/1 tsp finely grated lime rind

> COOK'S TIP
> To serve this dish as a main course, rather than an appetizer, make six large pasties instead of the 18 smaller ones suggested here.

1 Preheat the oven to 190°C/375°F/Gas 5. To make the filling, cut the fish into 2cm/¾in cubes and dust with the seasoned flour. Peel and devein the prawns and cut each one into four pieces.

2 Heat half of the oil and 15g/½oz/1 tbsp of the butter in a frying pan. Add the spring onions and fry them over a gentle heat for 2 minutes. Add the garlic and fry for about 5 minutes more, or until the onions are very soft but not coloured. Transfer to a large bowl.

3 Heat the remaining oil and a further 25g/1oz/2 tbsp of the butter in a clean pan. Fry the fish pieces briefly. As soon as they begin to turn opaque, use a slotted spoon to transfer them to the bowl with the spring onions.

4 Cook the prawns in the fat remaining in the pan. When they begin to change colour, lift them out and add them to the bowl of cooked fish.

5 Add the cooked rice to the fish and prawns, with the grated ginger, coriander and lime rind. Mix gently to combine, taking care not to break up the fish.

6 Dust the work surface with a little flour. Roll out the pastry and cut into 18 × 10cm/4in rounds. Place spoonfuls of filling just off-centre on the pastry rounds. Dot with a little butter. Dampen the edges of the pastry with a little of the beaten egg mixture, fold one side of the pastry over the filling and press the edges together firmly.

7 Place the turnovers on a lightly greased baking sheet. Decorate them with the pastry trimmings, if you like, then brush with more beaten egg and bake for 12–15 minutes, or until the pastry is well risen and golden. Serve hot, garnished with fresh coriander leaves and lime twists.

Tuna & Egg Galette

This flaky pastry tart combines soft-centred eggs and a slightly piquant fish filling with capers and lemon juice. It makes a wonderful dish for a summer supper and is a great buffet-table standby. It is also the ideal dish for a picnic lunch – leave the galette in its baking tray for easy transportation.

Serves 4

Ingredients
2 sheets of ready-rolled flaky or puff pastry, thawed if frozen
plain (all-purpose) flour, for dusting
beaten egg, to glaze
60ml/4 tbsp olive oil
175g/6oz tuna steak
2 onions, sliced
1 red (bell) pepper, seeded and chopped
2 garlic cloves, crushed
45ml/3 tbsp bottled capers, drained
5ml/1 tsp grated lemon rind
30ml/2 tbsp lemon juice
4 eggs
salt and ground black pepper
30ml/2 tbsp chopped fresh flat leaf parsley, to garnish

Cook's Tip
When eggs are cooked in this way, they can sometimes become hard on top. To keep the eggs soft, as is preferred in this recipe, it is advisable to cover the tart with lightly oiled foil.

1 Preheat the oven to 190°C/375°F/Gas 5. Lay one sheet of pastry on a lightly floured baking tray and cut to a 28 × 18cm/11 × 7in rectangle. Brush the whole sheet of pastry with beaten egg.

2 Cut the second sheet of pastry to the same size. Cut out a rectangle from the centre and discard, leaving a 2.5cm/1in border. Carefully lift the border on to the first sheet.

3 Brush the pastry border with beaten egg and prick the base with a fork. Bake the pastry case (pie shell) for about 15 minutes, or until golden and well risen.

4 Heat 30ml/2 tbsp of the oil in a frying pan and fry the tuna steak for about 3 minutes on each side, or until golden but still pale pink in the middle. Transfer to a plate and flake into small pieces.

5 Add the remaining oil to the pan, add the onions, red pepper and garlic and fry for 6–8 minutes, or until softened, stirring occasionally. Remove the pan from the heat and stir in the tuna, capers, lemon rind and juice. Season well.

6 Spoon the filling into the pastry case and level the surface, making shallow indentations for the eggs with the back of a spoon. Break the eggs into the filling and return the galette to the oven for about 10 minutes, or until the eggs have just cooked through. Garnish with chopped parsley and serve at once.

SMOKED SALMON QUICHE WITH POTATO PASTRY

The ingredients in this light but richly-flavoured quiche perfectly complement the melt-in-the-mouth pastry made with potatoes. Once tried, never forgotten.

SERVES 6

INGREDIENTS
275g/10oz smoked salmon
6 eggs, beaten
150ml/¼ pint/⅔ cup full cream (whole) milk
300ml/½ pint/1¼ cups double (heavy) cream
30–45ml/2–3 tbsp chopped fresh dill
30ml/2 tbsp bottled capers; chopped
salt and ground black pepper
salad leaves and chopped fresh dill, to serve

FOR THE PASTRY
115g/4oz floury maincrop potatoes, diced
225g/8oz/2 cups plain (all-purpose) flour, sifted
115g/4oz/8 tbsp butter, diced
½ egg, beaten
10ml/2 tsp chilled water

1 To make the pastry, boil the potatoes in a large pan of lightly salted water for 15 minutes, or until tender. Drain well through a colander and return to the pan. Mash the potatoes until smooth and set aside to cool completely.

2 Place the flour in a large bowl and rub in the butter to form fine crumbs. Using a wooden spoon, beat in the mashed potatoes and the beaten egg. Bring the mixture together, adding chilled water if needed to form a soft, smooth dough.

3 Roll out the pastry on a floured surface and use to line a deep 23cm/9in round, loose-based, fluted flan tin (quiche pan). Chill for 1 hour.

4 Preheat the oven to 200°C/400°F/Gas 6. Place a heavy baking sheet in the oven to preheat it. Chop the salmon into bitesize pieces and set aside.

5 To make the filling, beat together the eggs, milk and cream, then stir in the dill and capers and season with pepper. Add the chopped smoked salmon to the egg mixture and stir to combine.

6 Remove the pastry case (pie shell) from the refrigerator, prick the base well and pour the egg and salmon mixture into it. Bake on the hot baking sheet for 35–45 minutes, or until the filling is set and golden and the pastry is crisp. Serve warm with mixed salad leaves and some more dill.

VARIATIONS
- *These quantities can also be used to make six individual quiches, which are an ideal size to serve as a first course or a light lunch. Prepare them as above, but reduce the cooking time by about 15 minutes.*
- *For extra piquancy, sprinkle some finely grated fresh Parmesan cheese over the top of each quiche before baking in the oven.*

MUSSEL, LEEK, PEPPER & SAFFRON TARTS

Serve these vividly coloured little tarts as a first course, with a few salad leaves, such as watercress, rocket and frisée. Alternatively, cook the filling in one 23cm/9in tart shell and serve it as a main course with salad and fresh bread.

SERVES 6

INGREDIENTS

350g/12oz shortcrust (unsweetened) pastry, thawed if frozen
large pinch of saffron threads (about 15 threads)
15ml/1 tbsp hot water
30ml/2 tbsp olive oil
2 large leeks, sliced
2 large yellow (bell) peppers, halved, seeded, grilled (broiled) and peeled, then cut into strips
900g/2lb mussels, scrubbed and beards removed
2 large (US extra large) eggs
300ml/½ pint/1¼ cups single (light) cream
30ml/2 tbsp finely chopped fresh flat leaf parsley
salt and ground black pepper
salad leaves and bread (optional), to serve

> COOK'S TIP
> *Saffron is the dried stigmas of the saffron crocus. It is a very expensive spice but fortunately just a little goes a long way. It has an aromatic, slightly bitter taste. Mussels and saffron are a good combination, which is popular with restaurant chefs.*

1 Preheat the oven to 190°C/375°F/Gas 5. Roll out the pastry and use to line six 2.5cm/1in deep 10cm/4in tartlet tins (muffin pans). Prick the bases and line the sides with strips of foil. Bake for 10 minutes. Remove the foil and bake for another 5–8 minutes, or until lightly coloured. Remove from the oven. Reduce the temperature to 180°C/350°F/Gas 4.

2 Soak the saffron in the hot water for 10 minutes. Heat the oil in a large pan, add the leeks and fry over a medium heat for 6–8 minutes, or until softened and beginning to brown. Add the pepper strips and cook for another 2 minutes.

3 Bring 2.5cm/1in depth of water to a rolling boil in a large pan and add 10ml/ 2 tsp salt. Discard any open mussels that do not shut when tapped sharply, then throw the rest into the pan. Cover and cook over a high heat, shaking the pan occasionally, for about 4 minutes, or until the mussels open. Discard any mussels that do not open. Shell the mussels.

4 In a small bowl, beat together the eggs, cream and saffron liquid. Season well with salt and pepper and stir in the parsley.

5 Arrange the leeks, peppers and mussels in the pastry cases (pastry shells), add the egg mixture and bake for 20–25 minutes, or until risen and just firm. Serve at once with salad leaves for a first course, or with salad and bread for a main course.

Crab, Ricotta & Parmesan Cheese Tartlets

These wonderful, creamy tartlets have a delightfully subtle flavour. The delicate taste of crab works well with smooth, mild ricotta cheese and the addition of Parmesan cheese, mustard and lemon juice adds a slightly sharp edge. They are perfect picnic food and make a good light lunch or supper.

SERVES 4

INGREDIENTS

225g/8oz plain (all-purpose) flour, plus extra for dusting
115g/4oz butter, diced
about 60ml/4 tbsp iced water
225g/8oz ricotta cheese
15ml/1 tbsp grated onion
30ml/2 tbsp freshly grated Parmesan cheese
2.5ml/½ tsp mustard powder
2 eggs, plus 1 egg yolk
225g/8oz crab meat
30ml/2 tbsp chopped fresh flat leaf parsley
2.5–5ml/½–1 tsp anchovy essence (paste)
5–10ml/1–2 tsp lemon juice
salt and cayenne pepper
salad leaves, to garnish

1 Sift the flour and a good pinch of salt into a mixing bowl, add the diced butter and rub it in with your fingertips until the mixture resembles fine breadcrumbs. Gradually stir in enough iced water to make a firm dough.

2 Turn out the dough on to a floured surface and knead lightly. Roll out the pastry and use to line four 10cm/4in tartlet tins (muffin pans). Prick the bases with a fork, then chill for 30 minutes. Preheat the oven to 200°C/400°F/Gas 6.

3 Line the pastry cases (pastry shells) with baking parchment and fill with baking beans. Bake for 10 minutes, then remove the paper and beans. Return to the oven and bake for a further 10 minutes, or until the pastry is pale golden.

4 Place the ricotta, grated onion, Parmesan and mustard in a bowl and beat until soft. Gradually beat in the eggs and egg yolk until well mixed.

5 Gently stir in the crab meat and chopped parsley, then add the anchovy essence, lemon juice, and salt and cayenne pepper to taste.

6 Remove the tartlet cases from the oven and reduce the temperature to 180°C/ 350°F/Gas 4. Spoon the filling into the cases and bake for 20 minutes, or until set and golden brown. Serve hot with a garnish of salad leaves.

COOK'S TIPS

- *Use the meat from a freshly cooked crab, weighing about 450g/1lb, if you can. Otherwise, look out for frozen brown and white crab meat – the brown meat is from the shell, the white from the claws and legs.*
- *Ricotta is an Italian cheese made from the whey left over when making other cheeses. It has a delicate, smooth flavour and can be used for both savoury and sweet dishes.*

Everyday Main Courses

Fish and shellfish are perfect for everyday meals. They are extremely healthy and can be quick and easy to prepare. This chapter is full of simple dishes that can be whipped up for a healthy lunch or supper. Salmon Fishcakes and Sardine Frittata make simple and delicious mid-week suppers that will be popular with the whole family. Make classic dishes such as Baked Cod with Hollandaise Sauce and Plaice with Tomato Sauce, or try the aromatic flavours of Grilled Sole with Chive & Lemon Grass Butter and Trout with Tamarind & Chilli Sauce.

SALMON FISH CAKES

The secret of a good fishcake is to make it with freshly prepared fish and potatoes, home-made breadcrumbs and plenty of interesting seasoning. This recipe uses salmon but almost any fresh white or hot-smoked fish can be used.

SERVES 4

INGREDIENTS
450g/1lb cooked salmon fillet
450g/1lb freshly cooked potatoes, mashed
25g/1oz/2 tbsp butter, melted
10ml/2 tsp wholegrain mustard
15ml/1 tbsp each chopped fresh dill and chopped
  fresh flat leaf parsley
grated rind and juice of ½ lemon
15g/½oz/1 tbsp plain (all-purpose) flour
1 egg, lightly beaten
150g/5oz/1¼ cups dried breadcrumbs
60ml/4 tbsp sunflower oil
salt and ground black pepper
rocket (arugula) leaves and chives, to garnish
lemon wedges, to serve

1 Flake the cooked salmon, discarding any skin and bones. Put it in a bowl with the mashed potato, melted butter and wholegrain mustard, and mix well to combine. Stir in the chopped dill, parsley, lemon rind and juice. Season to taste with salt and ground black pepper.

2 Divide the mixture into eight portions and shape each into a ball, then flatten into a thick round. Dip the fish cakes first in flour, then in egg and finally in breadcrumbs, making sure that they are evenly coated.

3 Heat the oil in a frying pan until it is very hot. Fry the fish cakes in batches until golden brown and crisp all over. As each batch is ready, drain on kitchen paper and keep hot. Garnish with rocket leaves and chives, and serve with lemon wedges.

CRAB CAKES

These spicy crab cakes are made with fresh breadcrumbs instead of potatoes, which makes them light in texture. If you prefer, they can be grilled (broiled) instead of fried; brush with a little oil first.

SERVES 4

INGREDIENTS
450g/1lb mixed brown and white crab meat
30ml/2 tbsp mayonnaise or tartar sauce
2.5–5ml/½–1 tsp mustard powder
1 egg, lightly beaten
Tabasco sauce
45ml/3 tbsp chopped fresh flat leaf parsley
4 spring onions (scallions), finely chopped, plus extra to garnish
50–75g/2–3oz/1–1½ cups fresh breadcrumbs
sunflower oil, for frying
salt, ground black pepper and cayenne pepper
red onion marmalade or tomato chutney, to serve

1 Put the crab meat in a bowl and stir in the mayonnaise or tartar sauce. Add the mustard powder and egg, season with Tabasco, salt, ground black pepper and cayenne, and mix well.

2 Stir in the parsley, spring onions and 50g/2oz/1 cup of the breadcrumbs. The mixture should be just firm enough to hold together; depending on how much brown crab meat there is, you may need to add some more breadcrumbs.

3 Divide the mixture into eight portions, roll each into a ball and flatten slightly to make a thick, flat disc. Spread out the crab cakes on a platter and put in the refrigerator for 30 minutes before frying.

4 Pour the oil into a large frying pan to a depth of about 5mm/¼in. Fry the crab cakes in two batches until golden brown all over. Drain on kitchen paper and serve with red onion marmalade or tomato chutney.

Salt Cod Fritters with Aioli

Aioli is a fiercely garlicky, olive oil mayonnaise from Provence in the south of France and is a traditional accompaniment to salt cod. Here the salt cod is combined with potatoes to make tasty fritters.

SERVES 6

INGREDIENTS
450g/1lb salt cod
500g/1¼lb floury potatoes
300ml/½ pint/1¼ cups milk
6 spring onions (scallions), finely chopped
30ml/2 tbsp extra virgin olive oil
30ml/2 tbsp chopped fresh flat leaf parsley
juice of ½ lemon
2 eggs, beaten
60ml/4 tbsp plain (all-purpose) flour
90g/3½oz/1⅓ cups dry white breadcrumbs
vegetable oil, for shallow frying
salt and ground black pepper
lemon wedges and salad leaves, to serve

FOR THE AIOLI
2 large garlic cloves
2 egg yolks
300ml/½ pint/1¼ cups olive oil
lemon juice, to taste

1 Soak the salt cod in cold water for 24–36 hours, changing the water 5–6 times. The cod should swell as it rehydrates and a tiny piece should not taste unpleasantly salty when tried. Drain well.

2 Cook the potatoes, unpeeled, in a pan of boiling salted water for about 20 minutes, or until tender. Drain, then peel and mash the potatoes.

3 Poach the cod very gently in the milk with half the spring onions for about 10 minutes, or until it flakes easily. Remove the cod and flake it with a fork into a bowl, discarding bones and skin.

4 Add 60ml/4 tbsp of the mashed potato to the flaked cod and beat with a wooden spoon. Work in the olive oil, then gradually add the remaining potato. Beat in the remaining spring onions and the parsley. Season with lemon juice and pepper to taste – the mixture may need a little salt. Beat in 1 egg, then chill the mixture until firm.

5 Shape the mixture into 12–18 small round cakes. Coat them in flour, then dip them in the remaining egg and coat with the breadcrumbs. Chill the fish cakes until ready to fry.

6 Meanwhile, make the aioli. Place the garlic and a good pinch of salt in a mortar and pound to a paste with a pestle. Using a small whisk or a wooden spoon, gradually work in the egg yolks.

7 Add the olive oil, a drop at a time, until about half is incorporated. When the sauce is as thick as soft butter, beat in 5–10ml/1–2 tsp lemon juice, then continue adding oil until the aioli is very thick. Adjust the seasoning, adding lemon juice to taste.

8 Heat about 2cm/¾in depth of oil in a large, heavy frying pan. Add the fritters and cook over a medium-high heat for about 4 minutes. Turn them over and cook for a further 4 minutes on the other side, until crisp and golden. Drain on crumpled kitchen paper to soak up any excess oil, then serve with the aioli, lemon wedges and salad leaves.

COOK'S TIPS
- *Aioli traditionally has a sharp bite from the raw garlic. However, if you prefer a milder flavour, blanch the garlic once or twice in boiling water for about 3 minutes each time before using it.*
- *Try to find a thick, creamy white piece of salt cod, preferably cut from the middle of the fish rather than the tail and fin ends. Avoid thin, yellowish salt cod, as it will be too dry and salty.*
- *Mash potatoes by hand, never in a food processor, as this makes them gluey.*

Sardine Frittata

It may seem odd to cook sardines in an omelette, but they are surprisingly delicious this way. Serve the frittata with crisp sautéed potatoes and thinly sliced cucumber crescents.

Serves 4

Ingredients
4 fat sardines, cleaned, filleted and with heads removed
juice of 1 lemon
45ml/3 tbsp olive oil
6 large (US extra large) eggs
30ml/2 tbsp chopped fresh flat leaf parsley
30ml/2 tbsp chopped fresh chives
1 garlic clove, chopped
salt, ground black pepper and paprika

1 Open out the sardines and sprinkle the fish with lemon juice, a little salt and paprika. Heat 15ml/1 tbsp of the olive oil in a frying pan and fry the sardines for about 1–2 minutes on each side to seal them. Drain on kitchen paper, trim off the tails and set aside until required.

2 Separate the eggs. In a bowl, whisk the yolks lightly with the parsley, chives and a little salt and pepper. Beat the whites in a separate bowl with a pinch of salt until fairly stiff. Preheat the grill (broiler) to medium-high.

3 Heat the remaining olive oil in a frying pan, add the garlic and cook over a low heat until just golden. Gently mix together the egg yolks and whites and ladle half the mixture into the pan. Cook gently until just beginning to set on the base.

4 Lay the sardines on the frittata and sprinkle lightly with paprika. Pour over the remaining egg mixture and cook very gently until the frittata has browned underneath and is beginning to set on the top.

5 Put the pan under the grill and cook until the top of the frittata is golden brown and sizzling. Cut into wedges and serve hot.

Plaice with Tomato Sauce

This simple dish of fried plaice is perennially popular with children. It works equally well with flounder, lemon sole or dabs, which do not need skinning, or fillets of haddock and whiting.

Serves 4

Ingredients
25g/1oz/¼ cup plain (all-purpose) flour
2 eggs, beaten
75g/3oz/¾ cup dried breadcrumbs, preferably home-made
4 small plaice or flounder, black skin removed
15g/½oz/1 tbsp butter
15ml/1 tbsp sunflower oil
salt and ground black pepper
1 lemon, quartered, to serve

For the tomato sauce
30ml/2 tbsp olive oil
1 red onion, finely chopped
1 garlic clove, finely chopped
400g/14oz can chopped tomatoes
15ml/1 tbsp tomato purée (paste)
15ml/1 tbsp torn fresh basil leaves

1 First make the tomato sauce. Heat the olive oil in a large pan, and gently cook the onion and garlic for 5 minutes. Stir in the tomatoes and tomato purée, and simmer for 20–30 minutes, stirring occasionally. Season and stir in the basil.

2 Spread out the flour in a shallow dish, pour the beaten eggs into another and spread out the breadcrumbs in a third. Season the fish with salt and pepper. Hold a fish in your left hand and dip it first in flour, then in egg and finally in the breadcrumbs, patting the crumbs on with your dry right hand.

3 Heat the butter and oil in a frying pan until foaming. Fry the fish, one at a time, for about 5 minutes on each side, until golden brown but still juicy in the middle. Drain on kitchen paper and serve with lemon wedges and the tomato sauce.

SKATE WITH BLACK BUTTER

This classic dish is perfect for a family supper. The vinegar and capers give it a slightly piquant flavour, which goes very well with the hot, nutty butter. Despite the title of the recipe, the butter should be a rich golden brown. It should never be allowed to blacken, or it will taste unpleasantly bitter.

SERVES 4

INGREDIENTS
4 skate wings, about 225g/8oz each
60ml/4 tbsp red wine vinegar or malt vinegar
30ml/2 tbsp drained capers, chopped if large
30ml/2 tbsp chopped fresh flat leaf parsley
150g/5oz/⅔ cup butter
salt and ground black pepper
steamed leeks and plain boiled potatoes, to serve

1 Put the skate wings in a large, shallow pan, cover with cold water and add a pinch of salt and 15ml/1 tbsp of the red wine or malt vinegar.

2 Bring the water to the boil, skim the surface with a slotted spoon, then lower the heat and simmer gently for about 10–12 minutes, or until the skate flesh comes away from the bone easily. Carefully drain the fish and peel off the skin.

3 Transfer the skate to a warmed serving dish, season with salt and ground black pepper and sprinkle over the capers and parsley. Keep hot.

4 In a small pan, heat the butter until it foams and turns a rich nutty brown. Pour it over the skate. Pour the remaining vinegar into the pan and boil until reduced by about two-thirds. Drizzle over the skate and serve immediately with steamed leeks and plain boiled potatoes.

Herrings in Oatmeal with Bacon

This traditional Scottish dish is cheap and nutritious. For ease of eating, bone the herrings before coating them in the oatmeal. If you don't like herrings, use trout or mackerel instead. For extra colour and flavour, serve with oven-roasted tomatoes.

SERVES 4

INGREDIENTS
115–150g/4–5oz/1–1¼ cups medium oatmeal
10ml/2 tsp mustard powder
4 herrings, about 225g/8oz each, cleaned, boned, heads
  and tails removed
30ml/2 tbsp sunflower oil
8 rindless streaky (fatty) bacon rashers (strips)
salt and ground black pepper
lemon wedges, to serve

1 In a shallow dish, mix together the oatmeal and mustard powder with salt and pepper. Press the herrings into the seasoned oatmeal mixture one at a time to coat them thickly on both sides. Shake off any excess oatmeal mixture, place the herrings on a plate and set aside.

2 Heat the oil in a large frying pan and fry the bacon until crisp. Drain on kitchen paper and keep hot.

3 Put the herrings into the pan, two at a time, and fry them for 3–4 minutes on each side, until crisp and golden brown. Use tongs to turn the herrings so as not to dislodge the oatmeal. Serve the herrings with the streaky bacon rashers and lemon wedges.

Cajun Blackened Redfish

Paul Prudhomme, inventor of this dish, recommends it be cooked out of doors over a Butane flame as this fierce cooking method produces a lot of smoke. The fish takes on a wonderfully smoky flavour and, although cooking can be messy, the end result is simply delicious.

Serves 2

Ingredients
2 redfish fillets, not less than 2cm/³⁄4in thick
75g/3oz/6 tbsp butter
5ml/1 tsp paprika
2.5ml/½ tsp dried oregano
1.5ml/¼ tsp salt
good pinch each of garlic salt and cayenne
good grinding of black pepper
lime slices or lemon wedges and mixed salad, to serve

> Cook's Tip
> *Do not attempt this dish in a kitchen you can't ventilate; open the windows, turn on extractor fans. Use a really heavy cast-iron frying pan with a flat base – ridged ones hold the butter in the furrows, where it burns. Tackle the dish for just two at first, until you know what to expect.*

1 If using frozen redfish fillets, make sure that they are thoroughly thawed. Pat the fillets dry with kitchen paper and put them on a plate.

2 In a small pan, melt the butter and swirl in the paprika, oregano, salt, garlic salt and ground black pepper until well mixed. Pour the seasoned butter over the fish fillets and turn them in the butter to keep them coated on both sides until you are ready to cook.

3 Put a heavy frying pan over a medium-high heat and leave it there for 5 minutes. Be brave about heating the pan over a high heat until it develops a greyish-white smoky patina.

4 Turn the fillets once more in the butter and put them skin-side down on to the pan. Cook, pressing them down regularly with a metal spatula, for 2 minutes, or until the skin is crisp and very dark. Pour a little of the seasoned butter over the top of each fillet and turn them over. Cook for a further 2 minutes or so, again pressing down with the spatula.

5 Serve on hot plates, with the remaining seasoned butter poured over them, garnished with lime slices or lemon wedges and accompanied by a mixed salad.

SEA BASS WITH ORANGE CHILLI SALSA

The citrus salsa has a freshness that provides the perfect contrast to the wonderful flavour of fresh sea bass, and the colours contrast well too – the orange and green-speckled salsa with the bright white flesh.

SERVES 4

INGREDIENTS
4 sea bass fillets
salt and ground black pepper
fresh coriander (cilantro), to garnish

FOR THE SALSA
2 fresh green chillies
2 oranges or pink grapefruit
1 small onion

1 Make the salsa. Roast the chillies in a dry griddle pan until the skins are blistered, being careful not to let the flesh burn. Put them in a strong plastic bag and tie the top to keep the steam in. Set aside for 20 minutes.

2 Slice the top and bottom off each orange or grapefruit and cut off all the peel and pith. Cut between the membranes and put each segment in a bowl.

3 Remove the chillies from the bag and peel off the skins. Cut off the stalks, then slit the chillies, scrape out the seeds and discard. Chop the flesh finely. Cut the onion in half and slice it thinly. Add the onion and chillies to the orange or grapefruit segments and mix lightly. Season and chill.

4 Season the sea bass fillets. Line a large steamer with greaseproof (waxed) paper, allowing extra to hang over the sides to enable the fish to be lifted out after cooking. Place the empty steamer over a pan of water and bring to the boil.

5 Place the fish in a single layer in the steamer. Cover and steam for 8 minutes, or until just cooked. Garnish with fresh coriander and serve with the salsa.

GRILLED SOLE WITH CHIVE & LEMON GRASS BUTTER

Chives are at their best when barely cooked, and they make a delicious butter to serve with simple grilled fish. Sole is the ideal choice, but halibut, trout and swordfish are also good. Serve with steamed new potatoes and a simple vegetable dish.

SERVES 4

INGREDIENTS
115g/4oz/½ cup unsalted butter, softened, plus extra melted butter
5ml/1 tsp minced lemon grass
pinch of finely grated lime rind
1 kaffir lime leaf, very finely shredded (optional)
*45ml/3 tbsp chopped chives or chopped chive flowers, plus extra chives or chive
    flowers to garnish*
2.5–5ml/½–1 tsp Thai fish sauce (nam pla)
4 sole, skinned
salt and ground black pepper
lemon or lime wedges, to serve

1 Cream the butter with the lemon grass, lime rind, lime leaf, if using, and chives or chive flowers. Season to taste with Thai fish sauce, salt and pepper.

2 Chill the butter mixture to firm it for a short while, then form it into a roll and wrap in foil or baking parchment. Chill until firm. Preheat the grill (broiler).

3 Brush the fish with a little melted butter. Place it on the grill rack and season. Grill (broil) for about 5 minutes on each side, until firm and just cooked. Meanwhile, cut the chilled butter into thin slices. Serve the fish topped with slices of the butter. Serve immediately, garnished with chives. Offer lemon or lime wedges with the fish.

COOK'S TIP
Finer white fish fillets, such as plaice, can be cooked in this way, but reduce the cooking time slightly.

TROUT WITH TAMARIND & CHILLI SAUCE

Trout is a very economical fish, but can taste rather bland. This spicy Thai-inspired sauce really gives it a zing. If you like your food very spicy, add an extra chilli.

SERVES 4

INGREDIENTS
4 trout, about 350g/12oz each, cleaned
6 spring onions (scallions), sliced
60ml/4 tbsp soy sauce
15ml/1 tbsp stir-fry oil
30ml/2 tbsp chopped fresh coriander (cilantro)

FOR THE SAUCE
50g/2oz tamarind pulp
105ml/7 tbsp boiling water
2 shallots, roughly chopped
1 fresh red chilli, seeded and chopped
1cm/½in piece fresh root ginger, peeled and chopped
5ml/1 tsp soft light brown sugar
45ml/3 tbsp Thai fish sauce (nam pla)

1 Slash the trout diagonally four or five times on each side with a sharp knife and place in a shallow dish. Fill the cavities with spring onions and douse each fish with soy sauce. Carefully turn the fish over to coat both sides with the sauce. Sprinkle on any remaining spring onions and set aside until required.

2 Make the chilli sauce. Put the tamarind pulp in a small bowl and pour on the boiling water. Mash with a fork until soft. Tip into a food processor or blender, add the chopped shallots, fresh chilli, root ginger, sugar and Thai fish sauce and process to a coarse pulp.

3 Heat the oil in a large frying pan or wok and fry the trout, two at a time if necessary, for about 5 minutes on each side, until the skin is crisp and browned and the flesh cooked. Put on warmed plates and spoon over some of the sauce. Sprinkle with the coriander and serve with the remaining sauce.

GRILLED MACKEREL WITH SPICY DHAL

Oily fish such as mackerel are complemented by a tart or sour accompaniment, like these tamarind-flavoured lentils. Serve with fresh tomatoes, onion salad and flat bread.

SERVES 4

INGREDIENTS
250g/9oz/1 cup red lentils, or yellow split peas
1 litre/1¾ pints/4 cups water
30ml/2 tbsp sunflower oil
2.5ml/½ tsp each mustard seeds, cumin seeds, fennel seeds, and cardamom seeds
5ml/1 tsp ground turmeric
3–4 dried red chillies, crumbled
30ml/2 tbsp tamarind paste
5ml/1 tsp soft light brown sugar
30ml/2 tbsp chopped fresh coriander (cilantro)
4 mackerel, cleaned
salt and ground black pepper
fresh red chilli slices and finely chopped coriander, to garnish

1 Soak the yellow split peas overnight, if using. Rinse the lentils or split peas, drain thoroughly and put in a pan. Pour in the water and bring to the boil. Lower the heat, partially cover the pan and simmer for 30–40 minutes, stirring occasionally, until they are tender and mushy.

2 Heat the oil in a wok or shallow pan. Add the mustard seeds, then cover and cook for a few seconds, until they pop. Remove the lid, add the rest of the seeds, with the turmeric and chillies and fry for a few more seconds. Stir in the lentils or split peas, with salt to taste, then the tamarind paste and sugar. Bring to the boil, then reduce the heat and simmer for 10 minutes, or until thick. Add the coriander.

3 Meanwhile, heat a ridged griddle pan or the grill (broiler) until very hot. Make six diagonal slashes on either side of each fish. Season inside and out, then cook for 5–7 minutes on each side, or until the skin is crisp. Serve with the dhal and garnish with red chilli and chopped coriander.

Baked Cod with Hollandaise Sauce

Fresh fish topped with crunchy nuts and breadcrumbs needs little assistance other than a spoonful of this classic, lemon-flavoured egg and butter sauce.

Serves 4

Ingredients
4 cod steaks or cutlets
a little olive oil
a squeeze of lemon juice
15ml/1 tbsp fresh white breadcrumbs
15ml/1 tbsp roughly ground hazelnuts
salt and ground black pepper
a few sprigs of dill, to garnish
sautéed potatoes and mixed leaf salad, to serve

For the hollandaise sauce
30ml/2 tbsp lemon juice
2 egg yolks
115g/4oz/½ cup butter, melted and cooled slightly

1 Preheat the oven to 200°C/400°F/Gas 6. Brush both sides of the cod with oil and lemon juice. Season, then mix together the breadcrumbs, nuts and seasoning and press on to the fish. Place on a baking tray and bake for 15–20 minutes.

2 Meanwhile, prepare the hollandaise sauce. Simmer the lemon juice with 30ml/ 2 tbsp water in a small pan for a couple of minutes, or until reduced by at least half. Cool slightly.

3 Whisk in the egg yolks, then, over a very gentle heat, add the butter in a slow stream, whisking all the time. Keep whisking until glossy and thick, then season to taste. Keep warm over a pan of hot water. Top the fish with the sauce and garnish with dill. Serve with sautéed potatoes and a mixed leaf salad.

COCONUT BAKED RED SNAPPER

Adding one or two fresh red chillies to the coconut and lime marinade gives this dish
a really spicy flavour. Serve the baked snapper with plain boiled rice. This
combination evokes wonderful images of South-east Asia.

SERVES 4

INGREDIENTS
1 red snapper, about 1kg/2¼lb, scaled and cleaned
400ml/14fl oz/1⅔ cups coconut milk
105ml/7 tbsp dry white wine
juice of 1 lime
45ml/3 tbsp light soy sauce
1–2 fresh red chillies, seeded and finely sliced (optional)
60ml/4 tbsp chopped fresh flat leaf parsley
45ml/3 tbsp chopped fresh coriander (cilantro)
salt and ground black pepper

1 Lay the snapper in a shallow ovenproof dish and season with a little salt and plenty of pepper. Mix together the coconut milk, wine, lime juice, soy sauce and chillies, if using. Stir in the herbs and pour over the fish. Cover with clear film and marinate in the fridge for about 4 hours, turning the fish over halfway through.

2 Preheat the oven to 190°C/375°F/Gas 5. Take the fish out of the marinade and wrap loosely in foil, spooning over the marinade before sealing the parcel. Support the fish on a clean dish and bake for 30–40 minutes, or until the flesh comes away easily from the bone. Serve immediately.

COOK'S TIP
Use other types of snapper for this recipe, or try
trout. You can use one small fish per person instead
of one large fish, but be aware that small snapper
can be very bony, so if choosing small fish, it may be
best to buy trout.

THAI GREEN FISH CURRY

Any firm-fleshed fish can be used for this delicious curry; try exotic fish such as mahi mahi, hoki or swordfish, or humbler fish such as coley. Serve it with basmati or Thai fragrant rice and lime wedges.

SERVES 4

INGREDIENTS
40ml/2½ tbsp sesame oil
2 red onions, finely chopped
900g/2lb hoki fillets, skinned
400ml/14fl oz/1⅔ cups coconut milk
45ml/3 tbsp Thai fish sauce (nam pla)
50g/2oz fresh coriander (cilantro) leaves
50g/2oz fresh mint leaves
50g/2oz fresh basil leaves
6 spring onions (scallions), chopped
150ml/¼ pint/⅔ cup sunflower or groundnut oil
sliced fresh green chilli and finely chopped fresh coriander, to garnish
cooked basmati or Thai fragrant rice and lime wedges, to serve

FOR THE CURRY PASTE
4 garlic cloves, roughly chopped
5cm/2in piece fresh root ginger, peeled and roughly chopped
2 fresh green chillies, seeded and roughly chopped
grated rind and juice of 1 lime
5–10ml/1–2 tsp shrimp paste (optional)
5ml/1 tsp coriander seeds
5ml/1 tsp five-spice powder
40ml/2½ tbsp sesame oil

COOK'S TIPS
• Green curry paste can be bought in supermarkets and Asian stores. This makes a good substitute if you are in a hurry.
• The paste can be made in advance and stored in a small sealed container in the refrigerator.

1 First make the curry paste. Combine the garlic, fresh root ginger, green chillies, lime juice and shrimp paste (if using) in a food processor or blender. Add the coriander seeds and five-spice powder, with the sesame oil. Process to a fine paste, then set aside until required.

2 Heat a wok or large shallow pan, and pour in the sesame oil. When it is hot, stir-fry the red onions over a high heat for 2 minutes. Add the fish and stir-fry for 1–2 minutes to seal the fillets on all sides.

3 Lift out the red onions and fish and put them on a plate. Add the curry paste to the wok or pan and fry for 1 minute, stirring all the time.

4 Return the hoki fillets and red onions to the wok or pan, pour in the coconut milk and bring to the boil. Lower the heat, add the Thai fish sauce and simmer for 5–7 minutes, or until the fish is cooked through.

5 Meanwhile, place the herbs, spring onions, lime rind and oil in a food processor or blender and process to a coarse paste. Stir into the fish curry. Garnish with chilli and coriander and serve with rice and lime wedges.

FISH PIE

Flavourful mushrooms and a combination of fresh and smoked fish are coated in a parsley sauce and topped with buttery mashed potato, sliced tomatoes and cheese to make a very comforting pie.

SERVES 4

INGREDIENTS
450g/1lb cod or haddock fillets
225g/8oz undyed smoked cod or haddock fillets
300ml/½ pint/1¼ cups milk
½ lemon, sliced
1 bay leaf
1 fresh thyme sprig
4–5 black peppercorns
50g/2oz/¼ cup butter
25g/1oz/¼ cup plain (all-purpose) flour
30ml/2 tbsp chopped fresh flat leaf parsley
5ml/1 tsp anchovy essence (paste)
150g/5oz/2 cups shiitake or chestnut mushrooms, sliced
salt, ground black pepper and cayenne pepper

FOR THE TOPPING
450g/1lb potatoes, cooked and mashed with a little milk
50g/2oz/¼ cup butter
2 tomatoes, sliced
25g/1oz/¼ cup grated Cheddar cheese (optional)

VARIATION
This is a simple version, but you could add prawns or hard-boiled (hard-cooked) eggs to the fish mixture. Vary the potato topping by mixing in spring onions (scallions), or grated cheese or simply grating fresh Parmesan cheese on top.

1 Put the fish skin-side down in a shallow pan. Add the milk, lemon slices, bay leaf, thyme and peppercorns. Bring to the boil, then lower the heat and poach gently for about 5 minutes, or until just cooked. Strain off and reserve the milk. Remove the fish skin and flake the flesh, discarding any bones.

2 Melt half the butter in a small pan, stir in the plain flour and cook gently for 1 minute. Add the milk and boil, whisking, until smooth and creamy. Stir in the parsley and anchovy essence and season to taste.

3 Heat the remaining butter in a frying pan, add the sliced mushrooms and sauté until tender. Season and add to the flaked fish. Mix the sauce into the fish and stir gently to combine. Transfer the mixture to a casserole dish.

4 Preheat the oven to 200°C/400°F/Gas 6. Beat the mashed potato with the butter until very creamy. Season, then spread the topping evenly over the fish. Fork up the surface and arrange the sliced tomatoes around the edge.

5 Sprinkle the mashed potato topping with the grated cheese, if using. Bake for about 25 minutes, or until the topping is lightly browned.

KEDGEREE

This classic dish originated in India. It is best made with basmati rice, which goes well with the mild curry flavour, but long grain rice will work too.

SERVES 4

INGREDIENTS
450g/1lb undyed smoked haddock fillet
750ml/1¼ pints/3 cups milk
2 bay leaves
½ lemon, sliced
50g/2oz/¼ cup butter
1 onion, chopped
2.5ml/½ tsp ground turmeric
5ml/1 tsp mild Madras curry powder
2 green cardamom pods
350g/12oz/1¾ cups basmati or long grain rice, washed and drained
4 hard-boiled (hard-cooked) eggs (not too hard), roughly chopped
150ml/¼ pint/⅔ cup single (light) cream or Greek (US strained plain) yogurt (optional)
30ml/2 tbsp chopped fresh flat leaf parsley
salt and ground black pepper

1 Put the haddock in a shallow pan, add the milk, bay leaves and lemon slices, and poach gently for 8–10 minutes, or until the haddock flakes easily. Strain the milk into a jug (pitcher), discarding the bay leaves and lemon slices. Remove the skin from the haddock, and flake the flesh into large pieces. Keep hot until required.

2 Melt the butter in the clean pan, add the onion and cook over a low heat for about 3 minutes, until softened. Stir in the turmeric, Madras curry powder and cardamom pods and fry for 1 minute.

3 Add the rice to the pan, stirring well. Pour in the reserved milk, stir and bring to the boil. Lower the heat and simmer for 10 minutes, or until all the milk has been absorbed and the rice is tender. Season to taste. Gently stir in the fish and eggs, with the cream or yogurt, if using. Sprinkle with parsley and serve immediately.

SMOKED FISH SOUFFLÉ PUDDING

This superb dish is an interesting cross between a soufflé and a fish pie, substantial enough for a Sunday lunch or a winter supper. It's good to look at and easy to eat, so children will love it.

SERVES 4–5

INGREDIENTS
450g/1lb undyed smoked haddock or cod, soaked for 20 minutes
* in cold water*
350g/12oz cooked, peeled potatoes, kept warm
50g/2oz/4 tbsp butter
45ml/3 tbsp chopped fresh chives, plus extra to garnish
3 eggs, separated
15ml/1 tbsp lemon juice
salt and ground black pepper

1 Preheat the oven to 180°C/350°F/Gas 4. Drain the smoked haddock or cod, place in a large pan, cover in cold water and bring to simmering point. Poach the fish for 5–7 minutes, or until it flakes easily. Cool slightly, then drain well and remove the skin and bones. Flake the flesh.

2 Mash the potatoes thoroughly with the butter, chives, egg yolks and seasoning. Stir in the flaked fish and lemon juice. Whisk the egg whites until stiff and fold into the potato and fish mixture.

3 Spoon the fish mixture into a buttered, deep ovenproof dish and bake for about 35 minutes, or until well risen and golden brown on top.

COOK'S TIP
For a little extra flavour, add a splash of dry white vermouth or white wine to the fish poaching water. The alcohol disappears with cooking, so children can still enjoy this alternative.

PASTA & NOODLES

Fish and shellfish make natural partners for pasta and noodles. Italian recipes combine classic Mediterranean ingredients such as sardines, clams and tomatoes, while Asian recipes include local ingredients such as squid and hot red chillies. Pasta and noodles can be boiled and served with a sauce, combined with other ingredients and baked or stuffed with a fish or shellfish filling. Try simple classics, such as Linguine alle Vongole or Stir-fried Noodles in Seafood Sauce, for a quick and easy lunch or supper. Baked dishes such as Pappardelle, Sardine & Fennel Bake and Seafood Lasagne make hearty meals. Stuffed pasta such as Crab Ravioli takes a little time to prepare but tastes delicious.

Spaghetti with Bottarga

Although this may seem an unusual recipe, with bottarga (salted and air-dried mullet or tuna roe) as the principal ingredient, it is very well known in Sardinia – and also in Sicily and parts of southern Italy. It is simplicity itself to make and tastes very, very good, especially when sprinkled with rocket (arugula) or parsley.

SERVES 4

INGREDIENTS
350g/12oz fresh or dried spaghetti
about 60ml/4 tbsp olive oil
2–3 garlic cloves, peeled
60–90ml/4–6 tbsp grated bottarga
ground black pepper

1 Cook the pasta in a large pan of boiling salted water according to the instructions on the packet. Meanwhile, heat half the olive oil in a large pan. Add the garlic and cook gently, stirring, for a few minutes. Remove the pan from the heat, scoop out the garlic with a slotted spoon and discard.

2 Drain the pasta very well. Return the pan of garlic-flavoured oil to the heat and add the pasta. Toss well, season with pepper and moisten with the remaining oil, or more to taste. Divide the pasta among four warmed bowls, sprinkle the grated bottarga over the top and serve immediately.

COOK'S TIP
You can buy bottarga in Italian delicatessens. Small jars of ready-grated bottarga are convenient, but the best flavour comes from vacuum-packed slices of mullet bottarga. This is very easy to grate on a box grater. Keep any leftover bottarga tightly wrapped in the refrigerator, so that it does not taint other foods.

Spaghetti with Tuna, Olives, Anchovies & Mozzarella

Lightly cooked ripe tomatoes flavoured with white wine are mixed with tuna, anchovies and olives to make a pasta dish that is fresh, light and full of flavour. Serve it as soon as it is cooked to enjoy it at its best.

SERVES 4

INGREDIENTS
300g/11oz dried spaghetti
30ml/2 tbsp olive oil
6 ripe plum tomatoes, chopped
5ml/1 tsp granulated sugar
50g/2oz jar anchovies in olive oil, drained
about 60ml/4 tbsp dry white wine
200g/7oz can tuna in olive oil, drained
50g/2oz/½ cup pitted black olives, quartered lengthways
125g/4½oz mozzarella cheese, drained and diced
salt and ground black pepper
fresh basil leaves, to serve

1 Cook the spaghetti in a large pan of boiling salted water according to the instructions on the packet. Meanwhile, heat the oil in a medium pan. Add the tomatoes, sugar and pepper, and toss over a medium heat for a few minutes until the tomatoes soften and the juices run. Snip a few anchovies at a time into the pan of tomatoes, with kitchen scissors.

2 Add the wine, tuna and olives and stir once or twice until they are just evenly mixed into the sauce. Add the diced mozzarella cheese and heat through without stirring. Taste and add salt if necessary. Drain the pasta and tip it into a warmed serving bowl. Pour the sauce over the pasta, toss gently and sprinkle with basil leaves. Serve immediately.

PENNE WITH CREAM & SMOKED SALMON

This modern way of serving pasta is popular all over Italy. The three essential ingredients combine together beautifully, and the dish is very quick and easy to put together, making it the perfect light lunch.

SERVES 4

INGREDIENTS
350g/12oz/3 cups dried penne
115g/4oz thinly sliced smoked salmon
2–3 fresh thyme sprigs
25g/1oz/2 tbsp butter
150ml/¼ pint/⅔ cup single (light) cream
salt and ground black pepper

1 Cook the pasta in a large pan of boiling salted water according to the instructions on the packet. Meanwhile, using kitchen scissors, cut the smoked salmon into thin strips, about 5mm/¼in wide. Strip the leaves from the thyme sprigs.

2 Melt the butter in a large pan. Stir in the cream with about a quarter of the salmon and thyme leaves, then season with pepper. Heat gently for about 3 minutes, stirring all the time. Do not allow to boil. Taste the sauce for seasoning.

3 Drain the pasta and toss it thoroughly in the cream and salmon sauce. Divide among four previously warmed bowls and top with the remaining salmon and thyme leaves. Serve immediately.

Rigatoni with Prawns & Pernod

A contemporary recipe that is typical of those found on menus in the most innovative Italian restaurants. The Pernod and dill go well together in the creamy shellfish sauce, but you could use white wine and basil if the aniseed flavour is too much for you.

SERVES 4

INGREDIENTS
200ml/7fl oz/scant 1 cup double (heavy) cream
250ml/8fl oz/1 cup fish stock
350g/12oz/3 cups dried rigatoni
30–45ml/2–3 tbsp Pernod
*225g/8oz/1⅓ cups peeled, cooked prawns (shrimp), thawed and thoroughly dried
    if frozen*
30ml/2 tbsp chopped fresh dill, plus extra to garnish
salt and ground black pepper

1 Put the cream and the fish stock in a medium pan and bring to the boil. Lower the heat and simmer, stirring occasionally, for 10–15 minutes, or until reduced by about half. Meanwhile, cook the pasta in a large pan of boiling salted water according to the instructions on the packet.

2 Add the Pernod and prawns to the cream sauce, with salt and pepper to taste, if necessary. Heat the prawns through very gently. Drain the pasta and tip it into a warmed bowl. Pour the sauce over the pasta, add the dill and toss well. Serve immediately, sprinkled with chopped dill.

CONCHIGLIE WITH SCALLOPS & ROCKET

This is a very special modern dish composed of scallops, pasta and fresh rocket flavoured with roasted pepper, chilli and balsamic vinegar. It makes a substantial and impressive dinner party starter, or a main course for a light lunch.

SERVES 4

INGREDIENTS
8 large fresh scallops
300g/11oz/2¾ cups dried conchiglie
15ml/1 tbsp olive oil
15g/½oz/1 tbsp butter
120ml/4fl oz/½ cup dry white wine
90g/3½oz rocket (arugula) leaves, stalks trimmed
salt and ground black pepper

FOR THE VINAIGRETTE
60ml/4 tbsp extra virgin olive oil
15ml/1 tbsp balsamic vinegar
1 piece bottled roasted (bell) pepper, drained and finely chopped
1–2 fresh red chillies, seeded and chopped
1 garlic clove, crushed
5–10ml/1–2 tsp clear honey, to taste

COOK'S TIP
Make sure you use fresh scallops for this dish – they are available all year round in most fishmongers and from fish counters in supermarkets. Frozen scallops tend to be watery and tasteless, and often prove to be rubbery when cooked.

1 Cut each scallop into 2–3 pieces. If the pink corals are still attached, pull them off and cut each piece in half. Season the scallops and corals with salt and ground black pepper.

2 Cook the pasta according to the instructions on the packet. Meanwhile, to make the vinaigrette, put the oil, vinegar, chopped pepper and chillies into a jug (pitcher) with the garlic and honey and whisk well.

3 Meanwhile, heat the olive oil and butter in a non-stick frying pan until sizzling. Add half the scallops and toss over a high heat for 2 minutes. Remove to a dish with a slotted spoon and keep warm. Cook the remaining scallops in the same way.

4 Add the white wine to the liquid remaining in the pan and stir over a high heat until the mixture has reduced to a few tablespoons. Remove from the heat and put to one side and keep warm.

5 Drain the pasta and tip it into a warmed serving bowl. Add the rocket, warm scallops, the reduced cooking juices and the vinaigrette dressing and toss well to combine. Serve immediately.

TAGLIATELLE WITH SCALLOPS

Scallops and brandy make this a relatively expensive dish, but it is so delicious that you will find it well worth the cost. Serve it for a dinner party first course. Try to buy fresh scallops as they have a better texture than frozen ones, which tend to be watery.

SERVES 4

INGREDIENTS
200g/7oz scallops, sliced
30ml/2 tbsp plain (all-purpose) flour
40g/1½oz/3 tbsp butter
2 spring onions (scallions), cut into thin rings
½–1 small fresh red chilli, seeded and very finely chopped
30ml/2 tbsp finely chopped fresh flat leaf parsley
60ml/4 tbsp brandy
105ml/7 tbsp fish stock
275g/10oz fresh spinach-flavoured tagliatelle
salt and ground black pepper

1 Toss the scallops in the flour, then shake off the excess. Bring a pan of salted water to the boil, ready for cooking the pasta. Meanwhile, melt the butter in a large frying pan. Add the spring onions, chilli and half the parsley, and fry, stirring frequently, for 1–2 minutes over a medium heat. Add the scallops and toss over the heat for 1–2 minutes.

2 Pour the brandy over the scallops, then carefully set it alight with a match. As soon as the flames have died down, stir in the fish stock and salt and pepper to taste. Mix well. Simmer for 2–3 minutes, then cover the pan and remove it from the heat.

3 Add the pasta to the boiling salted water and cook it according to the instructions on the packet. Drain, add to the sauce and toss over a medium heat until mixed. Serve at once, in warmed bowls sprinkled with the remaining parsley.

LINGUINE ALLE VONGOLE

Use the smallest clams you can find for this Italian recipe. You will have great fun sucking them, rather noisily, out of their shells, but may find you need to eat this dish among family and close friends only. If you can't find linguine, use thin spaghetti.

SERVES 6 AS A FIRST COURSE, 4 AS A MAIN COURSE

INGREDIENTS

675g/1½lb small clams, scrubbed
45ml/3 tbsp olive oil
2 fat garlic cloves, finely chopped
15ml/1 tbsp anchovy essence (paste), or 4 drained canned anchovy fillets,
    finely chopped
400g/14oz can chopped tomatoes
30ml/2 tbsp finely chopped fresh flat leaf parsley
450g/1lb linguine
salt and ground black pepper

1 Put the clams in a large pan. Cover the pan and place it over a high heat for 3–4 minutes, shaking the pan occasionally, until all the clams have opened. Discard any that remain closed. Strain the clams, reserving the juices. Shell the clams, if you like.

2 Heat the oil in a pan, add the garlic and fry gently for 2 minutes, or until lightly coloured. Stir in the anchovy essence or chopped anchovy fillets, then add the tomatoes and the reserved clam juices. Add the parsley, bring to the boil, then lower the heat and simmer, uncovered, for 20 minutes, or until the sauce is well reduced and full of flavour. Season to taste.

3 Cook the linguine in plenty of lightly salted boiling water until just tender. Drain the pasta, then tip it back into the pan. Add the clams to the tomato and anchovy sauce, mix together well then pour the sauce over the linguine and toss until the pasta is well coated. Serve immediately.

Spaghetti al Cartoccio

This Italian recipe finishes the cooking in a paper parcel. When the parcel is opened, the most wonderful aroma wafts out. To serve as an appetizer, bake in two larger parcels. Whichever you choose, your guests will be impressed.

SERVES 4 AS A MAIN COURSE, 6 AS A FIRST COURSE

INGREDIENTS
500g/1¼lb mussels, scrubbed and beards removed
500g/1¼lb small clams, scrubbed
105ml/7 tbsp dry white wine
60ml/4 tbsp olive oil
2 fat garlic cloves, chopped
2 dried red chillies, crumbled
200g/7oz squid, cut into rings
200g/7oz raw peeled prawns (shrimp)
400g/14oz spaghetti
30ml/2 tbsp chopped fresh flat leaf parsley
5ml/1 tsp chopped fresh or 2.5ml/½ tsp dried oregano
salt and ground black pepper

FOR THE TOMATO SAUCE
30ml/2 tbsp olive oil
1 red onion, finely chopped
1 garlic clove, finely chopped
400g/14oz can chopped tomatoes
15ml/1 tbsp tomato purée (paste)
15ml/1 tbsp torn fresh basil leaves

1 Make the tomato sauce. Heat the oil in a pan and fry the onion and garlic over a low heat for 5 minutes. Stir in the tomatoes and tomato purée and simmer for 20–30 minutes, stirring occasionally. Season and add the basil.

2 Put the shellfish and wine in a large pan and bring to the boil. Put on the lid and cook for 4–5 minutes, shaking the pan occasionally, until all the shells have opened. Discard any that remain closed. Remove most of the cooked mussels and clams from the shells, leaving about a dozen of each in the shell. Strain the juices and set them aside.

3 Heat the olive oil in a frying pan, add the garlic and fry until lightly coloured. Add the chillies, then put in the squid and prawns and sauté for 2–3 minutes, or until the squid is opaque and the prawns have turned pink. Add the mussels and clams and their reserved juices, then stir in the tomato sauce. Set aside.

4 Preheat the oven to 240°C/475°F/Gas 9 or the grill (broiler) to hot. Cook the spaghetti in a pan of lightly salted boiling water for about 10 minutes, or until it is just tender. Drain very thoroughly, then return to the clean pan and stir in the seafood sauce, tossing to coat all the strands of spaghetti. Stir in the parsley and oregano, with some seasoning.

5 Cut out four 25cm/10in square pieces of baking parchment. Put a quarter of the spaghetti mixture into the middle of one piece and fold up the edges, pleating them to make a secure bag. Seal the sides first, then blow gently into the top to fill the bag with air. Fold over the top to seal. Make another three parcels with the other sheets of paper and the rest of the spaghetti mixture.

6 Place the parcels on a baking tray and cook in the oven or under the grill until the paper is browned and slightly charred at the edges. Transfer the parcels to serving plates and open them at the table so that you can enjoy the wonderful aromas before you tuck in.

CRAB RAVIOLI

This modern recipe for a dinner-party appetizer is spiked with chilli, which looks and tastes good with crab, but it is also good without.

SERVES 4 AS A FIRST COURSE

INGREDIENTS
300g/11oz/2¾ cups strong plain (all-purpose) flour (Italian tipo 00 if possible), sifted
3 eggs
5ml/1 tsp salt
90g/3½oz/7 tbsp butter
juice of 1 lemon

FOR THE FILLING
175g/6oz/¾ cup mascarpone cheese
175g/6oz/¾ cup crab meat
30ml/2 tbsp finely chopped fresh flat leaf parsley
finely grated rind of 1 lemon
pinch of crushed dried chillies (optional)
salt and ground black pepper

1 Make the pasta dough. Tip the flour on to the work surface and make a well in the centre. Keep the sides quite high so that when the eggs are added they will not run out of the well. Crack the eggs into the well, then add the salt. With a table knife or fork, mix the eggs and salt together, then gradually start incorporating the flour from the sides of the well. Try not to break the sides of the well.

2 As soon as the egg mixture is no longer liquid, dip your fingers in the flour and use them to work the ingredients together until they form a rough and sticky dough. Scrape up any dough that sticks to the work surface with a knife, then scrape this off the knife with your fingers. If the dough is too dry, add a few drops of cold water; if it is too moist, sprinkle a little flour over it.

3 Press the dough into a rough ball and knead it as you would bread. Push it away from you with the heel of your hand, then fold the end of the dough back on itself so that it faces towards you and push it out again. Continue folding the dough back a little further each time and pushing it out until you have folded it back all the way towards you and all the dough has been kneaded.

4 Give the dough a quarter turn anti-clockwise, then continue kneading, folding and turning for about 5 minutes if you intend using a pasta machine, or for 10 minutes if you will be rolling it out by hand. It should be smooth and elastic. If you are going to roll it out and cut it by hand, thorough kneading is essential.

5 Wrap the dough in clear film (plastic wrap) and leave to rest for 15–20 minutes at room temperature. It will then be ready to roll out.

6 Meanwhile, make the filling. Put the mascarpone in a bowl and mash it with a fork. Add the crab meat, parsley, lemon rind, crushed dried chillies (if using) and salt and pepper to taste. Stir well.

7 Using a pasta machine or a rolling pin, roll out one-quarter of the pasta into a 1 metre/39in strip. Cut the strip into two 50cm/20in lengths with a sharp knife (you can do this during rolling if the strip gets too long). With a 5cm/2½in round fluted cutter, cut out eight squares from each pasta strip.

8 Using a teaspoon, put a mound of filling in the centre of half the pasta rounds. Brush a little water around the edge, then top with the plain pasta rounds and press the edges to seal. To give the ravioli a decorative finish, press the edges with the tines of a fork.

9 Put the ravioli on floured dishtowels, sprinkle lightly with flour and leave to dry while repeating the process with the remaining dough to make 32 ravioli altogether. If you have any stuffing left, you can re-roll the pasta trimmings and make more ravioli.

10 Cook the ravioli in a large pan of boiling salted water for 4–5 minutes. Meanwhile, melt the butter and lemon juice in a small pan until sizzling. Drain the ravioli and divide them equally among four warmed bowls. Drizzle the lemon butter over the ravioli and serve immediately.

BUCKWHEAT NOODLES WITH SMOKED TROUT

The light, crisp texture of the pak choi balances the earthy flavours of the mushrooms, the buckwheat noodles and the smokiness of the trout.

SERVES 4

INGREDIENTS
350g/12oz buckwheat noodles
30ml/2 tbsp vegetable oil
115g/4oz fresh shiitake mushrooms, quartered
2 garlic cloves, finely chopped
15ml/1 tbsp grated fresh root ginger
225g/8oz pak choi (bok choy)
1 spring onion (scallion), finely sliced diagonally
15ml/1 tbsp dark sesame oil
30ml/2 tbsp mirin
30ml/2 tbsp soy sauce
2 smoked trout, skinned and boned
salt and ground black pepper
30ml/2 tbsp coriander (cilantro) leaves and 10ml/2 tbsp sesame seeds, toasted,
  to garnish

1 Cook the buckwheat noodles according to the instructions on the packet. Meanwhile, heat the oil in a large frying pan. Add the shiitake mushrooms, and sauté over a medium heat for 3 minutes. Add the garlic, ginger and pak choi, and continue to cook for 2 minutes.

2 Add the cooked noodles to the mushroom mixture with the spring onion, sesame oil, mirin and soy sauce. Toss, and season with salt and pepper to taste.

3 Break the smoked trout into bitesize pieces. Arrange the noodle mixture on individual serving plates. Place the smoked trout on top of the noodles. Garnish with coriander leaves and sesame seeds, and serve immediately.

Stir-fried Noodles in Seafood Sauce

This wonderful Chinese-style noodle dish is very quick to prepare, making it perfect for a summer's day. Lightly cooked spring vegetables combine perfectly with sweet crab meat and aromatic fresh ginger and garlic.

SERVES 6–8 AS A STARTER, 4 AS A MAIN COURSE

INGREDIENTS
225g/8oz Chinese egg noodles
8 spring onions (scallions), trimmed
8 asparagus spears
30ml/2 tbsp sunflower oil
5cm/2in piece fresh root ginger, peeled and cut into very fine matchsticks
3 garlic cloves, chopped
60ml/4 tbsp oyster sauce
450g/1lb crab meat (all white, or two-thirds white and one-third brown)
30ml/2 tbsp rice wine vinegar
15–30ml/1–2 tbsp light soy sauce

1 Put the noodles in a large pan or wok, cover with lightly salted boiling water, place a lid on top and leave for 3–4 minutes, or for the time suggested on the packet. Drain and set aside.

2 Cut off the green spring onion tops and slice them thinly. Set aside. Cut the white parts of the spring onions into 2cm/¾in lengths and quarter them lengthways. Cut the asparagus spears on the diagonal into 2cm/¾in pieces.

3 Heat the oil in a large pan or wok until very hot, then add the ginger, garlic and white spring onion batons. Stir-fry over a high heat for 1 minute. Add the oyster sauce, crab meat, rice wine vinegar and soy sauce to taste. Stir-fry for about 2 minutes, or until the crab and sauce are hot. Add the noodles and toss over the heat until heated through. At the last moment, toss in the spring onion tops and serve immediately.

SQUID & NOODLE CLAYPOT

SERVES 4

INGREDIENTS

675g/1½lb fresh squid
30ml/2 tbsp vegetable oil
3 slices fresh root ginger, finely shredded
2 garlic cloves, finely chopped
1 red onion, finely sliced
1 carrot, finely sliced
1 celery stalk, diagonally sliced
50g/2oz sugar snap peas, ends removed
5ml/1 tsp sugar
15ml/1 tbsp chilli bean paste
2½ml/½ tsp chilli powder
75g/3oz cellophane noodles, soaked in hot water until soft, then drained
120ml/4fl oz/½ cup chicken broth
15ml/1 tbsp oyster sauce
15ml/1 tbsp soy sauce
5ml/1 tsp sesame oil
salt
coriander (cilantro) leaves, to garnish

1 Prepare the squid. Holding the body in one hand, gently pull away the head and tentacles. Discard the head; trim and reserve the tentacles. Remove the transparent "quill" from inside the body and peel off the skin. Rub in a little salt, and wash thoroughly under cold running water. Cut the body of the squid into rings.

2 Heat the oil in a large clay pot or flameproof casserole. Add the ginger, garlic and onion, and fry for 1–2 minutes. Add the squid, carrot, celery and peas. Fry until the squid curls up. Season with salt and sugar, and stir in the chilli bean paste and powder. Transfer the mixture to a bowl, and set aside.

3 Add the noodles to the pot. Stir in the broth, oyster sauce and soy sauce. Cover, and cook over a medium heat for 10 minutes, or until the noodles are tender. Return the squid and vegetables to the pot. Cover, and cook for 5–6 minutes. Season. Just before serving, drizzle with sesame oil, and sprinkle with coriander.

Noodles with Sun-dried Tomatoes & Prawns

SERVES 4

INGREDIENTS

350g/12oz somen noodles
45ml/3 tbsp olive oil
20 uncooked king prawns (jumbo shrimp), peeled and deveined
2 garlic cloves, finely chopped
45–60ml/3–4 tbsp sun-dried tomato paste
salt and ground black pepper
handful of basil leaves and 30ml/2 tbsp sun-dried tomatoes in oil, drained and
 cut into strips, to garnish

1 Cook the noodles in a large pan of boiling salted water according to the instructions on the packet.

2 Heat half the oil in a large frying pan. Add the prawns and garlic, and fry over a medium heat for 3–5 minutes, or until the prawns turn pink and are firm to the touch. Stir in 15ml/1 tbsp of the sun-dried tomato paste, and mix well. Using a slotted spoon, transfer the prawns to a bowl, and keep hot.

3 Reheat the oil remaining in the pan. Stir in the rest of the oil with the remaining sun-dried tomato paste. You may need to add a spoonful or two of water if the mixture is very thick.

4 When the mixture starts to sizzle toss in the noodles. Add salt and pepper to taste, and mix well. Return the prawns to the pan, and toss to combine. Serve at once garnished with the basil and strips of sun-dried tomatoes.

COOK'S TIP
Make your own sun-dried tomato paste simply by processing bottled sun-dried tomatoes with their oil. You could also add a couple of anchovy fillets and some capers, if you like.

Pappardelle, Sardine & Fennel Bake

The wide, flat noodles called pappardelle are perfect for this Sicilian recipe. If you can't find them, any wide pasta such as maccheroncini or bucatini will do instead. The dish is also delicious made with fresh anchovies.

SERVES 6

INGREDIENTS
2 fennel bulbs, trimmed
a large pinch of saffron threads
12 sardines, backbones and heads removed
450g/1lb fresh or dried pappardelle
60ml/4 tbsp olive oil
2 shallots, finely chopped
2 garlic cloves, finely chopped
2 fresh red chillies, seeded and finely chopped
4 drained, canned anchovy fillets, or 8–12 pitted black olives, chopped
30ml/2 tbsp bottled, drained capers
75g/3oz/1 cup pine nuts
butter, for greasing
30ml/2 tbsp grated Pecorino cheese
salt and ground black pepper

> COOK'S TIP
> *Fennel has a distinct aniseed flavour. It is a classic flavouring for fish, especially oily fish since it counteracts the richness. Be sure to choose crisp, white bulbs, preferably with some leaves still attached since they are a good sign of its freshness.*

1 Preheat the oven to 200°C/400°F/Gas 6. Cut the fennel bulbs in half and place them in a pan of lightly salted boiling water, add the saffron threads and cook for about 10 minutes, or until tender. Drain, reserving the cooking liquid, and cut the fennel into small dice.

2 Finely chop the sardines, season with salt and ground black pepper and set aside until required.

3 Pour the reserved fennel liquid into a large pan and top it up with enough water to cook the pasta. Stir in a little salt, bring to the boil and add the pappardelle. Cook dried pasta for about 12 minutes; fresh pasta until it rises to the surface of the water. When the pasta is just tender, drain it.

4 While the pasta is cooking, heat the olive oil in a large pan, add the shallots and garlic and cook until lightly coloured. Add the chillies and sardines, and fry for 3 minutes. Stir in the fennel and cook gently for 3 minutes. If the mixture seems dry, add a little of the pasta water.

5 Add the anchovies or olives and cook for 1 minute, then stir in the capers and pine nuts, and season. Simmer for 3 minutes more, then turn off the heat.

6 Grease a shallow ovenproof dish and put in a layer of pasta, then make a layer of the sardine mixture. Continue until all the pasta and sardine mixture have been used, finishing with the fish. Sprinkle over the Pecorino and bake for 15 minutes, or until bubbling and golden brown. Serve piping hot.

SEAFOOD LASAGNE

This dish can be as simple or as elegant as you like. For a dinner party, dress it up with scallops, mussels or prawns and a really generous pinch of saffron in the sauce; for a family supper, use simple fish such as cod and smoked haddock. The lasagne can be prepared in advance and baked at the last moment.

SERVES 8

INGREDIENTS

350g/12oz monkfish
350g/12oz salmon fillet
350g/12oz undyed smoked haddock
1 litre/1¾ pints/4 cups milk
500ml/17fl oz/generous 2 cups fish stock
2 bay leaves or a good pinch of saffron threads
1 small onion, peeled and halved
75g/3oz/6 tbsp butter, plus extra for greasing
45ml/3 tbsp plain (all-purpose) flour
150g/5oz/2 cups mushrooms, sliced
grated nutmeg
225–300g/8–11oz no-precook lasagne
60ml/4 tbsp freshly grated Parmesan cheese
salt and ground black pepper
paprika and rocket (arugula) leaves, to serve

FOR THE TOMATO SAUCE

30ml/2 tbsp olive oil
1 red onion, finely chopped
1 garlic clove, finely chopped
400g/14oz can chopped tomatoes
15ml/1 tbsp tomato purée (paste)
15ml/1 tbsp torn fresh basil leaves

1 Make the tomato sauce. Heat the oil in a pan, add the onion and garlic and fry over a low heat for 5 minutes, or until softened and golden. Stir in the tomatoes and tomato purée and simmer for 20–30 minutes, stirring occasionally. Season with salt and pepper and stir in the basil.

2 Put all the fish in a shallow flameproof dish or pan with the milk, stock, bay leaves or saffron and onion. Bring to the boil over a medium heat, then poach for 5 minutes, or until almost cooked. Leave to cool.

3 When the fish is cool enough to handle, strain it, reserving the liquid. Remove the skin and any bones, and break the fish into large flakes. Put it to one side while you make the mushroom sauce.

4 Preheat the oven to 180°C/350°F/Gas 4. Melt the butter in a pan, stir in the flour and cook for 2 minutes, stirring. Gradually add the fish poaching liquid and bring to the boil, stirring. Add the mushrooms, cook for 2–3 minutes, then season to taste with salt, pepper and nutmeg.

5 Lightly grease a shallow ovenproof dish. Spoon a thin layer of the mushroom sauce over the base of the dish and spread it with a spatula. Stir the fish into the remaining mushroom sauce in the pan.

6 Add a layer of lasagne, then a layer of fish and mushroom sauce. Add another layer of lasagne, then spread over all the tomato sauce. Continue to layer the lasagne and fish, finishing with a layer of fish.

7 Sprinkle the grated Parmesan cheese evenly over the top of the lasagne. Bake for 30–45 minutes, or until bubbling and golden. Before serving, sprinkle a little paprika over the top and serve with rocket leaves.

COOK'S TIP
Use fresh lasagne, if it's available. Cook the sheets in a large pan of lightly salted boiling water for 3 minutes, then drain and spread out on a dishtowel until ready to layer with the sauce. Do not over-crowd the pan or the sheets will stick together.

RICE DISHES
& RISOTTOS

Many traditional rice dishes, such a Spanish paella and Italian risotto, are made with fish and shellfish. This chapter is full of classic dishes such as Seafood Paella and Risotto Nero, as well as contemporary dishes on a classic theme, such as Salmon Risotto with Cucumber & Tarragon and Creamy Fish Pilau with White Wine. As well as the classic rice dishes, there are many less well-known dishes that are just as good. Try Baked Trout with Rice, Sun-dried Tomatoes & Nuts, from Spain, Goan Prawn Curry with Southern-style Rice or North African Fish with Pumpkin Rice.

Baked Trout with Rice, Sun-dried Tomatoes & Nuts

The delicate flavour of salmon is set off perfectly by the flavoursome tomato, nut and rice stuffing in this wonderful Spanish recipe.

SERVES 4

INGREDIENTS

75g/3oz/¾ cup mixed unsalted cashew nuts, pine nuts, almonds and/or hazelnuts
25ml/1½ tbsp olive oil, plus extra for drizzling
1 small onion, finely chopped
10ml/2 tsp grated fresh root ginger
175g/6oz/1½ cups cooked white long grain rice (about 65g/2½oz raw rice)
4 tomatoes, peeled and very finely chopped
4 sun-dried tomatoes in oil, drained and chopped
30ml/2 tbsp chopped fresh tarragon, plus 2 fresh tarragon sprigs
2 fresh trout, each about 500g/1¼lb
salt and ground black pepper
mixed green leaf salad, to serve

1 Preheat the oven to 190°C/375°F/Gas 5. Spread out the nuts on a shallow baking tray and bake for about 3 minutes, or until golden, shaking the tray occasionally. Leave the nuts to cool, then chop them roughly.

2 Heat the oil in a small frying pan, add the onions and cook for 3–4 minutes until soft. Stir in the ginger, cook for 1 minute more, then spoon into a mixing bowl. Stir in the rice, fresh and sun-dried tomatoes, nuts and chopped tarragon. Season well.

3 Place each fish on a large piece of oiled foil and spoon the stuffing into the cavity. Add a sprig of tarragon and a drizzle of olive oil. Fold the foil over, and put the parcels in a roasting pan. Bake for 20–25 minutes. Serve with a green salad.

COOK'S TIP
The trout cooks more evenly and is easier to serve if you fillet it before cooking, because there are no bones to get in the way of the stuffing.

Smoked Salmon & Rice Salad Parcels

Feta, cucumber and tomatoes give a Greek flavour to these little smoked salmon-wrapped parcels. They can be made several hours in advance, so are perfect for entertaining.

SERVES 4

INGREDIENTS
175g/6oz/scant 1 cup mixed wild rice and basmati rice
8 smoked salmon slices, total weight about 350g/12oz
10cm/4in piece of cucumber, finely diced
225g/8oz feta cheese, finely cubed
8 cherry tomatoes, quartered
30ml/2 tbsp mayonnaise
10ml/2 tsp fresh lime juice
15ml/1 tbsp chopped fresh chervil
salt and ground black pepper
lime slices and fresh chervil, to garnish

1 Cook the rice according to the instructions on the packet. Drain, tip into a bowl and allow to cool. Line four large ramekins with clear film (plastic wrap), then line each ramekin with two slices of smoked salmon, leaving the excess hanging over the edges. Reserve any extra pieces of smoked salmon.

2 Add the cucumber, feta and tomatoes to the rice, and stir in the mayonnaise, lime juice and chervil. Mix together well. Season with plenty of pepper and salt (remember that both the feta and salmon are quite salty).

3 Spoon the rice mixture into the salmon-lined ramekins. Place any extra pieces of smoked salmon on top, then fold over the overlapping pieces of salmon so that the rice mixture is completely encased.

4 Chill the salmon parcels for at least 30 minutes, then invert each parcel on to a plate, using the clear film to ease them out of the ramekins. Carefully peel off the clear film, then garnish each parcel with slices of lime and a sprig of fresh chervil, and serve.

Rice Cakes with Herbs & Smoked Salmon

These elegant rice cakes are made using a risotto base. You could also use leftover long grain rice and add extra flavour with spring onions (scallions), if you prefer.

Serves 4

Ingredients
30ml/2 tbsp olive oil
1 onion, chopped
225g/8oz/generous 1 cup risotto rice
about 90ml/6 tbsp white wine
about 750ml/1¼ pints/3 cups fish or chicken stock
15g/½oz/¾ cup dried porcini mushrooms, soaked for 10 minutes
   in warm water to cover
15ml/1 tbsp chopped fresh flat leaf parsley
15ml/1 tbsp chopped fresh chives
5ml/1 tsp chopped fresh dill
1 egg, lightly beaten
about 45ml/3 tbsp ground rice, plus extra for dusting
oil, for frying
60ml/4 tbsp sour cream
175g/6oz thinly sliced smoked salmon
salt and ground black pepper
radicchio and oakleaf salad, tossed in French dressing, to serve

COOK'S TIP
If you want an impressive dish for a sophisticated occasion, garnish the rice cakes with roasted baby asparagus spears, lemon slices and dill.

1 Heat the olive oil in a pan, add the onion and fry for 3–4 minutes, or until soft. Add the rice and cook, stirring, until the grains are thoroughly coated in oil. Pour in the wine and stock, a little at a time, stirring constantly over a gentle heat until each quantity of liquid has been absorbed before adding more. This process will take 20–25 minutes.

2 Drain the soaked mushrooms and chop them into small pieces; strain and reserve the soaking liquid. When the rice is tender, and all the liquid has been absorbed, stir in the mushrooms, parsley, chives, dill and seasoning. Remove from the heat and set aside for a few minutes to cool.

3 Add the beaten egg to the rice mixture, then stir in enough ground rice to bind the mixture – it should be soft but manageable. Dust your hands with ground rice and shape the mixture into four patties, about 13cm/5in in diameter and 2cm/¾in thick.

4 Heat the oil in a large frying pan, add the rice cakes and fry, in batches if necessary, for 4–5 minutes, or until they are evenly browned on both sides. Drain on kitchen paper and cool slightly. Place each rice cake on a small serving plate and top with 15ml/1 tbsp sour cream. Twist two or three thin slices of smoked salmon on top, and serve with a dressed salad.

SALMON & RICE GRATIN

In this all-in-one supper dish salmon, eggs, rice and a spicy white sauce are topped with cheese and grilled until golden and bubbling. It is ideal for informal entertaining as it can be made ahead of time and reheated in a medium oven for about half an hour.

SERVES 6

INGREDIENTS
675g/1½lb fresh salmon fillet, skinned
1 bay leaf
a few parsley stalks
1 litre/1¾ pints/4 cups water
400g/14oz/2 cups basmati rice, soaked
30–45ml/2–3 tbsp chopped fresh flat leaf parsley, plus extra to garnish
175g/6oz/1½ cups Cheddar cheese, grated
3 hard-boiled (hard-cooked) eggs, chopped
salt and ground black pepper

FOR THE SAUCE
1 litre/1¾ pints/4 cups milk
40g/1½oz/⅓ cup plain (all-purpose) flour
40g/1½oz/3 tbsp butter
5ml/1 tsp mild curry paste or French mustard

1 Put the salmon in a wide, shallow pan. Add the bay leaf and parsley stalks, with salt and pepper. Pour in the water and bring to simmering point. Poach the fish for about 12 minutes, or until just tender.

2 Lift the fish out of the pan using a slotted spoon, then strain the liquid into another pan. Leave the fish to cool, then remove any visible bones and flake the flesh gently with a fork.

3 Drain the rice and add it to the pan containing the fish-poaching liquid. Bring to the boil, then lower the heat, cover and simmer for 10 minutes. Do not be tempted to lift the lid since this will allow the liquid to evaporate.

4 Remove the pan from the heat and, without lifting the lid, leave the rice to stand undisturbed for 5 minutes.

5 Meanwhile, make the sauce. Mix the milk, flour and butter in a pan. Bring to the boil over a low heat, whisking constantly until the sauce is smooth and thick. Stir in the curry paste or mustard, with salt and pepper to taste. Simmer for 2 minutes, then remove the pan from the heat.

6 Preheat the grill (broiler) and lightly grease a shallow baking dish. Stir the chopped parsley and rice into the sauce, with half the cheese. Using a large metal spoon, fold in the flaked fish and eggs. Spoon the mixture into the prepared baking dish and sprinkle with the rest of the cheese. Cook under the grill until the topping is golden brown and bubbling. Scatter the chopped parsley over the top and serve at once.

VARIATIONS
- *To make an extra spicy sauce, add a pinch of dried red chilli with the curry paste.*
- *This gratin would be equally delicious with prawns (shrimp) in place of the salmon.*
- *There are lots of other tangy, hard cheeses you can use instead of the Cheddar: try Lancashire, Red Leicester or Monterey Jack.*

Seared Scallops with Chive Sauce on Leek & Carrot Rice

Scallops are one of the most delicious shellfish and here they are partnered with a wonderful chive sauce and a pilaff of wild and white rice with sweet-tasting leeks and carrots and fresh chervil.

Serves 4

Ingredients

12–16 shelled scallops
45ml/3 tbsp olive oil
50g/2oz/⅓ cup wild rice
65g/2½oz/5 tbsp butter
4 carrots, cut into long, thin strips
2 leeks, cut into thick, diagonal slices
1 small onion, finely chopped
115g/4oz/⅔ cup long grain rice
1 fresh bay leaf
200ml/7fl oz/scant 1 cup white wine
450ml/¾ pint/scant 2 cups fish stock
60ml/4 tbsp double (heavy) cream
a little lemon juice
25ml/5 tsp chopped fresh chives
30ml/2 tbsp chervil sprigs
salt and ground black pepper

1 Lightly season the scallops, brush with 15ml/1 tbsp of the olive oil and set aside. Cook the wild rice in plenty of boiling water for about 30 minutes or according to the instructions on the packet, until tender, then drain.

2 Melt half the butter in a small frying pan, add the carrots and cook fairly gently for 4–5 minutes. Add the leeks and fry for another 2 minutes. Season with salt and pepper and add 30–45ml/2–3 tbsp water, then cover and cook for a few minutes more. Uncover and cook until the liquid has reduced. Set aside off the heat.

3 Melt half the rest of the butter with 15ml/1 tbsp of the remaining oil in a heavy pan. Add the onion and fry for 3–4 minutes, or until softened but not browned.

4 Add the long grain rice and bay leaf to the onion and cook, stirring constantly, until the rice looks translucent and the grains are coated with oil. Pour in half the wine and half the stock. Season with 2.5ml/½ tsp salt and bring to the boil. Stir, then cover and cook very gently for 15 minutes, or until the liquid is absorbed and the rice is cooked and tender.

5 Reheat the carrots and leeks gently, then stir them into the long grain rice mixture with the wild rice. Add seasoning to taste, if necessary. Meanwhile, pour the remaining wine and fish stock into a small pan and boil rapidly until reduced by about half.

6 Heat a heavy frying pan over a high heat. Add the remaining butter and oil. Sear the scallops for 1–2 minutes each side, then set aside and keep warm.

7 Pour the reduced stock into the pan and heat until bubbling, then add the cream and boil until thickened. Season with lemon juice, salt and pepper, then stir in the chives and scallops. Stir the chervil into the rice and spoon it on to plates. Arrange the scallops on top and spoon the sauce over the rice. Serve immediately.

COOK'S TIP
To shell a fresh scallop, hold it firmly with the flat-side up and insert a strong knife blade between the shells to cut the top muscle. Separate the two shells. Slide the knife blade under the skirt to cut the second muscle. Remove the scallop. The edible part is the round white part and the coral or roe, if present. You can use the skirt for stock, but discard everything else.

North African Fish with Pumpkin Rice

This is a dish of contrasts – the slightly sweet flavour of pumpkin, the mildly spicy fish, and the coriander and ginger mixture that is stirred in at the end – all bound together with well-flavoured rice to form a filling meal.

Serves 4

Ingredients
450g/1lb sea bass or other firm fish fillets
30ml/2 tbsp plain (all-purpose) flour
5ml/1 tsp ground coriander
1.5–2.5ml/¼–½ tsp ground turmeric
1 wedge of pumpkin, about 500g/1¼lb
30–45ml/2–3 tbsp olive oil
6 spring onions (scallions), diagonally sliced
1 garlic clove, finely chopped
275g/10oz/1½ cups basmati rice, soaked
550ml/18fl oz/2½ cups fish stock
salt and ground black pepper
fresh coriander (cilantro) sprigs, to garnish
lime or lemon wedges, to serve

For the flavouring mixture
45ml/3 tbsp finely chopped fresh coriander (cilantro)
10ml/2 tsp finely chopped fresh root ginger
½–1 fresh chilli, seeded and very finely chopped
45ml/3 tbsp lime or lemon juice

1 Remove and discard any skin or stray bones from the fish, and cut into 2cm/¾in chunks. Mix the flour, ground coriander, turmeric and a little salt and pepper in a plastic bag. Add the fish and shake for a few seconds so that the fish is evenly coated in the spice mixture. Set aside.

2 Make the flavouring mixture. Place the chopped fresh coriander, fresh root ginger and chilli in a small bowl. Add the lime or lemon juice and stir well to combine. Set aside.

3 Carefully cut away the skin from the pumpkin and scoop out the seeds. Cut the flesh into 2cm/¾in chunks.

4 Heat 15ml/1 tbsp of the oil in a flameproof casserole, add the spring onions and garlic and stir-fry for a few minutes until slightly softened. Add the pumpkin and cook over a fairly low heat, stirring frequently, for 4–5 minutes, or until the flesh just begins to soften.

5 Drain the rice, add it to the casserole and toss over a brisk heat for 2–3 minutes. Stir in the stock, with a little salt. Bring to simmering point, then lower the heat, cover and cook for 12–15 minutes, or until both the rice and the pumpkin are tender.

6 About 4 minutes before the rice and pumpkin are ready, heat the remaining oil in a frying pan. Fry the spiced fish over a medium-high heat for about 3 minutes until the outside is lightly browned and crisp, and the flesh is cooked but still moist.

7 Stir the coriander and ginger flavouring mixture into the rice and transfer to a warmed serving dish. Lay the fish pieces on top and serve immediately, garnished with coriander, and offer lime or lemon wedges for squeezing over the fish.

GOAN PRAWN CURRY WITH SOUTHERN-STYLE RICE

Make this curry as mild or as fiery as you wish. Goans traditionally like their seafood dishes fairly hot, but a milder curry is just as delicious, flavoured with herbs and spices and softened with coconut milk.

SERVES 4

INGREDIENTS
15g/½oz/1 tbsp ghee or butter
2 garlic cloves, crushed
450g/1lb small raw prawns (shrimp), peeled and deveined
4 green cardamom pods
4 cloves
1 cinnamon stick
15ml/1 tbsp mustard seeds
about 15ml/1 tbsp groundnut (peanut) oil
1 large onion, chopped
½–1 fresh red chilli, seeded and finely sliced
4 tomatoes, peeled, seeded and chopped
175ml/6fl oz/¾ cup fish stock or water
350ml/12fl oz/1½ cups coconut milk
45ml/3 tbsp fragrant spice mix (see Cook's Tip)
10–20ml/2–4 tsp cayenne pepper
salt

FOR THE RICE
350g/12oz/1¾ cups basmati rice, soaked and drained
5ml/1 tsp coriander seeds
5ml/1 tsp cumin seeds
30ml/2 tbsp urad dhal, rinsed (optional)
2.5ml/½ tsp ground turmeric
15ml/1 tbsp groundnut (peanut) oil
5ml/1 tsp brown mustard seeds
115g/4oz/1 cup cashew nuts
15g/½oz/1 tbsp ghee or butter

1 Melt the ghee or butter in a flameproof casserole, add the garlic and stir over a low heat for a few seconds. Add the prawns and stir-fry briefly to coat. Transfer to a plate and set aside in a cool place.

2 Place the cardamom pods, cloves and cinnamon stick in a dry frying pan and dry-fry for 2 minutes. Add the mustard seeds and cook for 1 minute. Heat the oil in the flameproof casserole, add the onion, chilli and the dry-fried spices and cook, stirring, for 3–4 minutes. Add the tomatoes, fish stock or water, coconut milk, fragrant spice mix, cayenne pepper and salt, to taste. Set aside.

3 Preheat the oven to 180°C/350°F/Gas 4. Cook the rice in a pan of lightly salted boiling water for 5 minutes, then drain well. Meanwhile, dry-fry the coriander and cumin seeds with the urad dhal, if using, for a few minutes. Add the turmeric and grind the mixture finely in a spice mill or in a mortar, using a pestle. Heat the oil in a frying pan, add the mustard seeds and cashew nuts and fry for a few minutes, then stir into the rice with the ground spice mix.

4 Spoon the rice mixture into the casserole and dot with ghee or butter. Cover tightly with foil before fitting the lid securely. Cook in the oven for 20 minutes.

5 About 10 minutes before the rice is ready, reheat the curry sauce and add the prawns. Simmer gently for 3–5 minutes, or until the prawns are cooked through. Spoon into a hot serving dish and serve with the rice.

COOK'S TIP
To make a fragrant spice mix, dry-fry 25ml/1½ tbsp coriander seeds, 15ml/1 tbsp black peppercorns, 5ml/1 tsp cumin seeds, 1.5ml/¼ tsp fenugreek seeds and 1.5ml/¼ tsp fennel seeds until aromatic, then grind finely in a mortar with a pestle. Alternatively, mix together ready-ground spices, in which case, use only 15ml/1 tbsp ground coriander along with the other ground spices.

CREAMY FISH PILAU WITH WHITE WINE

This dish is inspired by a fusion of cuisines – the method comes from India and uses that country's favourite rice, basmati, but the delicious wine and cream sauce is very much French in flavour. This rich and creamy dish is perfect for a special dinner and is sure to delight your guests.

SERVES 4–6

INGREDIENTS
450g/1lb fresh mussels, scrubbed and beards removed
350ml/12fl oz/1½ cups dry white wine
a sprig of fresh flat leaf parsley, plus 15ml/1 tbsp chopped, and extra sprigs, to garnish
675g/1½lb salmon fillet
225g/8oz scallops
about 15ml/1 tbsp olive oil
40g/1½oz/3 tbsp butter
2 shallots, finely chopped
225g/8oz/3 cups button (white) mushrooms, halved if large
275g/10oz/1½ cups basmati rice, soaked
300ml/½ pint/1¼ cups fish stock
150ml/¼ pint/⅔ cup double (heavy) cream
225g/8oz large cooked prawns (shrimp), peeled and deveined
salt and ground black pepper

> VARIATION
> *Any firm fish can be used in place of the salmon, if you like. Monkfish, cod and halibut will all give good results. More robustly flavoured fish, such as tuna or swordfish will also be delicious.*

1 Preheat the oven to 160°C/325°F/Gas 3. Discard any mussels that are broken or remain closed when you tap them sharply. Place the mussels in a pan with about 90ml/6 tbsp of the wine and the sprig of parsley. Cover and cook for 4–5 minutes, or until they have opened. Drain, reserving the cooking liquid. Remove the mussels from their shells, discarding any that have not opened.

2 Cut the salmon into bitesize pieces. Detach the corals, if any, from the scallops and cut the white scallop flesh into thick slices.

3 Heat half the olive oil and the butter in a frying pan and fry the shallots and mushrooms for 3–4 minutes, or until softened but not coloured. Transfer to a large bowl. Heat the remaining oil in the frying pan and cook the rice for 2–3 minutes, stirring, until it is coated in oil. Spoon the rice into a deep casserole.

4 Pour the stock, remaining wine and reserved mussel liquid into the frying pan, and bring to the boil. Remove the pan from the heat, stir in the cream and chopped parsley, and season lightly. Pour the stock mixture over the rice, then add the salmon and the scallop flesh, together with the mushroom mixture. Stir carefully to mix.

5 Cover the casserole tightly. Bake for 30–35 minutes, then add the scallop corals. Replace the cover and cook for 4 minutes more. Add the mussels and prawns, cover and cook for 3–4 minutes, or until the seafood is heated through and the rice is tender. Serve garnished with the extra parsley sprigs.

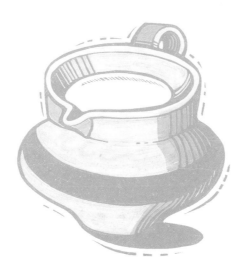

Seafood Paella

There are as many versions of paella as there are regions of Spain. Those from near the coast contain a lot of seafood, while inland versions add chicken or pork. Here the only meat is the chorizo, essential for an authentic flavour.

SERVES 4

INGREDIENTS
45ml/3 tbsp olive oil
1 Spanish onion, chopped
2 fat garlic cloves, chopped
150g/5oz chorizo sausage, sliced
300g/11oz small squid, cleaned
1 red (bell) pepper, seeded and cut into strips
4 tomatoes, peeled, seeded and diced, or 200g/7oz can tomatoes
500ml/17fl oz/generous 2 cups chicken stock
105ml/7 tbsp dry white wine
200g/7oz/1 cup short grain Spanish rice or risotto rice
a large pinch of saffron threads
150g/5oz/1 cup fresh or frozen peas
8 langoustines, in the shell, or 12 large cooked prawns
    (jumbo shrimp)
450g/1lb fresh mussels, scrubbed and beards removed
450g/1lb medium clams, scrubbed
salt and ground black pepper

COOK'S TIP
You can make a much more elaborate paella by adding the flesh of 1 small cooked lobster. Add it to the pan about 5 minutes before cooking is complete.

1 Heat the olive oil in a paella pan or wok, add the onion and garlic and cook, stirring, until translucent. Add the chorizo and fry until lightly golden.

2 If the squid are very small, leave them whole, otherwise cut the bodies into rings and the tentacles into pieces. Add the squid to the pan and sauté over a high heat for 2 minutes.

3 Add the pepper strips and tomatoes to the chorizo and squid and stir to mix. Cook gently for about 5 minutes, or until tender. Pour in the chicken stock and white wine, stir well and bring to the boil.

4 Stir in the rice and saffron threads and season well with salt and ground black pepper. Spread the contents of the pan evenly with the back of a wooden spoon. Bring the liquid back to the boil, then lower the heat slightly and simmer gently for about 10 minutes.

5 Discard any mussels that are broken or remain closed when you tap them sharply. Add the peas, langoustines or prawns, mussels and clams, stirring them gently into the rice, taking care not to squash them.

6 Cook the paella gently for a further 15–20 minutes, or until the rice is tender and all the mussels and clams have opened. If any remain closed, discard them. If the paella seems dry, add a little more hot chicken stock. Gently stir everything together and serve piping hot.

Salmon Risotto with Cucumber & Tarragon

This simple risotto is cooked all in one go, and is therefore simpler than the usual risotto. If you prefer to cook the traditional way, add the liquid gradually, adding the salmon about two-thirds of the way through cooking.

SERVES 4

INGREDIENTS
25g/1oz/2 tbsp butter
small bunch of spring onions (scallions), white parts only, chopped
½ cucumber, peeled, seeded and chopped
350g/12oz/1¾ cups risotto rice
1.2 litres/2 pints/5 cups hot chicken or fish stock
150ml/¼ pint/⅔ cup dry white wine
450g/1lb salmon fillet, skinned and diced
45ml/3 tbsp chopped fresh tarragon
salt and ground black pepper

1 Heat the butter in a large pan and add the spring onions and cucumber. Cook for 2–3 minutes without letting the spring onions colour.

2 Stir in the rice, then pour in the stock and wine. Bring to the boil, then lower the heat and simmer, uncovered, for 10 minutes, stirring occasionally.

3 Stir in the diced salmon and season to taste with salt and freshly ground black pepper. Continue cooking for a further 5 minutes, stirring occasionally, then switch off the heat. Cover and leave to stand for 5 minutes.

4 Remove the lid, add the chopped tarragon and mix lightly. Spoon into a warmed bowl and serve.

> COOK'S TIP
> *Carnaroli risotto rice would be excellent in this risotto, although it may not be easy to get hold of. Arborio rice is a good alternative.*

MONKFISH RISOTTO

The superb flavour of monkfish is accentuated with lemon grass in this sophisticated risotto. Chop only the bottom 5cm/2in of the lemon grass stalk.

SERVES 3–4

INGREDIENTS
30–45ml/2–3 tbsp seasoned flour
about 450g/1lb monkfish, cut into cubes
30ml/2 tbsp olive oil
40g/1½oz/3 tbsp butter
2 shallots, finely chopped
1 lemon grass stalk, finely chopped
275g/10oz/1½ cups risotto rice, preferably carnaroli
175ml/6fl oz/¾ cup dry white wine
1 litre/1¾ pints/4 cups simmering fish stock
30ml/2 tbsp chopped fresh flat leaf parsley
salt and ground black pepper
dressed salad leaves, to serve

1 Spoon the seasoned flour over the monkfish cubes in a large bowl. Toss the monkfish until thoroughly coated.

2 Heat 15ml/1 tbsp of the oil with half the butter in a frying pan. Add the monkfish cubes (discarding any excess flour) and fry over a medium to high heat for 3–4 minutes, or until cooked, turning occasionally. Transfer to a plate and set aside.

3 Heat the remaining oil and butter in a heavy pan, add the shallots and fry over a low heat for about 4 minutes, or until soft but not brown. Add the lemon grass and cook for 1–2 minutes more. Tip in the rice. Cook for 2–3 minutes, stirring, until the rice is coated with oil and is slightly translucent. Gradually add the wine and the hot stock, stirring and waiting until each ladleful has been absorbed before adding the next.

4 When the rice is about three-quarters cooked (after about 15 minutes), stir in the monkfish and parsley. Continue to cook the risotto, adding the remaining stock and stirring until the grains of rice are tender, but still retain a bit of "bite". Season with salt and black pepper.

Risotto Nero

If you happen to have some squid or cuttlefish complete with ink sac, retrieve the ink yourself to make this black risotto. Otherwise, you can buy sachets of squid or cuttlefish ink at good fishmongers and some delicatessens.

Serves 4

Ingredients
450g/1lb small cuttlefish or squid, with their ink, or 350g/12oz cuttlefish and
   4 sachets cuttlefish or squid ink
1.2 litres/2 pints/5 cups light fish stock
50g/2oz/¼ cup butter
30ml/2 tbsp olive oil
3 shallots, finely chopped
350g/12oz/1¾ cups risotto rice
105ml/7 tbsp dry white wine
30ml/2 tbsp chopped fresh flat leaf parsley
salt and ground black pepper

1 If the cuttlefish or squid contain ink, squeeze it out into a small bowl and set it aside. Cut the bodies into thin rings and chop the tentacles. Set aside.

2 Add the ink to the fish stock. Bring to the boil and lower the heat so that the liquid is at a gentle simmer. Heat half the butter and all the olive oil in a large pan. Add the chopped shallots and cook for about 3 minutes, or until they are soft and translucent.

3 Add the cuttlefish or squid to the pan and fry very gently for 5–7 minutes, or until tender. Add the rice and stir well to coat all the grains with fat. Pour in the wine and simmer until most of it has been absorbed by the rice. Add a ladleful of the hot stock and cook, stirring continuously, until it has been absorbed.

4 Continue cooking and stirring for 20–25 minutes, adding the remaining stock a ladleful at a time after the previous quantity has been absorbed.

5 Season to taste, then stir in the parsley. Beat in the remaining butter to make the risotto glossy. Spoon the risotto into four warmed dishes and serve.

TRUFFLE & LOBSTER RISOTTO

To capture the precious qualities of the fresh truffle, partner it with lobster and serve in a silky smooth risotto. Both truffle shavings and truffle oil are added towards the end of cooking to preserve their flavour. This is a truly opulent dish.

SERVES 4

INGREDIENTS
50g/2oz/4 tbsp unsalted butter
1 onion, chopped
350g/12oz/1¾ cups risotto rice, preferably carnaroli
1 fresh thyme sprig
150ml/¼ pint/⅔ cup dry white wine
1.2 litres/2 pints/5 cups simmering chicken stock
1 freshly cooked lobster
45ml/3 tbsp chopped mixed fresh flat leaf parsley and chervil
3–4 drops truffle oil
2 hard-boiled (hard-cooked) eggs
1 fresh black or white truffle
salt and ground black pepper

1 Melt the butter, add the onion and fry until soft. Add the rice and stir well to coat with butter. Add the thyme, then the wine and cook until the wine has been absorbed. Add the chicken stock a little at a time, stirring. Let each ladleful be absorbed before adding the next.

2 To prepare the lobster, twist off its tail, cut the underside with scissors and remove the white tail meat. Carefully break open the claws with a small kitchen hammer and remove the flesh. Cut half the meat into big chunks, then roughly chop the remainder.

3 Stir the chopped lobster meat into the risotto with half the chopped herbs and the truffle oil. Remove the pan from the heat, cover and leave to stand for 5 minutes. Divide among warmed plates and place the lobster chunks on top. Cut the hard-boiled eggs into wedges and arrange them around the lobster meat. Finally, shave fresh truffle over each portion and sprinkle with the remaining herbs. Serve immediately.

LIGHT &
HEALTHY DISHES

Fish and shellfish are rich in many essential nutrients, making them important to your everyday diet. This chapter is dedicated to dishes that are full of wholesome ingredients and use healthy cooking methods such as steaming, grilling and baking. Try light and delicious dishes such as Steamed Lettuce-wrapped Sole, Hoki Stir-fry and Oriental Fish en Papillote. For more substantial dishes that are just as healthy, try Roast Cod with Pancetta & Butter Beans, Smoked Haddock with Mustard Cabbage and Baked Sea Bass with Fennel.

Steamed Lettuce-wrapped Sole

If you can afford it, use Dover sole fillets for this recipe; if not, lemon sole, trout, plaice, flounder and brill are all excellent cooked this way.

SERVES 4

INGREDIENTS
15ml/1 tbsp sesame seeds
15ml/1 tbsp sunflower or groundnut (peanut) oil
10ml/2 tsp sesame oil
2.5cm/1in piece fresh root ginger, peeled and grated
3 garlic cloves, finely chopped
15ml/1 tbsp soy sauce or Thai fish sauce (nam pla)
juice of 1 lemon
2 spring onions (scallions), thinly sliced
2 large sole fillets, skinned, seasoned and halved lengthways
8 large, soft lettuce leaves
12 large fresh mussels, scrubbed and beards removed

1 Heat a heavy frying pan until hot. Add the sesame seeds and toast lightly but do not allow them to burn. Set aside in a bowl until required. Heat the oils in the frying pan over a medium heat. Add the ginger and garlic and cook until lightly coloured, then stir in the soy sauce or Thai fish sauce, lemon juice and spring onions. Remove the pan from the heat and stir in the toasted sesame seeds.

2 Lay the fish on a chopping board, skinned-side up and spread with the ginger mixture. Roll up each piece, starting at the tail end. Place on a baking sheet.

3 Using a sieve, plunge the lettuce leaves into boiling water and immediately remove them. Lay them on kitchen paper and gently pat them dry. Wrap each sole parcel in two lettuce leaves, making sure that the filling is well covered to keep it in place.

4 Arrange the fish parcels in a steamer basket, cover and steam over simmering water for 8 minutes. Discard any mussels that do not close when tapped sharply. Add the mussels to the steaming basket and steam for 2–4 minutes, or until opened. Discard any that remain closed. Put the parcels on individual warmed plates with the mussels and serve immediately.

SALMON EN PAPILLOTE WITH LEEKS & YELLOW PEPPERS

Cooking fish "en papillote" makes a lot of sense, ensuring that the fish retains its flavour while it cooks in its steamy parcel with aromatic ingredients. It is also excellent when entertaining, as the parcels may be prepared ahead of cooking.

SERVES 6

INGREDIENTS
25ml/1½ tbsp groundnut (peanut) oil
2 yellow (bell) peppers, seeded and thinly sliced
4cm/1½in fresh root ginger, peeled and finely shredded
1 large fennel bulb, finely sliced, feathery tops chopped and reserved
1 green chilli, seeded and finely shredded
2 large leeks, cut into 10cm/4in lengths and shredded lengthways
30ml/2 tbsp chopped chives
10ml/2 tsp light soy sauce
6 salmon fillet portions, each weighing 150–175g/5–6oz, skinned
10ml/2 tsp toasted sesame oil
salt and ground black pepper

1 Heat the oil in a large non-stick frying pan and cook the peppers, ginger and fennel for 5–6 minutes, or until they are softened but not browned. Add the chilli and leeks and cook for a further 2–3 minutes. Stir in half the chives and the soy sauce with seasoning to taste. Set aside to cool.

2 Preheat the oven to 190°C/375°F/Gas 5. Cut six 35cm/14in rounds of baking parchment or foil. Divide the vegetable mixture between the six rounds and place a portion of salmon on each. Drizzle with sesame oil and sprinkle with the remaining chives and the chopped fennel tops. Season with salt and pepper.

3 Fold the parchment or foil over to enclose the fish, rolling and twisting the edges together to seal the parcels completely. Place the parcels on a baking tray and bake for 15–20 minutes, or until the parcels are puffed up and, if made with paper, lightly browned. Transfer the parcels to warmed individual plates and serve immediately.

ORIENTAL FISH EN PAPILLOTE

The aromatic smell that wafts out of these fish parcels as you open them is deliciously tempting. If you don't like oriental flavours, use white wine, herbs and thinly sliced vegetables, or Mediterranean ingredients such as tomatoes, basil and olives.

SERVES 4

INGREDIENTS
2 carrots
2 courgettes (zucchini)
6 spring onions (scallions)
2.5cm/1in piece fresh root ginger, peeled
1 lime
2 garlic cloves, thinly sliced
30ml/2 tbsp teriyaki marinade or Thai fish sauce (nam pla)
5–10ml/1–2 tsp sesame oil
4 salmon fillets, about 200g/7oz each
ground black pepper
rice, to serve

1 Cut the carrots, courgettes and spring onions into matchsticks. Cut the ginger into thin matchsticks and put these in a small bowl. Using a zester, pare the lime thinly. Add the pared rind to the ginger, with the garlic. Squeeze the lime juice.

2 Place the teriyaki marinade or Thai fish sauce in a bowl and stir in the lime juice and sesame oil. Preheat the oven to 220°C/425°F/Gas 7. Cut out four rounds of baking parchment, each with a diameter of 40cm/16in. Season the salmon with pepper. Lay a fillet on one side of each paper round, about 3cm/1¼in off-centre. Scatter a quarter of the ginger mixture over each and pile a quarter of the vegetable matchsticks on top. Spoon a quarter of the teriyaki or Thai fish sauce mixture over the top.

3 Fold the bare side of the baking parchment over the salmon and roll over the edges of the parchment to seal each parcel very tightly.

4 Place the salmon parcels on a baking tray and cook in the oven for about 10–12 minutes, depending on the thickness of the fillets. Transfer the parcels to warmed individual plates and serve with rice.

SARDINES IN ESCABECHE

This spicy marinade, known as escabeche, is widely used in Spain and Portugal as a traditional means of preserving fish, poultry or game. It is also very tasty if you use it to flavour fish – especially lightly fried sardines.

SERVES 2–4

INGREDIENTS
16 sardines, cleaned
about 30ml/2 tbsp seasoned flour
30ml/2 tbsp olive oil
roasted red onion, green (bell) pepper and tomatoes, to serve

FOR THE MARINADE
90ml/6 tbsp olive oil
1 onion, sliced
1 garlic clove, crushed
3–4 bay leaves
2 cloves
1 dried red chilli
5ml/1 tsp paprika
120ml/4fl oz/½ cup wine or sherry vinegar
120ml/4fl oz/½ cup white wine
salt and ground black pepper

1 Cut the heads off the sardines and split them along the belly. Turn the sardines over so that the backbone is uppermost. Press down along the backbone to loosen it, then carefully lift out the backbone and as many remaining bones as possible.

2 Close the sardines up and dust them with seasoned flour. Heat the olive oil in a frying pan, add the sardines and fry for 2–3 minutes on each side. Remove from the pan and allow to cool, then place in a single layer in a large shallow dish.

3 Make the marinade. Add the oil to the pan. Add the onion and garlic and cook gently for 5–10 minutes, or until soft. Add the bay leaves, cloves, chilli and paprika, with pepper. Fry for 1–2 minutes, then stir in the vinegar and wine, and season with salt. Allow the marinade to bubble, then pour over the sardines. When cool, cover and chill overnight. Serve with roasted onion, pepper and tomatoes.

Smoked Haddock
with Mustard Cabbage

This simple dish takes less than twenty minutes to make and is quite delicious. The mustard butter complements Savoy cabbage and the robust flavour of the haddock perfectly. Sweet grilled tomatoes make the final touch to a wonderful dish.

SERVES 4

INGREDIENTS
1 Savoy cabbage
675g/1½lb undyed smoked haddock fillet
300ml/½ pint/1¼ cups milk
½ onion, peeled and sliced into rings
2 bay leaves
½ lemon, sliced
4 white peppercorns
4 ripe tomatoes
50g/2oz/¼ cup butter
30ml/2 tbsp wholegrain mustard
juice of 1 lemon
salt and ground black pepper
30ml/2 tbsp chopped fresh flat leaf parsley, to garnish

1 Cut the cabbage in half, remove the central core and thick ribs, then shred the cabbage. Cook in a pan of lightly salted boiling water, or steam over boiling water for about 10 minutes, or until just tender. Leave in the pan, undrained, or in the steamer until required.

2 Meanwhile put the haddock in a large shallow pan with the milk, onion and bay leaves. Add the lemon slices and peppercorns. Bring to simmering point, then cover and poach until the fish flakes easily when tested with the tip of a sharp knife. This will take 8–10 minutes, depending on the thickness of the fillets. Take the pan off the heat and set aside until needed. Preheat the grill (broiler).

3 Cut the tomatoes in half horizontally, season them with salt and pepper and grill (broil) until lightly browned. Now it is time to drain the cabbage, refresh under cold water and drain again.

4 Melt the butter in a shallow pan or wok, add the cabbage and toss over the heat for 2 minutes. Mix in the mustard and season to taste, then tip the cabbage into a warmed serving dish.

5 Drain the haddock. Carefully remove the skin and cut the fish into four pieces. Place on top of the cabbage with some onion rings and grilled tomato halves. Pour on the lemon juice, then sprinkle with chopped parsley and serve.

COOK'S TIPS
- *Try to choose firm tomatoes for this dish – plum tomatoes, or those sold on the vine, are especially good for grilling.*
- *Savoy is a dark, curly leaved cabbage that is full of vitamins and essential nutrients. Use other green cabbages, if you prefer, but choose one with a firm heart and plenty of dark outside leaves (although you will probably discard these, they keep the centre of the cabbage moist during storage).*

Roast Cod with Pancetta & Butter Beans

Thick cod steaks wrapped in pancetta and roasted make a superb supper dish when served on a bed of butter beans, with sweet and juicy cherry tomatoes on the side.

Serves 4

Ingredients
200g/7oz/1 cup butter (lima) beans, soaked overnight in cold water to cover
2 leeks, thinly sliced
2 garlic cloves, chopped
8 fresh sage leaves
90ml/6 tbsp fruity olive oil
8 thin slices of pancetta
4 thick cod steaks, skinned
12 cherry tomatoes
salt and ground black pepper

1 Drain the beans, tip them into a pan and cover with cold water. Bring to the boil and skim off any foam. Lower the heat, then stir in the leeks, garlic, 4 of the sage leaves and 30ml/2 tbsp of the oil. Simmer for 1–1½ hours until the beans are tender. Drain, return to the pan, season, stir in 30ml/2 tbsp oil and keep warm.

2 Preheat the oven to 200°C/400°F/Gas 6. Wrap two slices of pancetta around the edge of each cod steak, tying it on with kitchen string or securing it with a wooden cocktail stick (toothpick). Insert a sage leaf between the pancetta and the cod. Season the fish with salt and pepper.

3 Heat a heavy frying pan, add 15ml/1 tbsp of the remaining oil. Add the cod steaks two at a time and cook for 1 minute on each side to seal. Transfer them to an ovenproof dish and roast in the oven for 5 minutes.

4 Add the tomatoes to the dish and drizzle over the remaining olive oil. Roast for 5 minutes more, or until the cod steaks are cooked but still juicy. Serve them on a bed of butter beans with the roasted tomatoes.

Baked Sea Bass with Fennel

Sea bass has a wonderful flavour, but cheaper alternatives, such as snapper or bream can be used. Serve with crisply cooked green beans tossed in olive oil and garlic for a light and nutritious lunch.

Serves 4

Ingredients
4 fennel bulbs, trimmed
4 tomatoes, peeled and diced
8 drained, canned anchovy fillets, halved lengthways
a large pinch of saffron threads, soaked in 30ml/2 tbsp hot water
150ml/¼ pint/⅔ cup chicken or fish stock
2 red or yellow (bell) peppers, seeded and each cut into 12 strips
4 garlic cloves, chopped
15ml/1 tbsp chopped fresh marjoram
45ml/3 tbsp olive oil
1 sea bass, about 1.75kg/4–4½lb, scaled and cleaned
salt and ground black pepper
chopped fresh flat leaf parsley, to garnish

1 Preheat the oven to 200°C/400°F/Gas 6. Quarter the fennel bulbs lengthways. Cook in a pan of lightly salted boiling water for 5 minutes until barely tender. Drain and arrange in a shallow ovenproof dish. Season with pepper, then set aside.

2 Spoon the diced tomatoes and anchovy strips on top of the fennel. Stir the saffron and its soaking water into the chicken or fish stock and pour the mixture over the tomatoes. Lay the strips of pepper alongside the fennel and sprinkle with the garlic and marjoram. Drizzle 30ml/2 tbsp of the olive oil over the peppers and season with salt and pepper.

3 Bake the vegetables for 15 minutes. Season the prepared sea bass inside and out and lay it on top of the fennel and pepper mixture. Drizzle the remaining olive oil over the fish and bake for 30–40 minutes more, or until the sea bass flesh comes away easily from the bone when tested with the point of a sharp knife. Serve at once, garnished with the chopped parsley.

Seared Tuna Steaks with Red Onion Salsa

This contemporary dish contains a fantastic combination of flavours – fresh herbs, colourful fruits and vegetables combined to make a refreshing raw salsa to serve with the chilli-spiced tuna.

Serves 4

Ingredients
4 tuna steaks, each weighing about 175–200g/6–7oz
5ml/1 tsp cumin seeds, toasted and crushed
pinch of dried red chilli flakes
grated rind and juice of 1 lime
30–60ml/2–4 tbsp extra virgin olive oil
salt and ground black pepper
lime wedges and fresh coriander (cilantro) sprigs, to garnish

For the salsa
1 small red onion, finely chopped
200g/7oz red or yellow cherry tomatoes, roughly chopped
1 avocado, peeled, stoned (pitted) and chopped
2 kiwi fruit, peeled and chopped
1 fresh red chilli, seeded and finely chopped
15g/½oz fresh coriander (cilantro), chopped
5 fresh mint sprigs, leaves only, chopped
5–10ml/1–2 tsp Thai fish sauce (nam pla)
about 5ml/1 tsp muscovado (molasses) sugar

Cook's Tip
Salsa is a great sauce that goes extremely well with grilled fish. It is best made freshly and not too far in advance. Red onions are the ideal ingredient, both for their mild, sweet flavour and pretty colour.

1 Wash the tuna steaks and pat dry. Sprinkle with half the cumin, the dried chilli, salt, pepper and half the lime rind. Rub in 30ml/2 tbsp of the oil and set aside in a glass or china dish for about 30 minutes.

2 Meanwhile, make the salsa. Mix together the onion, tomatoes, avocado, kiwi fruit, fresh chilli, chopped coriander and mint. Add the remaining cumin, the rest of the lime rind and half the lime juice. Add Thai fish sauce and sugar to taste. Set aside for 15–20 minutes, then add more Thai fish sauce, lime juice and olive oil if you feel a little extra flavour is required.

3 Heat a ridged, cast iron griddle. Place the tuna steaks on the hot pan and cook, allowing about 2 minutes on each side for rare tuna or a little longer for a medium rare result.

4 Serve the seared tuna steaks garnished with lime wedges and fresh coriander sprigs. Serve the red onion salsa separately or spoon a little on to individual plates with the tuna.

Moroccan Spiced Mackerel

Mackerel is extremely good for you. The Moroccan spices in this recipe counteract the richness of the fish and give it a delicious aroma.

Serves 4

Ingredients
150ml/¼ pint/⅔ cup sunflower oil
15ml/1 tbsp paprika
5–10ml/1–2 tsp harissa or chilli powder
10ml/2 tsp ground cumin
10ml/2 tsp ground coriander
2 garlic cloves, crushed
juice of 2 lemons
30ml/2 tbsp chopped fresh mint leaves, plus extra mint sprigs to garnish
30ml/2 tbsp chopped fresh coriander (cilantro)
4 mackerel, cleaned
salt and ground black pepper
lemon wedges, to serve

1 In a bowl, whisk together the oil, spices, garlic and lemon juice. Season, then stir in the mint and coriander to make a spicy marinade.

2 Make two or three diagonal slashes on either side of each mackerel so that they may absorb the marinade. Pour the marinade into a shallow glass or china dish that is large enough to hold the fish in a single layer.

3 Put in the mackerel and turn them over in the marinade, spooning it into the slashes. Cover the dish with clear film (plastic wrap) and place in the refrigerator for at least 3 hours or more if you wish.

4 To cook the mackerel, preheat the grill (broiler) to medium-high. Transfer the fish to a rack set over a grilling pan and grill (broil) for about 5 minutes on each side, or until just cooked, turning the fish once and basting them several times with the marinade. Serve hot or cold with lemon wedges, garnished with mint.

Marrakesh Monkfish with Chermoula

Chermoula is a Moroccan spice mixture, which is used as a marinade for meat, poultry and fish. You will find your mouth watering in anticipation as you make it.

SERVES 4

INGREDIENTS
1 small red onion, finely chopped
2 garlic cloves, crushed
1 fresh red chilli, seeded and finely chopped
30ml/2 tbsp chopped fresh coriander (cilantro)
15ml/1 tbsp chopped fresh mint
5ml/1 tsp ground cumin
5ml/1 tsp paprika
generous pinch of saffron threads
60ml/4 tbsp olive oil
juice of 1 lemon
675g/1½lb monkfish fillets
salt
salad and pitta bread, to serve

1 To make the chermoula, mix the onion, garlic, chilli, coriander, mint, cumin, paprika, saffron, olive oil, lemon juice and salt in a bowl.

2 Pull off any pink membrane from the monkfish fillets, then cut the monkfish into cubes. Add the cubes to the spice mixture in the bowl. Mix well to coat, then cover and leave in a cool place for 1 hour. Thread the monkfish on to four skewers and place on a rack over a grill (broiling) pan. Spoon a little of the marinade over the fish skewers.

3 Grill the monkfish skewers, close to the heat, for about 3 minutes on each side, until cooked and lightly browned. Serve with a green, leafy salad and warm pitta bread.

SWORDFISH KEBABS

The firm, meaty flesh of swordfish is ideal for grilling. Here it is marinated in lemon juice, olive oil and paprika, before being threaded on to skewers with chunks of tomato, pepper and onion. A herby, olive oil sauce makes the perfect accompaniment.

SERVES 4

INGREDIENTS
900g/2lb swordfish, skinned
5ml/1 tsp paprika, plus extra to garnish
60ml/4 tbsp lemon juice
45ml/3 tbsp olive oil
6 fresh bay leaves
4 small tomatoes
2 green (bell) peppers, seeded and cut into 5cm/2in pieces
2 onions, each cut into 4 wedges
salt and ground white pepper
lettuce and cucumber salad and lime or lemon wedges, to serve

FOR THE SAUCE
120ml/4fl oz/½ cup extra virgin olive oil
juice of 1 lemon
60ml/4 tbsp finely chopped fresh flat leaf parsley

COOK'S TIP
To help prevent the onion from falling apart during the cooking, keep the root end intact when you prepare the onion. When you slice into it the root will hold the layers together.

1 Cut the swordfish into 5cm/2in cubes and place in a shallow dish. Mix together the paprika, lemon juice, olive oil and seasoning and pour over the fish. Crush 2 bay leaves over the fish.

2 Cover the fish with clear film (plastic wrap) and leave to marinate in the refrigerator for at least 2 hours. Carefully turn the fish cubes in the marinade once or twice to coat well.

3 Thread the fish cubes and vegetable pieces on to four large skewers and finish with a bay leaf. Place the skewers under a preheated grill (broiler) or over the hot coals of a barbecue, and cook, basting with any remaining marinade mixture from time to time. Turn the fish once during cooking.

4 Meanwhile, make the sauce. In a bowl whisk the extra virgin olive oil, lemon juice, chopped parsley, and salt and ground black pepper together until thickened, and pour into a jug (pitcher).

5 Arrange the swordfish kebabs on lettuce leaves and serve with the parsley oil sauce, a crisp lettuce and cucumber salad and lime or lemon wedges.

CHARGRILLED SWORDFISH WITH CHILLI & LIME SAUCE

Swordfish is a prime candidate for the barbecue or grill, as long as it is not overcooked. It tastes wonderful with a spicy sauce whose fire is tempered with crème fraîche. Chargrill some vegetables at the same time to accompany the fish.

SERVES 4

INGREDIENTS
2 fresh serrano chillies (or any other hot, red chilli)
4 tomatoes
45ml/3 tbsp olive oil
grated rind and juice of 1 lime
4 swordfish steaks
2.5ml/½ tsp salt
2.5ml/½ tsp ground black pepper
175ml/6fl oz/¾ cup crème fraîche

1 Roast the chillies in a dry griddle pan until the skins are blistered. Put in a strong plastic bag and tie the top. Set aside for 20 minutes, then peel off the skins. Cut off the stalks, then slit the chillies, scrape out the seeds and slice the flesh.

2 Cut a cross in the base of each tomato. Place them in a heatproof bowl and pour over boiling water to cover. After 3 minutes, lift the tomatoes out on a slotted spoon and plunge them into a bowl of cold water. Drain. Peel, then cut them in half and scoop out the seeds. Chop the flesh into 1cm/½in pieces.

3 Heat 15ml/1 tbsp of the oil in a small pan and add the strips of chilli, with the lime rind and juice. Cook for 2–3 minutes, then stir in the tomatoes. Cook for 10 minutes, stirring the mixture occasionally, until the tomato is pulpy.

4 Brush the steaks with oil and season. Barbecue or grill (broil) for 3–4 minutes, turning once. Stir the crème fraîche into the sauce, and heat through. Place the steaks on individual plates, pour over the sauce and serve immediately.

Chargrilled Shark Steaks with Herbs

Shark is very low in fat, with dense, well-flavoured flesh. Other close-textured fish like tuna and marlin work equally well in this recipe, which is ideal for a barbecue. Serve the fish with a tangy tomato salad.

Serves 4

Ingredients
45ml/3 tbsp olive oil
2 fresh bay leaves, chopped
15ml/1 tbsp chopped fresh basil
15ml/1 tbsp chopped fresh oregano
30ml/2 tbsp chopped fresh flat leaf parsley
5ml/1 tsp finely chopped fresh rosemary
5ml/1 tsp fresh thyme leaves
2 garlic cloves, crushed
4 pieces drained sun-dried tomatoes in oil, chopped
4 shark steaks, about 200g/7oz each
juice of 1 lemon
15ml/1 tbsp drained small capers in vinegar (optional)
salt and ground black pepper

1 Whisk the oil, herbs, garlic and sun-dried tomatoes in a bowl, then pour the mixture into a shallow glass or china dish that is large enough to hold the shark steaks in a single layer. Season the shark steaks with salt and pepper and brush the lemon juice over both sides. Lay the fish in the dish, turning the steaks to coat them all over. Cover and marinate in the refrigerator for 1–2 hours.

2 Heat a ridged griddle pan or barbecue until it is very hot. Lift the shark steaks out of the marinade, pat dry with kitchen paper and grill (broil) or cook on the barbecue for about 5 minutes on each side, or until they are cooked through. Pour the marinade into a small pan and bring to the boil. Stir in the capers, if you are using them. Spoon over the grilled shark steaks and serve immediately.

HOKI STIR-FRY

Any firm white fish, such as monkfish, hake or cod, can be used for this attractive stir-fry. Vary the vegetables according to what is available, but try to include at least three different colours. Shrimp-fried rice would be the perfect accompaniment.

SERVES 4–6

INGREDIENTS
675g/1½lb hoki fillet, skinned
pinch of five-spice powder
2 carrots
115g/4oz/1 cup small mangetouts (snow peas)
115g/4oz asparagus spears
4 spring onions (scallions)
45ml/3 tbsp groundnut (peanut) or stir-fry oil
2.5cm/1in piece fresh root ginger, peeled and cut into thin slivers
2 garlic cloves, finely chopped
300g/11oz beansprouts
8–12 small baby corn cobs
15–30ml/1–2 tbsp light soy sauce
salt and ground black pepper

1 Cut the hoki into fingersize strips and season with salt, pepper and five-spice powder. Cut the carrots diagonally into slices as thin as the mangetouts. Top and tail the mangetouts. Trim the asparagus spears and cut in half crossways. Trim the spring onions and cut them diagonally into 2cm/¾in pieces, keeping the white and green parts separate. Set aside.

2 Heat a wok, then pour in the oil. As soon as it is hot, add the ginger and garlic. Stir-fry for 1 minute, then add the white parts of the spring onions and cook for 1 minute more.

3 Add the hoki strips and stir-fry for 2–3 minutes, or until all the pieces of fish are opaque. Add the beansprouts. Toss them around to coat them in the oil, then put in the carrots, mangetouts, asparagus and baby corn. Continue to stir-fry for 3–4 minutes, by which time the fish should be cooked, but all the vegetables will still be crunchy. Add soy sauce to taste, toss everything quickly together, then stir in the green parts of the spring onions. Serve immediately.

STIR-FRIED FIVE-SPICE SQUID WITH BLACK BEAN SAUCE

Squid is perfect for stir-frying as it should be cooked quickly, and the spicy sauce makes the ideal accompaniment. Serve with rice or noodles.

SERVES 6

INGREDIENTS
450g/1lb small squid, cleaned
45ml/3 tbsp oil
2.5cm/1in piece fresh root ginger, grated
1 garlic clove, crushed
8 spring onions (scallions), cut diagonally into 2.5cm/1in lengths
1 red (bell) pepper, seeded and cut into strips
1 fresh green chilli, seeded and thinly sliced
6 mushrooms, sliced
5ml/1 tsp five-spice powder
30ml/2 tbsp black bean sauce
30ml/2 tbsp soy sauce
5ml/1 tsp granulated sugar
15ml/1 tbsp rice wine or dry sherry

1 Rinse the squid and pull away the outer skin. Dry on kitchen paper. Slit open and score the outside into a criss-cross pattern. Cut the squid into strips.

2 Heat a wok briefly and add the oil. When it is hot, stir-fry the squid quickly. Remove the squid strips from the wok with a slotted spoon and set aside. Add the ginger, garlic, spring onions, red pepper, chilli and mushrooms to the oil remaining in the wok and stir-fry for 2 minutes.

3 Return the squid to the wok and stir in the five-spice powder, black bean sauce, soy sauce, sugar and rice wine or sherry. Bring to the boil and cook for 1 minute.

COOK'S TIP
As with all stir-fried dishes it is important to have all the ingredients ready before you start to cook.

MALAYSIAN STEAMED TROUT WITH CHILLI, COCONUT & LIME

This simple dish can be prepared extremely quickly. Serve it on a bed of noodles accompanied by ribbons of colourful vegetables, to make a nutritious and filling meal.

SERVES 4

INGREDIENTS
8 pink trout fillets of even thickness, about 115g/4oz each, skinned
45ml/3 tbsp grated creamed coconut (coconut cream)
grated rind and juice of 2 limes
45ml/3 tbsp chopped fresh coriander (cilantro)
15ml/1 tbsp sunflower or groundnut (peanut) oil
2.5–5ml/½–1 tsp chilli oil
salt and ground black pepper
lime slices and coriander (cilantro) sprigs, to garnish

1 Cut four rectangles of baking parchment, about twice the size of the trout fillets. Place a fillet on each piece and season lightly.

2 Mix together the coconut, lime rind and coriander and spread a quarter of the mixture over each trout fillet. Place the other trout fillets on top. Mix the lime juice with the oils and drizzle the mixture over the trout.

3 Prepare a steamer. Fold up the edges of the paper and pleat them over the trout. Place the parcels in the steamer and steam over the simmering water for about 15 minutes until the trout is just cooked. Serve garnished with lime and coriander.

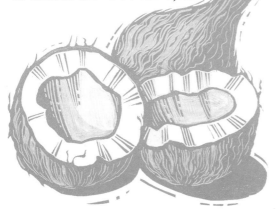

CHINESE-STYLE SCALLOPS & PRAWNS

Serve this light, delicate dish for lunch or supper accompanied by aromatic rice or fine rice noodles and stir-fried pak choi (bok choy). It makes a colourful blend that gives off a delicious aroma.

SERVES 4

INGREDIENTS
15ml/1 tbsp stir-fry or sunflower oil
500g/1¼lb raw tiger prawns (large shrimp), peeled
1 star anise
225g/8oz scallops, halved horizontally if large
2.5cm/1in piece fresh root ginger, grated
2 garlic cloves, thinly sliced
1 red (bell) pepper, seeded and cut into thin strips
115g/4oz/1¾ cups shiitake or button (white) mushrooms, thinly sliced
juice of 1 lemon
5ml/1 tsp cornflour (cornstarch), mixed to a paste with 30ml/2 tbsp cold water
30ml/2 tbsp light soy sauce
chopped fresh chives, to garnish
salt and ground black pepper

1 Heat the oil in a wok until very hot. Add the prawns and star anise and stir-fry over a high heat for 2 minutes. Add the scallops, ginger and garlic and stir-fry for 1 minute more, by which time the prawns should have turned pink and the scallops opaque. Season with a little salt and plenty of pepper, then remove from the wok using a slotted spoon. Discard the star anise.

2 Add the red pepper and mushrooms to the wok and stir-fry for 1–2 minutes. Pour in the lemon juice, cornflour paste and soy sauce, then bring to the boil and stir for 1–2 minutes, or until the sauce is smooth and slightly thickened.

3 Stir the prawns and scallops into the sauce, cook for a few seconds until heated through, then season with salt and ground black pepper and serve garnished with the chopped chives.

ELEGANT DISHES FOR ENTERTAINING

If you want to impress your guests, there is no better food to serve than fish or shellfish. This chapter is dedicated to sumptuous, elegant dishes that look wonderful and taste divine. Simple yet memorable dishes include Hake au Poivre with Red Pepper Relish, Roast Monkfish with Garlic, Sole with Wild Mushrooms and Grilled Langoustines with Herbs. For the ultimate treat try Fillets of Halibut with Oysters in a creamy champagne sauce, aromatic Scallops with Garlic & Coriander or John Dory with Coconut Curry Sauce served on a fresh banana leaf.

Hake au Poivre
with Red Pepper Relish

This fish version of the classic steak au poivre is quite delicious. Thick, juicy hake steaks are encrusted with peppercorns and served with a sweet, piquant relish. Cod or monkfish can be used instead of hake.

SERVES 4

INGREDIENTS
30–45ml/2–3 tbsp mixed dried peppercorns (black, white, pink and green)
4 hake steaks, about 175g/6oz each
30ml/2 tbsp olive oil

FOR THE RELISH
2 red (bell) peppers
15ml/1 tbsp olive oil
2 garlic cloves, chopped
4 ripe tomatoes, peeled, seeded and quartered
4 drained, canned or bottled anchovy fillets, chopped
5ml/1 tsp drained, bottled capers
15ml/1 tbsp balsamic vinegar, plus extra to garnish
12 fresh basil leaves, shredded, plus a few extra to garnish
salt and ground black pepper

> COOK'S TIP
> *Vary the quantity of peppercorns according to your personal taste. Their colour indicates their strength – starting with green as the mildest and working up through pink, white and black.*

1 Put the mixed peppercorns in a mortar and crush them coarsely with a pestle. Alternatively, put them in a plastic bag and crush them with a rolling pin. Season the hake steaks lightly with salt, then coat them evenly on both sides with the crushed peppercorns. Set the coated fish steaks aside while you make the red pepper relish.

2 To make the relish, cut the red peppers in half lengthways, remove the core and seeds from each and cut the flesh into 1cm/½in wide strips. Heat the olive oil in a wok or shallow pan that has a lid. Add the peppers and stir-fry them for about 5 minutes, or until they are slightly softened. Stir in the chopped garlic, tomatoes and anchovies, then cover the pan and simmer the mixture very gently for about 20 minutes, or until the peppers are very soft.

3 Tip the contents of the pan into a food processor or blender and process to a coarse purée. Transfer the purée to a warmed bowl and season to taste. Stir in the capers, balsamic vinegar and basil. Keep the relish hot.

4 Heat the olive oil in a frying pan, add the hake steaks and fry them, in batches if necessary, for 5 minutes on each side, turning them once or twice, until they are just cooked through.

5 Place the fish on individual plates and spoon a little red pepper relish on to each plate. Garnish with fresh basil leaves and a little extra balsamic vinegar. Serve the rest of the relish separately.

SEA BASS WITH GINGER & LEEKS

This wonderful fish is always a treat. Its mild flavour goes perfectly with the light and delicious flavours of sweet, juicy leeks and aromatic fresh ginger.

SERVES 4

INGREDIENTS

1 sea bass, about 1.4–1.5kg/3–3½lb, scaled and cleaned
8 spring onions (scallions)
60ml/4 tbsp teriyaki marinade or dark soy sauce
30ml/2 tbsp cornflour (cornstarch)
juice of 1 lemon
30ml/2 tbsp rice wine vinegar
5ml/1 tsp ground ginger
60ml/4 tbsp sunflower or groundnut (peanut) oil
2 leeks, shredded
2.5cm/1in piece fresh root ginger, peeled and grated
105ml/7 tbsp chicken or fish stock
30ml/2 tbsp rice wine or dry sherry
5ml/1 tsp caster (superfine) sugar
salt and ground black pepper

COOK'S TIP
You can use whole fish or thick fillets for this recipe, which is also excellent made with red bream or porgy, snapper, pomfret or butterfish and trevally. You can serve the fish with fried rice and stir-fried Chinese green vegetables, if you like, or with boiled new potatoes and a green salad.

---

1 Make several diagonal slashes on either side of the sea bass so it can absorb the flavours, then season the fish inside and out with salt and ground black pepper. Trim the spring onions, cut them in half lengthways, then slice them diagonally into 2cm/¾in lengths. Put half of the spring onions in the cavity of the fish and reserve the rest for later use.

2 In a large, shallow dish, mix together the teriyaki marinade or dark soy sauce, the cornflour, lemon juice, vinegar and ground ginger to make a smooth, runny paste. Turn the fish in the marinade to coat it thoroughly, working it into the slashes, then leave it to marinate for 20–30 minutes, turning it several times.

3 Heat a wok or frying pan that is large enough to hold the sea bass comfortably. Add the oil, then the leeks and grated ginger. Fry gently, stirring frequently, for about 5 minutes, or until the leeks are tender. Remove the leeks and ginger with a slotted spoon and drain on kitchen paper, leaving the oil in the wok or pan.

4 Lift the sea bass out of the marinade and lower it carefully into the hot oil. Fry over a medium heat for 2–3 minutes on each side. Stir the stock, rice wine or sherry and sugar into the marinade, with salt and pepper to taste. Pour the mixture over the fish. Return the leeks and ginger to the wok or pan, together with the reserved spring onions. Cover and simmer for about 15 minutes, or until the fish is cooked through. Serve at once.

Roast Monkfish with Garlic

Monkfish tied up and cooked in this way is known in French as a gigot, *because it resembles a leg of lamb. The combination of monkfish and garlic is superb. For a contrast in colour, serve it with vibrant, fresh green beans.*

SERVES 4–6

INGREDIENTS
1kg/2¼lb monkfish tail
14 fat garlic cloves
5ml/1 tsp fresh thyme leaves
30ml/2 tbsp olive oil
juice of 1 lemon
2 bay leaves
salt and ground black pepper

1 Preheat the oven to 220°C/425°F/Gas 7. Remove any membrane from the monkfish tail and cut either side of the central bone to form two fillets. Peel 2 of the garlic cloves and cut them into thin slivers. Scatter a quarter of these and half the thyme leaves over the cut side of one of the fillets, then place the other fillet on top. Use fine kitchen string to tie them into a neat shape. Pat dry with kitchen paper.

2 Make incisions on either side of the fish and push in the remaining garlic slivers. Heat half the olive oil in a frying pan that can safely be used in the oven. When the oil is hot, put in the monkfish and cook it for about 5 minutes, or until evenly browned. Season with salt and pepper, sprinkle with lemon juice and scatter over the remaining thyme.

3 Tuck the bay leaves under the monkfish, arrange the remaining, unpeeled garlic cloves around it, and drizzle the remaining olive oil over the fish and the garlic. Transfer the frying pan to the oven and roast the monkfish for 20–25 minutes, or until the flesh is cooked through.

4 Remove the string and cut the monkfish into 2cm/¾in thick slices. Serve with the soft, roasted garlic.

Baked Sea Bream

Herbed potatoes form an aromatic base for sea bream baked with sweet, juicy tomatoes. If you prefer to use filleted fish rather than a whole sea bream, choose a chunky fillet, like cod, and roast it skin-side up.

SERVES 4–6

INGREDIENTS
8 ripe tomatoes
10ml/2 tsp caster (superfine) sugar
200ml/7fl oz/scant 1 cup olive oil
450g/1lb new potatoes
1 lemon, sliced
1 bay leaf
1 fresh thyme sprig
8 fresh basil leaves
1 sea bream, about 1kg/2¼lb, cleaned and scaled
150ml/¼ pint/⅔ cup dry white wine
30ml/2 tbsp fresh white breadcrumbs
2 garlic cloves, crushed
15ml/1 tbsp finely chopped fresh flat leaf parsley
salt and ground black pepper

1 Preheat the oven to 240°C/475°F/Gas 9. Cut the tomatoes in half lengthways and arrange them in a single layer in an ovenproof dish, cut-side up. Sprinkle with sugar, salt and pepper and drizzle over a little of the olive oil. Roast the tomatoes for about 35 minutes, or until they are soft and lightly browned. Meanwhile, cut the potatoes into 1cm/½in slices. Par-boil for 5 minutes, then drain and set aside.

2 Grease an ovenproof dish with oil. Arrange the potatoes in a single layer and place the lemon slices over; scatter on the bay leaf, thyme and basil. Season and drizzle with half the remaining oil. Lay the fish on top, season then pour the wine and the rest of the oil over the top. Arrange the tomatoes around the fish. Combine the breadcrumbs, garlic and parsley; sprinkle over the fish. Bake for 30 minutes and garnish with chopped parsley or basil.

FILLETS OF BRILL IN RED WINE

Forget the old maxim that red wine and fish do not go well together. Robust red wine adds colour and richness to this excellent dish. Sole, halibut and John Dory are also delicious cooked in this way.

SERVES 4

INGREDIENTS
4 fillets of brill, about 175–200g/6–7oz each, skinned
150g/5oz/⅔ cup chilled butter, diced, plus extra for greasing
115g/4oz shallots, thinly sliced
200ml/7fl oz/scant 1 cup robust red wine
200ml/7fl oz/scant 1 cup fish stock
salt and ground white pepper
fresh chervil or flat leaf parsley leaves, to garnish

1 Preheat the oven to 180°C/350°F/Gas 4. Season the fish on both sides with salt and pepper. Generously butter a flameproof dish, which is large enough to take all the brill fillets in a single layer without overlapping. Spread the shallots over the base and lay the fish fillets on top. Season.

2 Pour in the red wine and fish stock, cover the dish and bring the liquid to just below boiling point. Transfer the dish to the oven and bake for 6–8 minutes, or until the brill is just cooked. Using a metal spatula, carefully lift the fish and shallots on to a serving dish, cover with foil and keep hot.

3 Transfer the flameproof dish to the hob (stovetop) and bring the cooking liquid to the boil over a high heat. Boil the liquid rapidly until it has reduced by half. Lower the heat and whisk in the diced, chilled butter, one piece at a time, to make a smooth, shiny sauce. Season with salt and ground white pepper to taste, set aside and keep hot.

4 Divide the shallots among four warmed plates and lay the brill on top. Pour the sauce over and around the fish. Garnish with the chervil or flat leaf parsley and serve immediately.

SOLE WITH WILD MUSHROOMS

If possible, use chanterelles for this dish; their glowing orange colour combines really wonderfully with the saffron-scented cream sauce. Boiled new potatoes make the perfect accompaniment to this dish.

SERVES 4

INGREDIENTS
4 Dover sole fillets, about 115g/4oz each, skinned and halved lengthways
50g/2oz/4 tbsp butter
500ml/17fl oz/generous 2 cups fish stock
150g/5oz/2 cups chanterelles or oyster mushrooms
a large pinch of saffron threads
150ml/¼ pint/⅔ cup double (heavy) cream
1 egg yolk
salt and ground white pepper
finely chopped fresh flat leaf parsley, to garnish

1 Preheat the oven to 200°C/400°F/Gas 6. Place the sole on a board with the skinned side uppermost. Season, then roll up. Grease an ovenproof dish just large enough to hold the sole in a single layer. Arrange the sole in it, then pour over the stock. Cover with foil and bake for 12–15 minutes, or until cooked through.

2 Meanwhile, clean the chanterelles and wipe with a damp cloth. Halve or quarter any large ones. Heat the remaining butter in a frying pan until foaming, and sauté the mushrooms for 4 minutes, or until just tender. Season and keep hot.

3 Remove the fish fillets from the liquid and place them on a warmed serving dish. Keep hot. Strain the liquid into a small pan, add the saffron, set over a very high heat and boil until reduced to about 250ml/8fl oz/1 cup. Stir in the cream.

4 Beat the egg yolk in a bowl, pour on a little of the sauce and stir well. Stir the mixture into the sauce in the pan and cook, stirring, over a very low heat for 1–2 minutes, or until slightly thickened. Season. Stir the mushrooms into the sauce and pour it over the sole fillets. Garnish with parsley and serve at once.

John Dory with Coconut Curry Sauce

This excellent combination of flavours also works well with other flat fish like halibut and brill, or more exotic species like mahi-mahi or orange roughy. Serve the fish with pilau rice and mango chutney. This dish looks wonderful arranged on fresh banana leaves, if you can find some.

Serves 4

Ingredients
4 John Dory fillets, each about 175g/6oz, skinned
15ml/1 tbsp sunflower oil
25g/1oz/2 tbsp butter
salt and ground black pepper
15ml/1 tbsp fresh coriander (cilantro) leaves, 4 banana leaves (optional), and
*   1 small mango, peeled and diced, to garnish*

For the curry sauce
30ml/2 tbsp sunflower oil
1 carrot, chopped
1 onion, chopped
1 celery stick, chopped
white part of 1 leek, chopped
2 garlic cloves, crushed
50g/2oz creamed coconut, crumbled or 60ml/4 tbsp coconut cream
2 tomatoes, peeled, seeded and diced
2.5cm/1in piece fresh root ginger, grated
15ml/1 tbsp tomato purée (paste)
5–10ml/1–2 tsp mild curry powder
500ml/17fl oz/generous 2 cups chicken or fish stock

1 Make the curry sauce. Heat the sunflower oil in a large pan and add the carrot, onion, celery, leek and garlic. Cook over a gently heat for about 5 minutes, or until soft but not brown. Add the coconut, tomatoes and fresh ginger. Cook for about 2 minutes, then stir in the tomato purée and curry powder to taste. Add the chicken or fish stock, stir and season with salt and black pepper.

2 Bring the sauce to the boil, then lower the heat, cover the pan and cook over the lowest heat for about 50 minutes. Stir occasionally to prevent the sauce sticking to the base of the pan. Leave the sauce to cool.

3 Pour the cooled sauce into a food processor or blender and process until smooth. Return to a clean pan and reheat very gently, adding a little water if it is too thick in consistency.

4 Season the fish fillets with salt and pepper. Heat the oil in a large frying pan, add the butter and heat until sizzling. Put in the fish fillets and fry for about 3 minutes on each side, or until pale golden and cooked through. Drain on kitchen paper to remove the excess fat.

5 If you have banana leaves, place these on individual warmed plates and arrange the fillets on top. Pour the sauce around the fish and scatter the finely diced mango over the top. Garnish with coriander leaves and serve immediately.

COOK'S TIPS
- *Creamed coconut is sold in blocks and can be sliced and then crumbled for use in recipes. The coconut sauce should be cooked over a very low heat, so use a heat diffuser if you have one.*
- *The curry sauce should be subtle so choose a very mild curry powder to avoid overpowering the delicate flavours of the other ingredients.*

Fillets of Halibut with Oysters

In this luxurious dish, fillets of haddock sit atop a pretty pile of vegetable julienne and are surrounded by oysters and a creamy Champagne sauce. It is perfect for special occasions.

Serves 4

Ingredients

12 oysters
115g/4oz/½ cup butter
2 carrots, cut into julienne strips
200g/7oz celeriac, cut into julienne strips
white part of 2 leeks, cut into julienne strips
375ml/13fl oz/generous 1½ cups Champagne or dry white sparkling wine (about ½ bottle)
105ml/7 tbsp whipping cream
1 halibut, about 1.75kg/4–4½lb, filleted and skinned
salt and ground white pepper

> Cook's Tip
> *It is worth buying a whole halibut and asking the fishmonger to fillet and skin it for you. Keep the head, bones and trimmings for stock. Sole, brill and flounder can all be substituted for the halibut.*

1 Using an oyster knife, open the oysters over a bowl to catch the juices, then carefully remove them from their shells, discarding the shells, and place them in a separate bowl. Set aside until required.

2 Melt 25g/1oz/2 tbsp of the butter in a shallow pan, add the vegetable julienne and cook over a low heat until tender but not coloured. Pour in half the Champagne or sparkling wine and cook very gently until all the liquid has evaporated. Keep the heat low so that the vegetables do not colour.

3 Strain the oyster juices into a small pan and add the whipping cream and the remaining Champagne or sparkling wine. Place over a medium heat and cook, stirring, until the mixture has reduced to the consistency of thin cream.

4 Dice half the remaining butter and whisk it into the sauce, one piece at a time, until smooth. Season with salt and white pepper to taste, then pour the sauce into a blender and process until velvety smooth.

5 Return the sauce to the pan, bring it to just below boiling point, then add the oysters. Poach gently for about 1 minute. Keep warm, but do not allow to boil.

6 Season the halibut fillets with salt and pepper. Heat the remaining butter in a large frying pan until foaming, then add the fillets and fry over a medium heat for about 3 minutes on each side, or until cooked through and golden.

7 Cut each halibut fillet into three pieces and arrange on warmed individual plates. Pile the vegetable julienne on top, place three oysters around the halibut fillets on each plate and pour the sauce around the edge. Serve immediately.

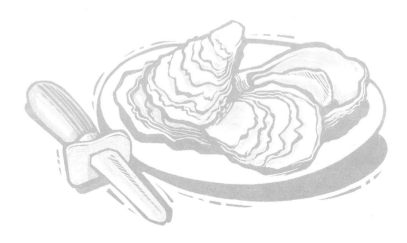

Scallops with Garlic & Coriander

Hot chilli sauce and lime are popular ingredients in many fish recipes, not only because they taste delicious together but also because they are so readily available.

Serves 4

Ingredients
20 scallops
2 courgettes (zucchini)
75g/3oz/6 tbsp butter
15ml/1 tbsp vegetable oil
4 garlic cloves, chopped
30ml/2 tbsp hot chilli sauce
juice of 1 lime
small bunch of fresh coriander (cilantro), finely chopped

1 If you have bought scallops in their shells, open them. Hold a scallop shell in the palm of your hand, with the flat side uppermost. Insert the blade of a knife close to the hinge that joins the shells and prise them apart. Run the blade of the knife across the inside of the flat shell to cut away the scallop. Only the whole, white adductor muscle and the orange coral are eaten, so pull away and discard all other parts. Rinse the scallops under cold running water.

2 Cut the courgettes in half, lengthways, then into four pieces. Melt the butter in the oil in a large frying pan. Add the courgettes and fry until soft. Remove from the pan. Add the garlic and fry until golden. Stir in the hot chilli sauce.

3 Add the scallops to the sauce. Cook, stirring constantly, for 1–2 minutes only. Stir in the lime juice, chopped coriander and the courgette pieces. Serve immediately on warmed plates.

Cook's Tip
Oil can withstand higher temperatures than butter, but butter gives fried food added flavour. Using a mixture, as here, provides the perfect compromise.

LOBSTER THERMIDOR

This classic French dish makes a small amount of lobster go a long way. Ideally use a live crustacean and cook it yourself, but a boiled lobster from the fishmonger will do. Serve with steamed rice and mixed salad leaves.

SERVES 2

INGREDIENTS
1 large lobster, about 1kg/2¼lb, boiled
45ml/3 tbsp brandy
25g/1oz/2 tbsp butter
2 shallots, finely chopped
115g/4oz/1½ cups button (white) mushrooms, thinly sliced
15ml/1 tbsp plain (all-purpose) flour
105ml/7 tbsp fish or shellfish stock
120ml/4fl oz/½ cup double (heavy) cream
5ml/1 tsp Dijon mustard
2 egg yolks, beaten
45ml/3 tbsp dry white wine
45ml/3 tbsp freshly grated Parmesan cheese
salt, ground black pepper and cayenne pepper

1 Split the lobster in half lengthways; crack the claws. Discard the stomach sac; keep the coral for another dish. Keeping each half-shell intact, extract the meat from the tail and claws, then cut into large dice. Place in a shallow dish, sprinkle over the brandy, then cover and set aside. Dry the half-shells and set them aside.

2 Melt the butter in a pan, add the shallots and cook over a low heat. Add the mushrooms and cook until tender. Stir in the flour and a pinch of cayenne and stir for 2 minutes. Gradually add the stock, stirring until the sauce boils and thickens. Stir in the cream and mustard. Cook until it is smooth and thick. Season to taste. Pour half the sauce on to the egg yolks, stir well and return the mixture to the pan. Stir in the wine; adjust the seasoning, being generous with the cayenne.

3 Preheat the grill (broiler) to medium-high. Stir the diced lobster and the brandy into the sauce. Arrange the lobster half-shells in a grill (broiling) pan and divide the mixture among them. Sprinkle with Parmesan and grill until browned.

Grilled Langoustines with Herbs

This simple cooking method enhances both the delicate colour and flavour of the langoustines. Try to find live langoustines for this recipe. Choose the largest you can find (or afford), and allow 5–6 per serving. Lobster and crayfish are also delicious cooked this way.

SERVES 4 AS A MAIN COURSE, 6 AS A FIRST COURSE

INGREDIENTS
60ml/4 tbsp extra virgin olive oil
60ml/4 tbsp hazelnut oil
15ml/1 tbsp each finely chopped fresh basil, chives, chervil, flat leaf parsley
  and tarragon
pinch of ground ginger
20–24 large langoustines, preferably live
salt and ground black pepper
lemon wedges and rocket (arugula) leaves, to serve

1 Preheat the grill (broiler) to very hot. Mix together the olive and hazelnut oils in a small bowl. Add the herbs, a pinch of ground ginger, and salt and pepper to taste. Whisk thoroughly until slightly thickened and emulsified.

2 If you are using live langoustines immerse them in a large pan of boiling water for 1–2 minutes, then drain and leave them to cool. Split the langoustines lengthways using a large, sharp knife and arrange them on a foil-lined grill (broiler) pan. Spoon over the herb-flavoured oil.

3 Grill (broil) for 8–10 minutes, basting the langoustines two or three times until they are cooked and lightly browned. Arrange the langoustines on a warmed serving dish, pour the juices from the grill pan over and serve immediately with lemon wedges and rocket leaves.

GRILLED SQUID WITH CHORIZO

Tender, fried squid and spicy chorizo sausage are tossed with grilled tomatoes and tiny new potatoes in a lemony dressing to make a delicious summer salad.

SERVES 6

INGREDIENTS
24 small squid, cleaned
150ml/¼ pint/⅔ cup extra virgin olive oil
300g/11oz cooking chorizo, cut into 12 slices
3 tomatoes, halved and seasoned with salt and pepper
24 cooked new potatoes, halved
a handful of fresh rocket (arugula) leaves
juice of 1 lemon
salt and ground black pepper

1 Separate the body and tentacles of the squid and cut the bodies in half lengthways if they are large. Pour half the oil into a bowl, season with salt and pepper, then toss all the squid in the oil. Heat a ridged griddle pan or grill (broiler) to very hot.

2 Cook the prepared squid bodies for about 45 seconds on each side, or until the flesh is opaque and tender, then transfer to a plate and keep hot. Cook the tentacles for about 1 minute on each side, then transfer them to the plate. Grill the chorizo slices for about 30 seconds on each side, or until golden brown, then set them aside with the squid. Grill the tomato halves for 1–2 minutes on each side, until they are softened and browned.

3 Place the potatoes and rocket in a large bowl. Pour the lemon juice into a bowl and whisk in the remaining oil. Season. Reserve 30ml/2 tbsp of this dressing in a jug (pitcher). Pour the dressing over the potatoes and rocket, toss lightly and divide among six plates. Pile a portion of the squid, tomatoes and chorizo on each salad, and drizzle over the reserved dressing. Serve at once.

VEGETABLE-STUFFED SQUID

Shirley Conran famously said that life is too short to stuff a mushroom. The same might be said of squid, except that the result is so delicious that it makes the effort seem worthwhile. Small cuttlefish can be prepared in the same way.

SERVES 4

INGREDIENTS
4 medium squid, or 12 small squid, skinned and cleaned
75g/3oz/6 tbsp butter
50g/2oz/1 cup fresh white breadcrumbs
2 shallots, chopped
4 garlic cloves, chopped
1 leek, finely diced
2 carrots, finely diced
150ml/¼ pint/⅔ cup fish stock
30ml/2 tbsp olive oil
30ml/2 tbsp chopped fresh flat leaf parsley
salt and ground black pepper
saffron rice, to serve

1 Preheat the oven to 220°C/425°F/Gas 7. Cut off the tentacles and side flaps from the squid and chop these finely. Set the chopped squid and the squid bodies aside.

2 Melt half the butter in a large frying pan that can be used in the oven. Add the breadcrumbs and fry until they are golden brown, stirring to ensure that they brown evenly. Transfer the breadcrumbs to a bowl and set aside until required.

3 Heat the remaining butter in the frying pan and add the chopped and diced vegetables. Fry until softened but not browned, then stir in the fish stock and cook until the stock has reduced and the vegetables are very soft. Season to taste with salt and ground black pepper and transfer to the bowl with the breadcrumbs. Mix lightly together.

4 Heat half the olive oil in the frying pan, add the chopped squid and fry over a high heat for 1 minute. Remove the squid with a slotted spoon and stir it into the vegetable mixture. Stir in the parsley.

5 Put the stuffing mixture into a piping bag, or use a teaspoon to stuff the squid tubes with the mixture. Do not overfill them, as the stuffing will swell lightly during cooking. Secure the openings with wooden cocktail sticks (toothpicks), or sew up with fine kitchen thread.

6 Heat the remaining olive oil in the frying pan, place the stuffed squid in the pan and fry until they are sealed on all sides and golden brown. Transfer the frying pan to the oven and roast the squid for 20 minutes.

7 Unless the squid are very small, carefully cut them into three or four slices and arrange on a bed of saffron rice. Spoon the cooking juices over and around the squid, and serve immediately.

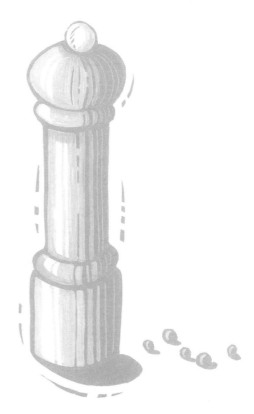

OCTOPUS STEW

This rustic stew is a perfect dish for entertaining, as it tastes even better if made a day in advance. It is important to tenderize the meat – apparently Greek fishermen do this by bashing their catch against the rocks numerous times. Serve with a colourful salad of baby chard, rocket (arugula) and radicchio.

SERVES 4–6

INGREDIENTS
1kg/2¼lb octopus, cleaned
45ml/3 tbsp olive oil
1 large red onion, chopped
3 garlic cloves, finely chopped
30ml/2 tbsp brandy
300ml/½ pint/1¼ cups dry white wine
800g/1¾lb ripe plum tomatoes, peeled and chopped, or two 400g/14oz cans
    chopped tomatoes
1 fresh red chilli, seeded and chopped (optional)
450g/1lb small new potatoes
15ml/1 tbsp chopped fresh rosemary
15ml/1 tbsp fresh thyme leaves
1.2 litres/2 pints/5 cups fish stock
30ml/2 tbsp fresh flat leaf parsley leaves
salt and ground black pepper

FOR THE GARLIC CROÛTES
1 fat garlic clove, peeled
8 thick slices of baguette or ciabatta
30ml/2 tbsp olive oil

1 Cut the octopus into large pieces, put these in a pan and pour in cold water to cover. Season with salt, bring to the boil, then lower the heat and simmer for 30 minutes to tenderize. Drain and cut into bitesize pieces.

2 Heat the oil in a large, shallow pan. Fry the onion for 2–3 minutes, or until lightly coloured, then add the garlic and fry for 1 minute more. Add the octopus and fry for 2–3 minutes, stirring and tossing to colour it lightly on all sides.

3 Pour the brandy over the octopus and ignite it. When the flames have died down, add the wine, bring to the boil and bubble gently for about 5 minutes. Stir in the tomatoes, with the chilli, if using, then add the potatoes, rosemary and thyme. Simmer for 5 minutes.

4 Pour in the fish stock and season well. Cover the pan and simmer for about 20 minutes, stirring occasionally. The octopus and potatoes should be very tender and the sauce should have thickened slightly. At this stage, you can leave the stew to cool, then put it in the refrigerator overnight.

5 Preheat a medium-hot grill (broiler). To make the garlic croûtes, cut the garlic clove in half and rub both sides of the slices of baguette or ciabatta with the cut side. Crush the garlic, stir it into the oil and brush the mixture over both sides of the bread. Grill on both sides until the croûtes are golden brown and crisp.

6 To serve the stew, reheat it gently if it has been in the refrigerator overnight, check the seasoning and stir in the parsley leaves. Serve piping hot in individual warmed bowls accompanied by the warm garlic croûtes.

SAUCES FOR
FISH & SHELLFISH

There is little more delicious than grilled or poached fish served with a simple sauce. This chapter contains classic sauces that can be served with plain, simply cooked fish. Never-fail Mayonnaise and Mustard & Dill Sauce are perfect for serving with cold fish such as poached salmon. Roasted Garlic & Olive Oil Dressing can be drizzled over hot or cold fish or a simple fish salad for delicious results. There is also a selection of hot sauces, such as Hollandaise Sauce, Green Peppercorn Sauce and Beurre Blanc, that will go wonderfully with hot, freshly cooked fish.

ROASTED GARLIC & OLIVE OIL DRESSING

Garlic that has been roasted tastes sweet and is milder than you would expect. This dressing is perfect served with simply cooked fish for a light lunch or supper, or drizzle it over raw fillets or whole fish before grilling (broiling).

SERVES 4

INGREDIENTS
1 whole head of garlic
120ml/4fl oz/½ cup extra virgin olive oil
salt and ground black pepper

1 Preheat the oven to 180°C/350°F/Gas 4. Place the garlic in an oiled baking tray and roast it for 30 minutes. Leave the garlic to cool, then lay it on its side and slice off the top third with a sharp knife.

2 Hold the garlic over a bowl and dig out the flesh from each clove with the point of the knife. When all the flesh has been added to the bowl, pour in the oil and add salt and plenty of black pepper. Mix well.

NEVER-FAIL MAYONNAISE

Some people find classic mayonnaise difficult to make, but this simple processor version takes away the mystique. The essential thing is to have all of the ingredients at room temperature before you start. This recipe contains raw eggs so should be avoided by the young, elderly, pregnant women and those with a compromised immune system. If this is a concern, use bought mayonnaise instead.

SERVES 4–6

INGREDIENTS
1 egg, plus 1 egg yolk
5ml/1 tsp Dijon mustard
juice of 1 large lemon
175ml/6fl oz/³⁄₄ cup olive oil
175ml/6fl oz/³⁄₄ cup grapeseed, sunflower or corn oil
salt and ground white pepper

1 Put the whole egg and yolk in a food processor or blender and process for 20 seconds. Add the Dijon mustard, half the lemon juice, and a generous pinch of salt and ground white pepper. Process for about 30 seconds more, or until the mixture is thoroughly combined.

2 With the motor running, pour in the oils through the feeder tube in a thin, steady stream. Process until the oils are incorporated and the mayonnaise is pale, thick and creamy. Check for seasoning and add more lemon juice and salt and white pepper if necessary.

Mustard & Dill Sauce

This fresh-tasting sauce makes a wonderful alternative to mayonnaise and is good with any cold, smoked or raw, marinated fish.

Serves 4

Ingredients
1 egg yolk
30ml/2 tbsp Dijon mustard
2.5–5ml/½–1 tsp soft dark brown sugar
15ml/1 tbsp white wine vinegar
90ml/6 tbsp sunflower or light olive oil
30ml/2 tbsp finely chopped fresh dill
salt and ground black pepper

1 Put the egg yolk in a small bowl and add the mustard with a little sugar to taste. Beat with a wooden spoon until smooth. Stir in the vinegar, then gradually whisk in the sunflower or olive oil, a little at a time, mixing well after each addition.

2 When the oil has been completely amalgamated, season the sauce with salt and plenty of freshly ground black pepper, then stir in the finely chopped dill. Chill for about an hour before serving.

Watchpoint
The very young, the elderly, pregnant women and those in ill-health or with a compromised immune system are advised against consuming raw eggs or dishes containing raw eggs.

BUERRE BLANC

Legend has it that this exquisite sauce was invented by a cook who forgot to put egg yolks into a béarnaise sauce. Whether or not this is true does not matter: this light, buttery sauce goes perfectly with poached or grilled fish.

SERVES 4

INGREDIENTS
3 shallots, very finely chopped
45ml/3 tbsp dry white wine or court-bouillon
45ml/3 tbsp white wine or tarragon vinegar
115g/4oz/½ cup chilled unsalted (sweet) butter, diced
lemon juice (optional)
salt and ground white pepper

1 Put the shallots in a small pan with the wine or court-bouillon and vinegar. Bring to the boil and cook over a high heat for a few minutes until only about 30ml/2 tbsp of the liquid remains. Remove the pan from the heat and leave to cool until the liquid is just lukewarm.

2 Whisk the chilled butter into the cooled shallot mixture, one piece at a time, to make a pale, creamy sauce (ensure that each piece is completely melted before adding the next). Taste the sauce, then season with salt and ground white pepper and add a little lemon juice if you like.

3 If you are not serving the sauce immediately, keep it warm in the top of a double boiler set over barely simmering water. (Do not let the sauce get too hot or it will separate. Make sure that the base of the top pan in the double boiler does not touch the simmering water.)

HOLLANDAISE SAUCE

This rich, piquant sauce goes well with any poached fish. Serve it warm. As the egg yolks are barely cooked, do not serve to children, the elderly or anyone with a compromised immune system.

SERVES 4

INGREDIENTS
115g/4oz/½ cup unsalted (sweet) butter
2 egg yolks
15–30ml/1–2 tbsp lemon juice, white wine vinegar or tarragon vinegar
salt and ground white pepper

1 Melt the butter in a small pan. Put the egg yolks and 15ml/1 tbsp lemon juice or vinegar in a bowl. Add salt and pepper, and whisk until completely smooth.

2 Pour the melted butter in a steady stream on to the egg yolk mixture, beating vigorously with a wooden spoon to make a smooth sauce. Alternatively, put the mixture in a food processor or blender and add the butter in a slow, steady stream through the feeder tube, with the motor running. Taste the sauce and add more seasoning and lemon juice or vinegar if necessary.

GREEN PEPPERCORN SAUCE

This piquant sauce is delicious served with all kinds of fish and shellfish, but it is especially good with pan-fried salmon fillets.

SERVES 4

INGREDIENTS
15g/½oz/1 tbsp butter
2 or 3 shallots, finely chopped
15ml/1 tbsp brandy (optional)
60ml/4 tbsp dry white wine
90ml/6 tbsp fish or chicken stock
125ml/4fl oz/½ cup whipping cream
30–45ml/2–3 tbsp green peppercorns in brine, rinsed
salt and ground black pepper

1 Melt the butter in a heavy pan over a medium heat. Add the shallots and cook for about 1–2 minutes, stirring occasionally, until just softened.

2 Add the brandy, if using, and the white wine, then add the stock and boil to reduce by three-quarters, stirring occasionally.

3 Reduce the heat, then add the cream and half the peppercorns, crushing them slightly with the back of a wooden spoon. Cook very gently for 4–5 minutes, or until the sauce is thickened, then strain and stir in the remaining peppercorns. Keep the sauce warm over a very low heat, stirring occasionally.

CRAWFISH SAUCE

This sauce, also known as Nantua sauce, is perfect for using up the shells left over from shellfish recipes. It can be made with other crustaceans, such as lobster, rock lobster or large prawns (shrimp). Use it to enhance any white fish or shellfish.

SERVES 4

INGREDIENTS
1 cooked crawfish or crayfish, about 450g/1lb
40g/1½oz/3 tbsp butter
15ml/1 tbsp olive oil
45ml/3 tbsp brandy
500ml/17fl oz/generous 2 cups fish or shellfish stock
15ml/1 tbsp plain (all-purpose) flour
45ml/3 tbsp double (heavy) cream
2 egg yolks
salt and ground white pepper

1 Remove the tail meat from the crawfish and keep for another recipe. Break up the shells and legs and crush them coarsely in a food processor.

2 Melt 25g/1oz/2 tbsp of the butter in the oil in a pan, add the shells and cook for about 3 minutes, stirring frequently. Add the brandy and stock, bring to the boil, then simmer for 10 minutes.

3 Mash the remaining butter with the flour. Whisk the paste into the sauce, a small piece at a time, and cook gently until thickened. Season, then strain through a fine sieve. Stir in the cream and bring back to just below boiling point.

4 Beat the egg yolks lightly in a bowl and mix in a couple of spoonfuls of the hot sauce. Return the mixture to the pan and cook gently until slightly thickened. Adjust the seasoning and serve at once.

PARSLEY SAUCE

When this classic herb sauce is well made it is delicious. Serve it with poached cod, haddock or any white fish. If possible, use the poaching liquid from fish to enhance the flavour of the sauce.

SERVES 4

INGREDIENTS
50g/2oz/¼ cup butter
45ml/3 tbsp plain (all-purpose) flour
300ml/½ pint/1¼ cups milk
300ml/½ pint/1¼ cups poaching liquid from fish (or an
   extra 300ml/½ pint/1¼ cups milk)
60ml/4 tbsp double (heavy) cream
lemon juice to taste
90ml/6 tbsp chopped fresh flat leaf parsley
salt and ground black pepper

1 Melt half the butter in a small pan, add the flour and cook, stirring, for about 2 minutes to make a smooth roux. Take the pan off the heat, add a couple of spoonfuls of milk and stir in until completely absorbed.

2 Continue to add small quantities of milk and poaching liquid, if available, stirring until the sauce has the consistency of double cream. Add the rest of the milk and poaching liquid and whisk to break down any lumps.

3 Return the pan to the heat and bring the sauce to the boil, then lower the heat and simmer gently for about 5 minutes, stirring frequently. Stir in the cream and lemon juice to taste, and season with salt and pepper. If the sauce is at all lumpy at this stage, whisk it thoroughly with a hand-held blender or a whisk. Stir in the chopped parsley, then whisk in the remaining butter and serve hot.

Shopping for Fish & Shellfish

AUSTRALIA
De Costi Seafoods
Sydney Fish Markets
Gipps Street
Pyrmont NSW 2009
Tel: (02) 9692 9188

The Fish Factory
363 Lytton Road
Colmslie QLD 4170
Tel: (07) 3399 9888

Poulos Bros
21–29 Bank Street
Pyrmont NSW 2009
Tel: (02) 9692 8411
www.poulosbros.
   com.au

Queen Victoria
   Markets
513 Elizabeth Street
Melbourne VIC 3000
Tel: (03) 9320 5822
www.qvm.com.au

Sydney Fish Markets
Gipps Street
Pyrmont NSW 2009
Tel: (02) 9660 3652
www.sydneyfishmarket.
   com.au

CANADA
Bill's Lobster and Fish
   Market
600 Gerrard Street East
Toronto
Ontario M4M 1Y2
Tel: (416) 778 0943
www.billslobster.com

Codfather Seafood Ltd
1915 Denmar Road
Unit 151
Pickering
Ontario L1V 3E1
Tel: (905) 619 2560
Fax: (775) 361 5812
www.CodfatherSeafood.
   com

NEW ZEALAND
New Zealand Fishing
   Industry Board
Private Bag 24 901
Manners Street Post Office
Wellington
Tel: (04) 385 4005/8115
www.seaford.co.nz

UNITED KINGDOM
B & M Seafoods
250 Kentish Town Road
London NW5 2AA
Tel: 020 7485 0346

Chalmers and Gray
67 Nottinghill Gate
London W11 3JS
Tel: 020 7221 6177

Corney, J. A. Ltd (kosher)
16 Hallswelle Parade
Finchley Road
London NW11 0DL
Tel: 020 8455 9588

Cornwall Fish
17 Station Approach
West Byfleet
Surrey KT14 6NF
Tel: 01932 355550/1

Covent Garden
   Fishmongers
Phil Diamond
37 Turnham Green
   Terrace
London W4 1RG
Tel: 020 8995 9273

Dagon's Ltd
16 Granvill Arcade
Brixton Market
London SW9 8PR
Tel: 020 7274 1665

Fortnum and Mason
181 Piccadilly
London W1
Tel: 020 734 8040

France Fresh Fish
99 Stroud Green Road
London N4 3PX
Tel: 020 7263 9767

Good Harvest Fish and
   Meat Market (Chinese
   fish and shellfish)
14 Newport Place
London WC2H 7PR
Tel: 020 7437 0712

Harrods Food Hall
87 Brompton Road
Knightsbridge
London SW1X 7XL
Tel: 020 7730 1234

Harvey Nichols Food Hall
109–125 Knightsbridge
London SW1X 7RJ
Tel: 020 7235 5000

HM Seafoods Ltd
2 The Parade
Loxwood
West Sussex RH14 0SB
Tel: 01403 753250

John Blagdens
65 Paddington Street
London W1M 3RR
Tel: 020 7935 8321

John Nicholson
  Fishmongers
108 Manor Road
Wallington
Surrey SN6 0DW
Tel: 020 8647 3922

Loaves and Fishes
52 Thoroughfare
Woodbridge
Suffolk IP12 1AL
Tel: 01394 385650

Manta Ray Seafoods
24 Hildreth Street
London SW12 9RQ
Tel: 020 8673 4678

Newnes, C. J.
  (exotic fish)
73 Billingsgate Market
Trafalgar Way
London E14 5TQ
Tel: 020 7515 0793

Ramus Seafoods
Ocean House
132–136 Kings Road
Harrogate
North Yorkshire
  HG1 5HY
Tel: 01423 563271
Fax: 01423 531040

The Seafood Store
15 Downing Street
Farnham
Surrey GU9 7PB
Tel: 01252 715010

Selfridges
400 Oxford Street
London W1A 1AB
Tel: 020 7629 1234

Steve Hatt
88–90 Essex Road
London N1 8LU
Tel: 020 7226 3963

UNITED STATES
Alioto-Lazio Fish
  Company
440 Jefferson Street
San Francisco CA 94100
Tel: (888) 673 5868

Balducci's
424 Sixth Avenue
New York NY 10011
Tel: (212) 673 2600

Big Tom's Seafood
  Market
4031 Thomas Drive
Panama Beach FL 32408
Tel: (850) 235 2926
www.bigtomseafood.com

Citarella
1313 Third Avenue
New York NY 10021
Tel: (212) 874 0383

Eli's Manhattan
1411 Third Avenue
New York NY 10028
Tel: (212) 717 8100

Flanders Fish Market
22 Chesterfield Road
East Lyme CT 06333
Tel: (800) 638 8189

The Fishery
250 Center Street
Auburn Maine 04210
Tel: (800) 515 5627
www.mk.net/~fishery

Fitts Seafoods
1175 Edgewater N.W.
Salem OR 97304
Tel: (503) 364 6724
www.fitts.net

George's Ultimate Seafood
112 Green Street
Worcester MA 01604
Tel: (508) 755 8331

Katch Seafood
765 Fish Dock Road
Homer AK 99603
Tel: (800) 368 7400
www.efish.com

Leo's Live Seafood
4098 Legoe Bay Road
Lummi Island WA 98262
Tel: (360) 758 7318
www.leoslive.com

Long Wharf Seafood
17 Connell Highway
Newport RI 02840
Tel: (401) 846 6320
www3.edgenet.net/lws

Robert's Quality Seafood
7722 Merrill Road
Jacksonville FL 32099
Tel: (904) 744 0200

INDEX

C